The Complete Colorado Campground Guide

ACKNOWLEDGMENTS

We would like to thank the following agencies for their cooperation and assistance in making this guide possible:

Colorado State Parks
Colorado Division of Wildlife
Bureau of Land Management
National Park Service
Boulder Mountain Parks
National Forest Service
Larimer County Parks
Hinsdale County

Front Cover:
Photo Courtesy of Durango
Chamber of Commerce
Cover Design:
Ken Grasman - Denver
Inside Photos
Rocky Mountain National Park

Editor & Publisher
Jack O. Olofson

Contributing Editor
Don Schuchardt

Staff
Dody Olofson
Sarah Ellison

OUTDOOR BOOKS & MAPS, INC.

11270 County Road 49
Hudson, CO 80642
1(800) 952-5342 FAX (303) 536-4641

ISBN 0-930657-23-3
UPC 7 27832 39104 4

Over 500

National Forests, ...
State Wildlife Areas, ...
Management and Other Campgrounds

Information:
- **Directions**
- **Fee - Max. Length of Unit - Elevation**
- **U.S.G.S. 7.5' Topographic Map Name**
- **Name and Phone Numbers of Managing Agency**
- **Reservation Requirement**
- **Regulations and Restrictions**

Trip Planning!
Outdoor Books & Maps publishes a wide range of Colorado outdoor recreation guides for outdoor enthusiasts. Informative guides for 4-Wheel Drive, boating, hiking, biking, fishing and camping. Trip planning guides with maps, directions and information for visitors to state parks, national parks, national forests, national monuments and state wildlife areas.

Each guide covers a specific outdoor activity and includes topics such as safety, regulations, wildlife viewing and historical information.

Fresh!
We update our publications before each printing, contacting and working with city, state, county and federal agencies that manage Colorado's recreation areas. Cooperation with these agencies assures a fresh guide that contains updated trip planning and recreation information.

We Listen!
Recommendations from controlling agencies, consumers and merchants determines the content and format of our guides, your comments and recommendations are welcome.

For a free catalog call 1 (800) 952-5342.

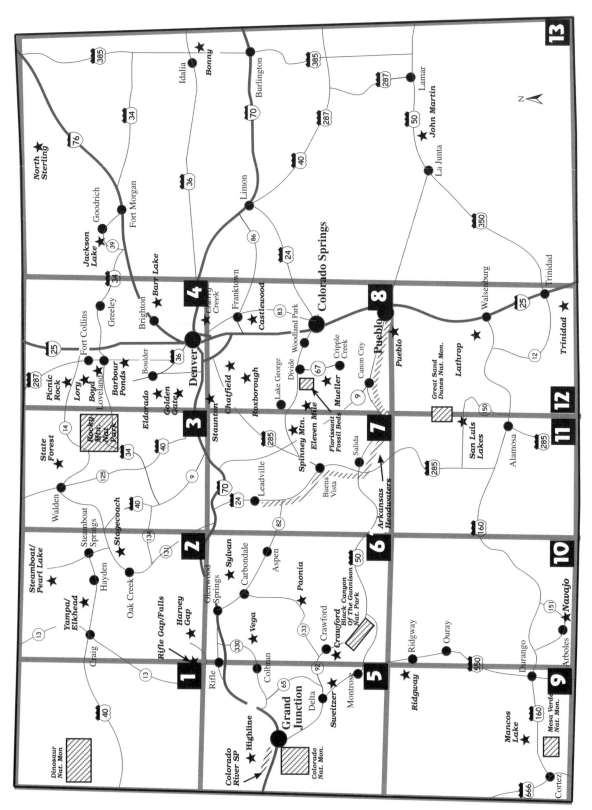

GENERALIZED COLORADO MAP DEPICTING BOOK SECTIONS

★ **State Park**

10 **Book Section Number**

Table of Contents

> NATIONAL FOREST, COLORADO DIVISION OF WILDLIFE, COUNTY AND CITY CAMPGROUNDS ARE LISTED IN EACH SECTION FOLLOWING THE NATIONAL PARKS AND STATE PARKS SHOWN IN THIS INDEX

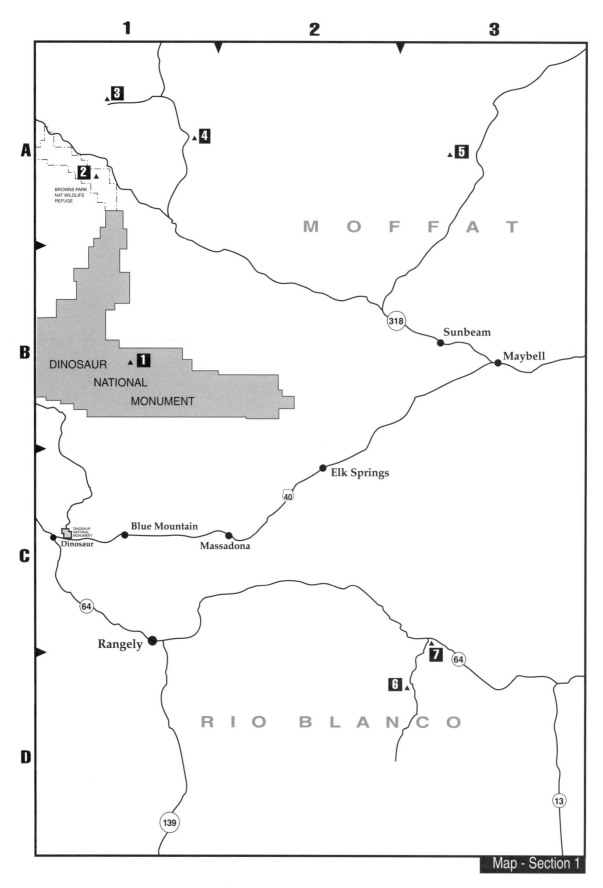

DINOSAUR NATIONAL MONUMENT

BROWNS PARK NAT WILDLIFE REFUGE

M O F F A T

Sunbeam

Maybell

Elk Springs

Blue Mountain

Massadona

DINOSAUR NATIONAL MONUMENT

Dinosaur

Rangely

R I O   B L A N C O

Map - Section 1

HOW TO USE THIS GUIDE

The Complete Guide to Colorado Campgrounds divides the state into 13 sections. A locator map in front of each section locates each campground by number. Open to the text section that follows the locator map and match the number on the bar heading to the number on the locator map. Within each section campgrounds are listed in alphabetical order by: National parks, State Parks, Division of Wildlife and Bureau of Land Management properties and National Forests.

BAR HEADING:

The bar heading is a fast reference tool - categories noted on the bar heading are:

No: Number shown on map. Represents approximate geographical location of campground.

Name: Name of campground.

Fee: $ - Indicates if you are required to pay to camp. NOTE: Many non-fee National Forest campgrounds are soon to be concessionaire operated and will charge fees.

No. Of Units: Campsites available

Max. Length: Recommended maximum length of camping unit. (State Parks have a limited number of spaces for units of any length - Call first).

Elev: Elevation of campground site.

Restrooms: Restrooms located on or near campground sites.

Drinking Water: Drinking water available on or near campground site.

Agency: Government agency that manages the campground.

Information: Below the bar heading is general information, including directions, activities, agency phone numbers, etc.

NOTE: Location mileages shown can be approximate, some distances calculated with a map planimeter.

Map No.	Name	Map Loc.	Fee	No. of Units	Max. Length	Elev.	Toilets	Water	Agency
4	**Irish Canyon**	A-1	0	3	30'	6,000'	Yes	No	Bureau of Land Management

NOTE: Information contained in this guide has been carefully compiled and edited, however, campgrounds are closed and opened annually. Please use the phone numbers shown with each campground to verify the information. Outdoor Books & Maps, Inc. is not responsible for the content other than for its intended use, which is for general trip planning reference material.

MAPS:

Contact the controlling agencies for a large scale maps of the area you wish to visit. U.S. Forest Service maps will show adjacent Bureau of Land Management and Division of Wildlife properties.

U.S. Forest Service:1" = 2 miles scale maps show roads, towns, campgrounds, rivers, trails and other physical features for a specific forest. Forest Service map are sold at Forest Service offices and some map stores.

U.S. Geological Survey: (7 1/2') 1" = 2000 feet scale topographic maps shows detailed topography, elevations, water, trails and other physical features. These topographic maps are sold by name, each campground has the topographic map name in the text under the bar heading. These maps can be purchased at U.S.G.S. maps sales, map stores.

Colorado Camping and Recreation Guide: 28" X 42" four color U.S.G.S. State map with campgrounds, towns, roads, rivers, and recreation information for state parks, national forests and national parks. (Outdoor Books & Maps -- ISBN 0-930657-31-4)

CONTENT SECTION 1

TEXT SYMBOLS

Handicapped accessible - Handicapped accessible facilities vary from site to site - Call first.

® Campgrounds on a reservation system. See page 89 for phone numbers.

TH Trailhead.(Trailhead in vicinity of campground.)

FDT Forest designated trail.

Map No.	Campground Name	Map Loc.	Fee	No. of Units	Max. Length	Elev.	Toilets	Water	Agency
1	**Dinosaur National Monument**	B-1	$	151	35'	4,800'	Yes	Yes	National Parks Service

Dinosaur National Monument is the legacy of rivers, past and present. Here, preserved in the sands of an ancient river, is a time capsule from the worlds of dinosaurs; the fossil hone deposit that gives the park its past. The remote and rugged land around it, created by today's rivers, is a secret of the present, known to few travelers.

Stand on the tip of Harpers Comer and look down at the rivers far below; your gaze is spanning time as well as space. In the rocks beneath you are fossils of sea creatures two or three times older than the dinosaurs. Upheavals that began about the time that the last dinosaur died jolted these shelf's far above sea level and downward cutting rivers stranded them on this promontory in the sky.

Seen in this context, the Age of Dinosaurs is but a brief chapter in a long story, and only a paragraph about the dinosaurs themselves are written in the rocks here. Not until about midpoint of dinosaur history, about 145 million years ago, did a suitable habitat develop here- a low-lying plain crossed by several large rivers and many intermittent streams, clad in a variety of ferns, cycads, clubmosses, and clumps of tall conifers. This was home to dinosaurs such as Apatosaursus (better known as Brontosaurus), Dipledocus, Stegosaurus, and other vegetarians, and to the sharp toothed carnivores. Allosaurus was the largest at this time who preyed upon them. Most of their skeletons decayed without a trace, but in at least one spot, river flood waters washed a great number of carcasses and bones onto a sandbar. There, mixed with the remains of turtles, crocodiles, and clams that lived in the river, the bones were preserved in the sand. This layer itself was not very thick, but thousands more meters of sediments piled up on top of it as the sea crept in and out during the last part of dinosaur times. Dissolved silica percolating through the strata turned the ancient riverbed into hard sandstone and mineralized the bones buried within it.

When the Rocky Mountains to the east began to rise, this area went a long for the ride. Here, the mountain-building did not push up the rock layers from below, but instead it squeezed them from the sides, warping and tilting them, sometimes cracking and shifting them along fault lines. Rain, frost, wind and gravity slowly but steadily wore away layer after layer of the uppermost strata, revealing the older rocks beneath. In this way, a bit of the long-buried riverbed and its fossil treasure began to show up on the top of a jagged ridge.

Not far from the ridge, the prehistoric Fremont people carved elaborate drawings into the cliffs about 1000 AD. Fur trader William H. Ashley floated down the Green River not far from that ridge in 1825. Explorer scientist John Wesley Powell followed the same route in 1869. But it remained for Earl Douglass to take a close enough look at the ridge to notice what was weathering out on its surface. Douglass, a paleontologist from the Carnegie Museum in Pittsburgh, Penn. had not come here by accident. He knew that similar rocks in Colorado and Wyoming had yielded great dinosaur finds, and he began to search this area in 1908. On August 17, 1909, he wrote in his diary: "At last in the top of the ledge I saw eight of the tail bones of a Brontosaurus in exact position. It was a beautiful sight." Those were the first of thousands of bones, including several nearly complete skeletons that Douglass and his workers removed from this single ridge. Many of them are now on display in the Carnegie Museum.

The quarry site was designated a national monument in 1915, and though Douglass continued to excavate for several more years, he did not remove everything. Today, the remainder of the bone-bearing layer forms one wall of the Dinosaur Quarry building. Here the fossil bones are still being exposed in, but not removed from, the sandstone face, creating a unique exhibit of the bones in their natural setting. In the summer you can watch the Quarry paleontologist's as they expose the fossils in high relief.

The canyons of the Green and Yampa Rivers were added to the original park in 1938, but isolated from main-traveled routes and perhaps overshadowed by the uniqueness of the Quarry, they have remained relatively unexplored. A few hardy souls settled in the canyons around the turn of the century, but most of the land is still wilderness.

Erosion has stripped away the "younger" rocks from most of the canyon country, accentuating the contrast, in both time and environments, between past and present. Land that was once a sea floor, where coral's and shellfish thrived, is now far away from moist ocean winds, and a semi-desert climate prevails. The temperature can vary by nearly 85°C (155°F) between January and July, and though snow cloaks the ground in winter, it contains little water. Rain, when it comes, is often in the form of brief, localized thundershowers, drenching the ground in one place and filling the gullies with flash floods, while dust devils rise in the hot breeze nearby. In this setting, life must be tolerant of extremes. Good looks, as humans rate them, are not very important in the desert. Most of the dry basin-and-plateau land of the park is covered with sagebrush, greasewood, and saltbush, graduating into "pygmy forests" of pinyon pine and juniper at the higher elevations. Drab as these plants may seem to our eyes, they are beautifully adapted for their special tasks: conserving water, resisting extreme temperatures, and eking out a living from unaware neighbors.

Within this arid setting, the rivers and their canyons are linear oases, in which the green of cottonwoods and boxelders seems all the more vivid in contrast to the surroundings.

Boaters drifting along a quiet stretch of water may be startled by the sound of a flock of Canada geese taking wing, or by the sight of a bighorn sheep high on a cliff. And around the next bend might be a surprise of another kind, as the river plunges madly into a foaming rapid. Roar-bounce-splash! - who would have expected this in the middle of the desert?

Perhaps the unexpected is what Dinosaur National Monument is all about, a gallery of dinosaur bones in solid rock, the whisper of flowing water heard from sun-baked canyon rim and the aroma of Douglass fir on the mountain slopes. Time and the river have long been at work on this land. Take time to discover its secrets.

Campgrounds

Split Mountain (35 sites, $) and Green River (99 sites, $), Gates of Lodore (17 sites) and Deerlodge (10 sites) can accommodate tents and RV vehicles. There are no hook-ups or sanitary dump stations. Firewood can be bought at some sites. Primitive campgrounds are Echo Park (15 sites) and Rainbow Park (2 sites). Drinking water is available at Green River, Split Mountain and Gates of Lodore. Vehicle based camping is limited to these designated campgrounds. Wood gathering is prohibited at all campgrounds.

Hiking

There are only a few trails in this rugged, high-desert park, but they provide the most intimate look at the landscape. Check with a ranger for information about trails and back-country permits. For any hiking always carry plenty of water and let someone know where your going and when you will be back.

Fishing

The muddy water of the rivers limits fishing. A state fishing license required. A number of endangered fish species inhabit these rivers. Check with a ranger for detailed information and conditions.

Regulations

The park belongs to everyone. Do not collect or disturbing rock, fossil, plant or artifact. Wildlife may not be hunted, trapped or injured. Do not feed any wildlife. Pets must be or otherwise physically restrained at all times, they are not allowed in public buildings, with hikers or on the rivers. Firearms must be sealed, cased, broken down or otherwise packed to prevent their use. Camp or picnic at designated sites and dispose of all trash in garbage cans. Never leave a campfire unattended, be sure it is out cold before you leave or go to bed. All vehicles, including four-wheel drive and motor bikes must stay on the roads. Off-road driving destroys plants and animals and leaves scars that are hard to heal.

Open for use: Year round
Contact:: Dinosaur National Monument
　　　　　PO Box 210
　　　　　Dinosaur, CO 81610
　　　　　(970) 374-3000

Map No.	Campground Name	Map Loc.	Fee	No. of Units	Max. Length	Elev.	Toilets	Water	Agency
2	**Browns Park National Wildlife Refuge**	A-1	0	Dispersed	Open	5,700'	Yes	Yes	US Fish & Wildlife Service

LOCATION: 59 mi. NW of Maybell on Hwy 318. FACILITIES: None. ACTIVITIES: Hunting, Fishing, Wildlife observation. OPEN FOR USE: May to October. CONTACT: U.S. Fish and Wildlife Service, Browns Park National Wildlife Refuge (970) 365-3613. NOTE: Green River, Rafting and excellent spring fishing.
7.5' TOPOGRAPHIC MAP: Lodore School (CALL FIRST).

Map No.	Campground Name	Map Loc.	Fee	No. of Units	Max. Length	Elev.	Toilets	Water	Agency
3	**Browns Park State Wildlife Area**	A-1	0	Dispersed	Open	8,100'	Yes	Yes	Colorado Division of Wildlife

LOCATION: 41 mi. NW of Maybell on Hwy 318, 17 mi. N on Cty Rd. 10, 9 mi. W on Cty Rd 72 to fork, left 4 mi. to unit. 2,226 acres all units. FACILITIES: None. ACTIVITIES: Hunting, Fishing, Camping, Wildlife observation. OPEN FOR USE: Year Round.
CONTACT: Colorado Division of Wildlife, (970) 255-6100. NOTE: Two camping areas Wiggins and Beaver Creek. No. 4

Map No.	Campground Name	Map Loc.	Fee	No. of Units	Max. Length	Elev.	Toilets	Water	Agency
4	**Irish Canyon**	A-1	0	3	30'	6,000'	Yes	Yes	Bureau of Land Management

LOCATION: 1 mi W of Maybell on Hwy 40, turn right (NW) on Hwy 318 for about 45 mi to Cty Rd 10 N. Turn right (N) on Cty Rd 10 N for 8 mi to the site. FACILITIES: None. ACTIVITIES: Hunting, Hiking, Archaeological rock art viewing. OPEN FOR USE: Year round. CONTACT: Little Snake Resource Area (970) 826-5000. NOTE: Scenic, arid, canyon campsites - Capacity 18 people. 7.5' TOPOGRAPHIC MAP: Irish Canyon. (CALL FIRST).

Map No.	Campground Name	Map Loc.	Fee	No. of Units	Max. Length	Elev.	Toilets	Water	Agency
5	**Little Snake State Wildlife Area**	A-3	0	Dispersed	Open	6,900'	Yes	Yes	Colorado Division of Wildlife

LOCATION:17 mi N of Maybell on Cty Rd 19. Cty Rd 19 runs through property from this point. 4,860 acres. FACILITIES: None. ACTIVITIES: Camping, Hunting, Hiking, Wildlife observation. OPEN FOR USE: Camping prohibited except in self contained units and prohibited during big game season. CONTACT: Colorado Division of Wildlife, (970) 255-6100. 7.5' TOPOGRAPHIC MAP: The Nipple.

Map No.	Campground Name	Map Loc.	Fee	No. of Units	Max. Length	Elev.	Toilets	Water	Agency
6	**Piceance State Wildlife Area**	D-3	0		Open	6,000'	Yes	Yes	Colorado Division of Wildlife

LOCATION: 20 mi. W of Meeker on Hwy 64.9 mi. S on Cty Rd 5. FACILITIES: None. ACTIVITIES: Hunting, Fishing, Hiking, Wildlife observation. OPEN FOR USE: Year round. CONTACT: Colorado Division of Wildlife, (970) 255-6100. 7.5' TOPOGRAPHIC MAP: Barcus Creek Southeast. *Designated camping.*

Map No.	Campground Name	Map Loc.	Fee	No. of Units	Max. Length	Elev.	Toilets	Water	Agency
7	**Rio Blanco Lake State Wildlife Area**	C-3	0		Open	6,000'	Yes	Yes	Colorado Division of Wildlife

LOCATION: 20 mi. W of Meeker on Hwy 64 to State Property. 383 acres. FACILITIES: Boat ramp. ACTIVITIES: Hunting, Fishing, Power boating, Waterskiing, Wildlife observation. OPEN FOR USE: Year Round. CONTACT: Colorado Division Of Wildlife (970) 255-6100. NOTE: 120 acre Rio Blanco Lake - trout and warm water fishing. 7.5' TOPOGRAPHIC MAP: White River City. *Designated camping.*

Colorado Peaks over 14,000 feet elevation

Name	Elevation
Mt. Elbert	14,433 feet
Mt. Massive	14,421 feet
Mt. Harvard	14,420 feet
Blanca Peak	14,345 feet
La Plata Peak	14,336 feet
Uncompahgre Peak	14,309 feet
Crestone Peak	14,294 feet
Mt. Lincoln	14,286 feet
Grays Peak	14,270 feet
Mt. Antero	14,269 feet
Torreys Peak	14,267 feet
Quandary Peak	14,265 feet
Castle Peak	14,265 feet
Mt. Evans	14,264 feet
Longs Peak	14,255 feet
Mt. Wilson	14,246 feet
Mt. Cameron	14,239 feet
Mt. Shavano	14,229 feet
Mt. Princeton	14,197 feet
Mt. Belford	14,197 feet
Mt. Yale	14,196 feet
Crestone Needle	14,191 feet
Mt. Bross	14,172 feet
Kit Carson Mountain	14,165 feet
El Diente Peak	14,159 feet
Maroon Peak	14,156 feet
Tabernauche Peak	14,155 feet
Mt. Oxford	14,153 feet
Mt. Sneffels	14,150 feet
Mt. Democrat	14,148 feet
Capitol Peak	14,130 feet
Pikes Peak	14,110 feet
Snowmass Mountain	14,092 feet
Mt. Eolus	14,083 feet
Windom Peak	14,082 feet
Challenger Point	14,080 feet
Mt. Columbia	14,073 feet
Culebra Peak	14,069 feet
Missouri Mountain	14,067 feet
Humboldt Peak	14,064 feet
Mt. Bierstadt	14,060 feet
Sunlight Peak	14,059 feet
Handies Peak	14,048 feet
Mt. Lindsey	14,042 feet
Ellingwood Point	14,042 feet
Little Bear Peak	14,037 feet
Mt. Sherman	14,036 feet
Red Cloud Peak	14,034 feet
Pyramid Peak	14,018 feet
Wilson Peak	14,017 feet
Wetterhorn Peak	14,017 feet
San Luis Peak	14,014 feet
North Maroon Peak	14,014 feet
Mt. of the Holy Cross	14,005 feet
Huron Peak	14,005 feet
Sunshine Peak	14,001 feet

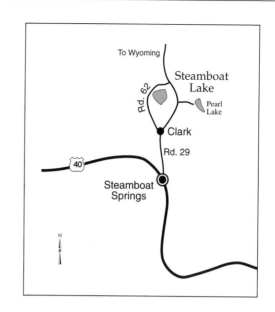

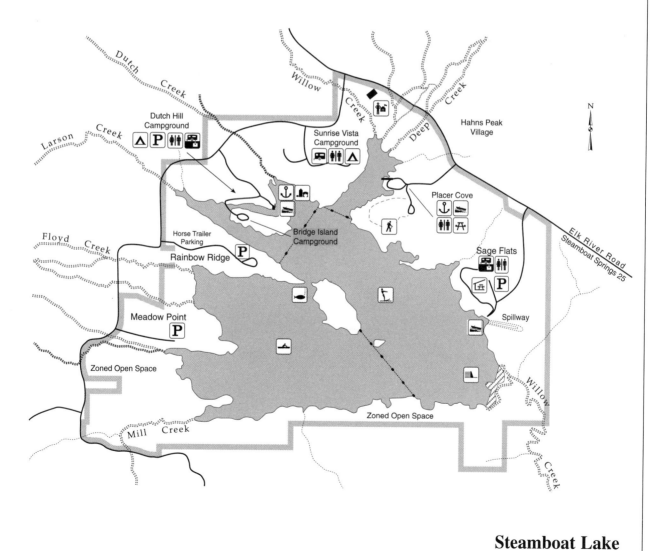

Steamboat Lake

See Page 12

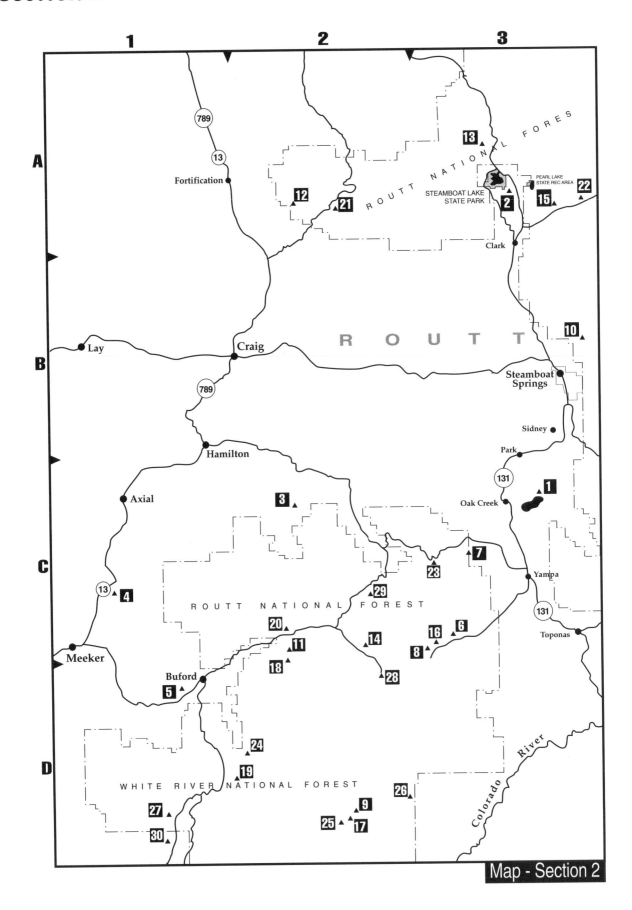

Map - Section 2

Stagecoach State Park

See text page 12

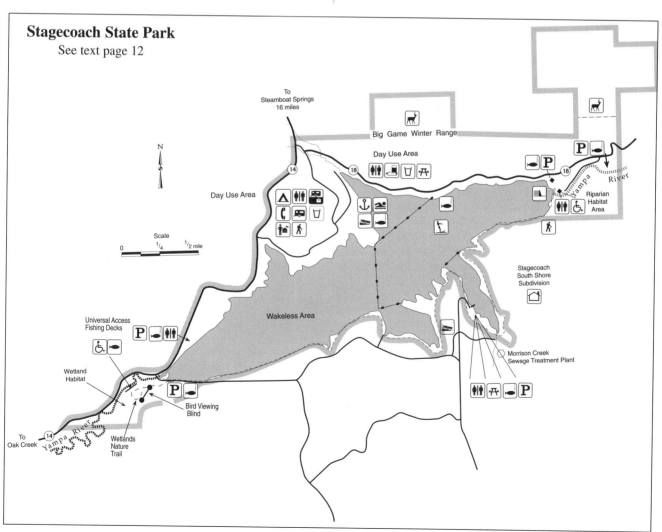

Map No.	Name	Map Loc.	Fee	No. of Units	Max. Length	Elev.	Toilets	Water	Agency
1	**Stagecoach State Park ®**	C-3	$	92	35'	7,210'	Yes	Yes	Colorado State Parks

Located approximately 16 miles south of Steamboat Springs on County Road 14. Stagecoach (775 acres) is nestled in the lower elevation of the river valley. Native grasses, shrubs and flowering plants are the dominant vegetation types in the park. Visitors enjoy views of Flattop Mountains to the southwest, and to the north, the cliff face of Blacktail Mountain.

Wagon wheels and ore cars are two symbols of the area's rich history. Stagecoaches traveled over Yellow Jacket Pass, now County Road 14, on their way to Oak Creek or Steamboat Springs. The fertile upper Yampa Valley attracted early ranchers, farmers and coal miners. Many of the reservoir's campgrounds and picnic areas are named after early coal mines and mining camps. The valley also attracted land developers, who visualized a resort community in the area.

Camping
The parks Junction City, Pinnacle, Harding Spur and McKinley campgrounds have a total of 92 campsites which can accommodate tents campers or trailers. Pull-through sites are located at Pinnacle and Junction City campgrounds. Junction City has electrical hookups. Only one camping unit per site is allowed. Campground users must have both a camping permit and park pass. Please display camping permit in the plastic holder at the campsite. A holding tank dump station is provided for your convenience. See map page 11.

Fishing
The reservoir is known for its fast growing, hard fighting rainbow trout, northern pike and the occasional brown or brook trout. Ice fishing permitted in winter months. Boat Ramp and Marina.

Other Activities
Picnicking, Water Skiing, Personal Watercraft, Boating, Hunting, Swimming and Hiking Trail.

For more information contact:
Stagecoach State Park
P.O. Box 98
Oak Creek, CO, 80467 (970) 736-2436

Map No.	Name	Map Loc.	Fee	No. of Units	Max. Length	Elev.	Toilets	Water	Agency
2	**Steamboat Lake/ Pearl Lake State Park ®**	A-3	$	222	35'	8,000'	Yes	Yes	Colorado State Parks

Located 27 miles north of Steamboat Springs on Routt County Road 129 (Elk River Road). Nestled in a valley at the foot of majestic Hahn's Peak, only a few miles west of the Continental Divide, Steamboat Lake State Recreation Area (508 acres land/190 acres lake) offers visitors one of the most beautiful settings in Colorado, no matter what the season. Routt National Forest is adjacent to the park, providing additional recreational opportunities, while the bright lights of Steamboat Springs are only 27 miles away for visitors who want an occasional night on the town.

Two sparkling man-made lakes-Steamboat and Pearl - are principle features of the 1550 acre park. Steamboat Lake (1553 acres) was completed in 1967 and filled in 1968. Pearl Lake (190 acres) was completed in 1962.

Camping
The park's Sunrise Vista, Dutch Hill and Pearl Lake campgrounds have a total of 222 campsites, which can accommodate tents and campers or trailers. There are some pull-through sites in each campground. Only one camping unit per site is allowed. Campground users must have both a camping permit and parks pass. Display the camping permit in the plastic holders at the campsites. A holding tank dump station is located at the Sage Flat Area for your convenience.

Fishing
The coves of Steamboat Lake are well known for their good-sized rainbow trout. Cutthroat trout dwell in Pearl Lake, where only fly and lure fishing is permitted. Ice fishing is allowed during winter months. Boat Ramp and Marina.

Other Activities
Picnicking, Water Sports, Hunting, and Nature Trail.

Handicapped Accessible:
Steamboat: Visitors center, restrooms, swimming, hunting, picnic tables, camping and fishing.
Pearl: Restrooms, picnic tables, camping and fishing. Some facilities accessible with assistance.

For information contact;
Steamboat Lake/Pearl Lake State Park
PO Box 750
Clark, CO 80428
(970) 879-3922

Map No.	Campground Name	Map Loc.	Fee	No. of Units	Max. Length	Elev.	Toilets	Water	Agency
3	**Indian Run State Wildlife Area**	C-2	0	Dispersed	Open	6,700'	Yes	Yes	Colorado Division of Wildlife

LOCATION: 12 mi. SE of Hamilton on Hwy 317, 6 mi. S on Cty Rd 67. (2,039 acres.). FACILITIES: None. ACTIVITIES: Fishing, Camping, Hunting, Hiking, Wildlife Observation. OPEN FOR USE: Year Round. CONTACT: Colorado Division of Wildlife (970) 255-6100. NOTE: On South Fork of Williams Fork. 7.5' TOPOGRAPHIC MAP: Pagoda.

Map No.	Campground Name	Map Loc.	Fee	No. of Units	Max. Length	Elev.	Toilets	Water	Agency
4	**Jensen State Wildlife Area**	C-1	0		Open	7,500'	Yes	Yes	Colorado Division of Wildlife

LOCATION: 9 mi NE of Meeker on Hwy 13, State Prop. Boundary at Hwy 13 and Cty Rd 30. (5,955 acres.) FACILITIES: None.ACTIVITIES: Hunting, Camping, Wildlife Observation. OPEN FOR USE: July 16 thru Nov. 30. CONTACT: Colorado Division of Wildlife (970) 255-6100. 7.5' TOPOGRAPHIC MAP: Nine Mile Gap. *Designated camping*.

Map No.	Campground Name	Map Loc.	Fee	No. of Units	Max. Length	Elev.	Toilets	Water	Agency
5	**Oak Ridge State Wildlife Area**	D-1	0	Dispersed	Open	6,995'	Yes	Yes	Colorado Division of Wildlife

LOCATION: 2 mi. NE of Meeker on Hwy 13, 18 mi. E on Cty Rd 8, N on unit access road. FACILITIES: Boat ramp, ACTIVITIES: Hunting, Fishing, Hiking, Wildlife Observation. OPEN FOR USE: July 16 through Nov. 30. CONTACT:Colorado Division of Wildlife (970) 878-4493. NOTE: Big Beaver Reservoir, White River - Cold water fishing. 7.5' TOPOGRAPHIC MAP: Big Beaver Reservoir.*Designated camping*.

Map No.	Campground Name	Map Loc.	Fee	No. of Units	Max. Length	Elev.	Toilets	Water	Agency
6	**Bear Lake**	C-3	$	29	60'	9,600'	Yes	Yes	Routt National Forest

LOCATION: 31 mi. SW of Steamboat on Hwy 131 to Yampa, 7 mi. SW on Cty Rd 7, 5-6 mi. SW on FDR 900. FACILITIES: Tables, Grills, Pets OK, ACTIVITIES: Hunting, Fishing, Hiking, Hand propelled Boating. OPEN FOR USE: June through mid-Sept. CONTACT: Yampa Ranger District (970) 638-4516. NOTE: Bear Reservoir. 7.5' TOPOGRAPHIC MAP: Orno Peak. *BEAR RIVER DISPERSED CAMPING:* Fee, 32 units, 60 feet max. length El. 9800' Mandall Lake TH. FDT 1121.

Map No.	Campground Name	Map Loc.	Fee	No. of Units	Max. Length	Elev.	Toilets	Water	Agency
7	**Chapman Reservoir**	C-3	$	12	40'	9,400'	Yes	Yes	Routt National Forest

LOCATION: S of Oak Creek 3 mi. N Hwy 131, W on Cty Rd 15/FDR 16, 8 mi. to FDR 940 1 mi. to Res. FACILITIES: Tables, Grills, Pets OK. ACTIVITIES: Hunting, Fishing. OPEN FOR USE: June through mid-October. CONTACT: Yampa Ranger District (970) 638-4516. NOTE: Near Flat Tops Wilderness. 7.5' TOPOGRAPHIC MAP: Sand Point.

Map No.	Campground Name	Map Loc.	Fee	No. of Units	Max. Length	Elev.	Toilets	Water	Agency
8	**Cold Springs**	C-3	$	5	40'	10,400'	Yes	Yes	Routt National Forest

LOCATION: 31 mi. SW of Steamboat Springs on Hwy 131 to Yampa, 7 mi. SW on Cty Rd 7, 8-9 mi. SW on FDR 900. FACILITIES: Boat ramp, Tables, Grills, Pets OK. ACTIVITIES: Fishing, Hiking. OPEN FOR USE: June through Oct. CONTACT: Yampa Ranger District (970) 638-4516. NOTE: Near Stillwater Reservoir. Trailhead to Flat Tops Wilderness. East Fork TH FDT 1119, 0.5 mi SW. 7.5' TOPOGRAPHIC MAP: Devils Causeway.

Map No.	Campground Name	Map Loc.	Fee	No. of Units	Max. Length	Elev.	Toilets	Water	Agency
9	Deep Lake	D-2	$	45	36'	10,460'	Yes	Yes	White River National Forest

LOCATION: 17 mi. E of Glenwood Springs on I-70 to Dotsero, 2 mi. N on Cty Rd. 301, 26-27 mi. NW on FDR 600. FACILITIES: Boat Ramp, Tables, Grills. ACTIVITIES: Hunting, Fishing, Hiking. OPEN FOR USE: July through late Oct. CONTACT: Eagle Ranger District (970) 328-6388. NOTE: On Deep Lake. 7.5' TOPOGRAPHIC MAP: Deep Lake.

Map No.	Campground Name	Map Loc.	Fee	No. of Units	Max. Length	Elev.	Toilets	Water	Agency
10	Dry Lake	B-3	$	8	20'	8,000'	Yes	Yes	Routt National Forest

LOCATION: 2 mi. N of Steamboat Springs on Strawberry Park Road, 2 mi. N on Cty Rd 36, 2 mi. E on FDR 60. FACILITIES: Tables, Grills, Pets OK. ACTIVITIES: Hunting, Hiking. OPEN FOR USE: Mid-July through late Oct. CONTACT: Hahns Peak/Bears Ears Ranger District (970) 879-1870. 7.5' TOPOGRAPHIC MAP: Rocky Peak.

Map No.	Campground Name	Map Loc.	Fee	No. of Units	Max. Length	Elev.	Toilets	Water	Agency
11	East Marvine	C-2	$	7	50'	8,500'	Yes	Yes	White River National Forest

LOCATION: 2 mi. E of Meeker on Hwy 13, 29 mi. NE on FDR 110. FACILITIES: Tables, Grills, Pets OK. ACTIVITIES: Fishing, Hiking Trails (Flat Tops Wilderness). OPEN FOR USE: Mid-May through mid-Nov. CONTACT: Blanco Ranger District (970) 878-4039. 7.5' TOPOGRAPHIC MAP: Lost Park. NOTE: E. Marvine TH, FDT 1822.

Map No.	Campground Name	Map Loc.	Fee	No. of Units	Max. Length	Elev.	Toilets	Water	Agency
12	Freeman Reservoir	A-2	$	17	22'	8,800'	Yes	Yes	Routt National Forest

LOCATION: 13 mi. NE of Craig on Hwy 13, 9 mi. NE on FDR 110. FACILITIES: Tables, Grills, Boat ramp, Pets OK. ACTIVITIES: Fishing, Hiking - Near trail #1144, 4-Wheel Drive Roads. OPEN FOR USE: Mid-June through mid-Nov. CONTACT: Hahns Peak/Bears Ears Ranger District (970) 879-1870. NOTE: On 14 acre Freeman Reservoir - Cold water fishing. 7.5' TOPOGRAPHIC MAP: Freeman Reservoir. ♿

Map No.	Campground Name	Map Loc.	Fee	No. of Units	Max. Length	Elev.	Toilets	Water	Agency
13	Hahns Peak Lake®	A-3	$	26	30'	8,500'	Yes	Yes	Routt National Forest

LOCATION: 28-29 mi. N of Steamboat Springs on Cty Rd 129, 2-3 mi. W on FDR 486. FACILITIES: Tables, Grills, Boat ramp, Pets OK. ACTIVITIES: Hunting, Fishing, Hiking, Boating. OPEN FOR USE: Mid-June through late Oct. CONTACT: Hahns Peak/Bears Ear Ranger District (970) 879-1870. NOTE: 38 acre lake (No motorized boats or rafts.) 7.5' TOPOGRAPHIC MAP: Hahns Peak. ♿

Map No.	Campground Name	Map Loc.	Fee	No. of Units	Max. Length	Elev.	Toilets	Water	Agency
14	Himes Peak	C-2	$	11	36'	9,000'	Yes	Yes	White River National Forest

LOCATION: 2 mi. E of Meeker on Hwy 13, 41 mi. E on Cty Rd 8, 5 mi. SE on FDR 205. FACILITIES: Tables, Grills, Pets OK. ACTIVITIES: Fishing, Trailhead (Flat Tops Wilderness). OPEN FOR USE: Late May through mid-Nov. CONTACT: Blanco Ranger District (970) 878-4039. NOTE: On North Fork White River. Big Fish/Boulder Lake, FDT 1819/2262. 7.5' TOPOGRAPHIC MAPS: Ripple Creek/Devils Causeway.

Map No.	Campground Name	Map Loc.	Fee	No. of Units	Max. Length	Elev.	Toilets	Water	Agency
15	**Hinman Park**	A-3	$	13	22'	7,600'	Yes	Yes	Routt National Forest

LOCATION:1-2 mi. NW of Steamboat Springs on Hwy 40, 16-17 mi. NE on Cty Rd 129, 4 mi. NE on FDR 400, 1/2 mi. SW on FDR 440. FACILITIES:Tables, Grills, Pets OK. ACTIVITIES: Hunting, Fishing, Hiking, Trails nearby (Mt. Zirkel Wilderness, Hinman Lake). OPEN FOR USE: June through mid-Nov. CONTACT: Hahns Peak/Bears Ears Ranger District (970) 879-1870. NOTE: Hinman Creek and Elk River join at campground. FDT 1100A. 7.5' TOPOGRAPHIC MAP: Farwell Mountain.

Map No.	Campground Name	Map Loc.	Fee	No. of Units	Max. Length	Elev.	Toilets	Water	Agency
16	**Horseshoe**	C-3	$	7	40'	10,000'	Yes	Yes	Routt National Forest

LOCATION: 7 mi. SW of Yampa on Cty Rd 7, 8-9 mi. SW on FDR 900. FACILITIES: Tables, Grills, Pets OK. ACTIVITIES: Hunting, Fishing, Hiking Trails. OPEN FOR USE: Mid-June through October. CONTACT: Yampa Ranger District (970) 638-4516. NOTE: Near Stillwater Reservoir. 7.5' TOPOGRAPHIC MAP: Orno Peak.

Map No.	Campground Name	Map Loc.	Fee	No. of Units	Max. Length	Elev.	Toilets	Water	Agency
17	**Klines Folly**	D-2	$	4	20'	10,750'	Yes	No	White River National Forest

LOCATION:17 mi. E of Glenwood Springs on I-70, 2 mi. N on Cty Rd 301, 24-25 mi. NW on FDR 600. FACILITIES: Tables, Grills, Pets OK. ACTIVITIES: Fishing. OPEN FOR USE: Mid-June through October. CONTACT: Eagle Ranger District (970) 328-6388. NOTE: Near Heart Lake and Deep Creek. 7.5' TOPOGRAPHIC MAP: Deep Lake.

Map No.	Campground Name	Map Loc.	Fee	No. of Units	Max. Length	Elev.	Toilets	Water	Agency
18	**Marvine**	C-2	$	18	60'	8,500'	Yes	Yes	White River National Forest

LOCATION: 2 mi. E of Meeker on Hwy 13, 29 mi. E on Cty Rd 8, 4-5 mi. SE on Cty Rd 12. FACILITIES: Tables, Grills, Pets OK. ACTIVITIES: Hunting, Fishing, Trailhead (Marvine Lakes and Flat Tops Wilderness). OPEN FOR USE: Late May through mid-Nov. CONTACT: Blanco Ranger District (970) 878-4039. 7.5' TOPOGRAPHIC MAP: Lost Park.

Map No.	Campground Name	Map Loc.	Fee	No. of Units	Max. Length	Elev.	Toilets	Water	Agency
19	**Meadow Lake**	D-1	$	10	16'	9,600'	Yes	Yes	White River National Forest

LOCATION: 9 mi. NW of New Castle on Cty Rd 245, 20-21 mi. N on FDR 245, 3-4 mi. E on FDR 601, left on FDR 823 3 mi. to CG. FACILITIES: Tables, Grills, Boat Dock, Pets OK. ACTIVITIES: Hunting, Fishing, Hiking, 4-Wheeling. OPEN FOR USE: Mid-June through mid-Nov. CONTACT: Rifle Ranger District (970) 625-2371. NOTE: Near Meadow Lake. 7.5' TOPOGRAPHIC MAP: Meadow Creek Lake.

Map No.	Campground Name	Map Loc.	Fee	No. of Units	Max. Length	Elev.	Toilets	Water	Agency
20	**North Fork®**	C-2	$	40	60'	8,000'	Yes	Yes	White River National Forest

LOCATION : 2 mi. E of Meeker on Hwy 13, 31 mi. E on Cty Rd 8. FACILITIES: Tables (Groups to 50 people), Grills, Pets OK. ACTIVITIES: Fishing, Camping, Hiking. OPEN FOR USE: Mid-May through mid-Nov. CONTACT: Blanco Ranger District (970) 878-4039. NOTE: On North Fork White River. 7.5' TOPOGRAPHIC MAP: Lost Park.

Map No.	Campground Name	Map Loc.	Fee	No. of Units	Max. Length	Elev.	Toilets	Water	Agency
21	**Sawmill Creek**	A-2	$	6	21'	9,000'	Yes	No	Routt National Forest

LOCATION: 13 mi. NE of Craig on Hwy 13, 12-13 mi. NE on FDR 110. FACILITIES: Tables, Grills, Pets OK. ACTIVITIES: Hunting, Fishing, Hiking - Near trail #1144. OPEN FOR USE: Mid-June through mid-Nov. CONTACT: Hahns Peak/Bears Ears Ranger District (970) 879-1870. NOTE: A 3 mile 4-wheel drive to Angel Spring. 7.5' TOPOGRAPHIC MAP: Buck Point.

Map No.	Campground Name	Map Loc.	Fee	No. of Units	Max. Length	Elev.	Toilets	Water	Agency
22	**Seedhouse**	A-3	0	25	25'	8,000'	Yes	Yes	Routt National Forest

LOCATION: NW of Steamboat Springs on Hwy 40 to Cty Rd 129, N 17 mi. to FDR 400, 7 mi. E. FACILITIES: Tables, Grills. ACTIVITIES: Hiking, Fishing. OPEN FOR USE: June through mid-Nov. CONTACT: Hahns Peak/Bears Ears Ranger District (970) 879-1870. NOTE: On Middle Fork Elk River - Near Trailhead to Mount Zirkel Wilderness. FDT 1101. *Note: Group Campground reopened 2001 ®.*

Map No.	Campground Name	Map Loc.	Fee	No. of Units	Max. Length	Elev.	Toilets	Water	Agency
23	**Sheriff Reservoir**	C-3	$	5	20'	9,800'	Yes	Yes	Routt National Forest

LOCATION: 3 mi. S of Oak Creek on Hwy 131, W on Cty Rd 15/FDR 16, 10 mi., S on FDR 959, 2.5 mi. to Res. FACILITIES: Tables, Grills. ACTIVITIES: Hiking, Fishing. OPEN FOR USE: June through mid-Nov. CONTACT: Yampa Ranger District (970) 638-4516. NOTE: Trailhead to Flat Tops Wilderness. 7.5' TOPOGRAPHIC MAP: Dunkley Pass.

Map No.	Campground Name	Map Loc.	Fee	No. of Units	Max. Length	Elev.	Toilets	Water	Agency
24	**South Fork**	D-2	$	16	60'	8,000'	Yes	Yes	White River National Forest

LOCATION: 2 mi. E of Meeker on Hwy 13, 18 mi. E on Cty Rd 8, 9-10 mi. S on Cty Rd 10. FACILITIES: Tables, Grills, some Barrier Free Access, Pets OK. ACTIVITIES: Fishing, Hiking (FDT 1827 to Flat Tops Wilderness). OPEN FOR USE: Mid-May through mid-Nov. CONTACT: Blanco Ranger District (970) 878-4039. 7.5' TOPOGRAPHIC MAP: Meadow Creek Lake.

Map No.	Campground Name	Map Loc.	Fee	No. of Units	Max. Length	Elev.	Toilets	Water	Agency
25	**Supply Basin**	D-2	$	6	20'	10,750'	Yes	Yes	White River National Forest

LOCATION:17 mi. E of Glenwood Springs on I-70, 2 mi. N on Cty Rd 301, 25-26 mi. NW on FDR 600. FACILITIES: Tables, Grills, Trails. ACTIVITIES: Hunting, Fishing, Hiking, Roads nearby great for 4 WD and Mtn Biking. OPEN FOR USE: July through late Oct.. CONTACT: Eagle Ranger District (970) 328-6388. NOTE: Near Heart Lake and Deep Creek. 7.5' TOPOGRAPHIC MAP: Deep Lake.

Map No.	Campground Name	Map Loc.	Fee	No. of Units	Max. Length	Elev.	Toilets	Water	Agency
26	**Sweetwater Lake**	D-2	$	10	20'	7,700'	Yes	Yes	White River National Forest

LOCATION: 18 mi. E of Glenwood Springs to Dotsero on I-70, 7 mi. N on Cty Rd 37, 10 mi. NW on Cty Rd 17, S on FDR 607. FACILITIES: Tables, Grills, Boat ramp, Trails. ACTIVITIES: Hunting, Fishing, Hiking. OPEN FOR USE: May through mid-Nov. CONTACT: Eagle Ranger District (970) 328-6388. NOTE: 80 acre lake. Trailhead FDT's 1832, 1855, 1856, 1866, 2042 to Flat Tops Wilderness. 7.5' TOPOGRAPHIC MAP: Sweetwater Lake.

Map No.	Campground Name	Map Loc.	Fee	No. of Units	Max. Length	Elev.	Toilets	Water	Agency
27	**Three Forks**	D-1	$	4	16'	7,600'	Yes	No	White River National Forest

LOCATION: 3 mi. N of Rifle on Hwy 13, 10 mi. NE on Hwy 325 through Rifle State Park on Cty Rd 217, 5 mi. on gravel road to CG. ACTIVITIES: Rock Climbing, Hunting, Fishing, Hiking. OPEN FOR USE: Mid June through mid Nov. CONTACT: Rifle Ranger District (970) 625-2371. 7.5' TOPOGRAPHIC MAP: Triangle Park. ***Construction 2001- call first.***

Map No.	Campground Name	Map Loc.	Fee	No. of Units	Max. Length	Elev.	Toilets	Water	Agency
28	**Trappers Lake**	D-2	$		36'	9,900'	Yes	Yes	White River National Forest
a.	**Bucks**			10					
b.	**Cutthroat**			14	*See Map page 18*				
c.	**Shepards Rim** (+Overflow)			20					
d.	**Trapline**			13					

LOCATION: 2 mi. E of Meeker on Hwy 13, 41 mi. E on Cty Rd 8, 10 mi. SE on FDR 205. FACILITIES: Tables, Grills, Dump Station, Firewood must be gathered, Pets OK. ACTIVITIES: Hunting, Fishing, Hiking Trails, Horse Trails. OPEN FOR USE: Mid-June through mid Nov. CONTACT: Blanco Ranger District (970) 878-4039. NOTE: 300 acre lake, artificial lures and flies only, no motorized boats. Wall Lake and Scott Bay Trailheads nearby, Carhart FDT 1815, Stillwater FDT 1814. 7.5' TOPOGRAPHIC MAPS: Trappers Lake, Devils Causeway.

Map No.	Campground Name	Map Loc.	Fee	No. of Units	Max. Length	Elev.	Toilets	Water	Agency
29	**Vaughn Lake**	C-2	$	6	36'	9,500'	Yes	No	Routt National Forest

LOCATION: S of Oak Creek 5-6 mi., W on FDR 16 28-30 mi. FACILITIES: Tables, Grills, Boat ramp, Pets OK on leash. ACTIVITIES: Hunting, Fishing, Boating, Hiking. OPEN FOR USE: Mid-June through mid-Nov. CONTACT: Yampa Ranger District (970) 638-4516. 7.5' TOPOGRAPHIC MAP: Pagoda Peak.

Map No.	Campground Name	Map Loc.	Fee	No. of Units	Max. Length	Elev.	Toilets	Water	Agency
30	**Blue Spruce**	D-1	$	30	50'	7,250'	Yes	Yes	City of Rifle

LOCATION: 3 mi. N of Rifle on Hwy 13, 10 mi. NE on Hwy 325 to Rifle Falls State Park, N 2 mi. FACILITIES: Water available at fish hatchery. ACTIVITIES: Hiking, Rock Climbing. OPEN FOR USE: May 15 through Sept. CONTACT: Rifle Mountain Park (970) 625-6221. 7.5' TOPOGRAPHIC MAP: Triangle Park.

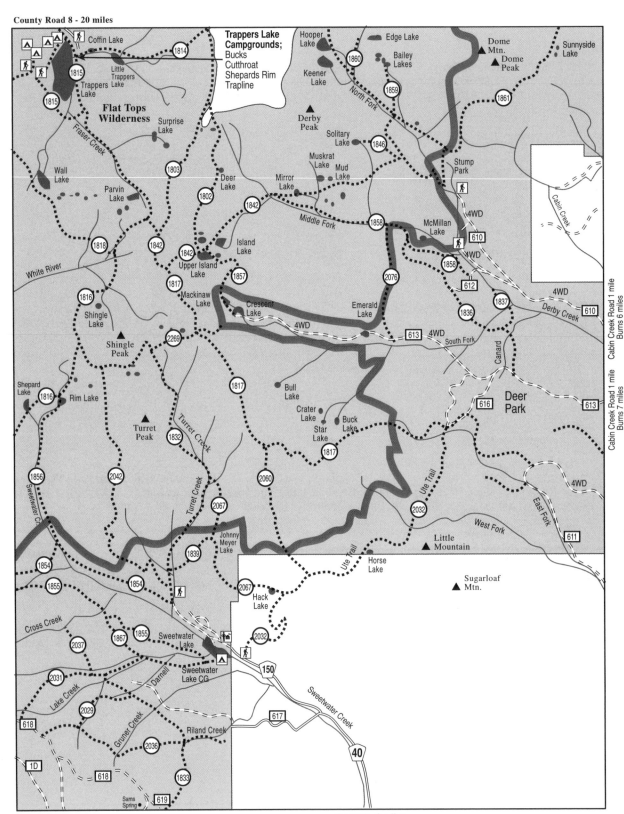

County Road 8 - 20 miles

Coffin Lake

Trappers Lake Campgrounds;
Bucks
Cutthroat
Shepards Rim
Trapline

Hooper Lake

Edge Lake

Dome Mtn.

Dome Peak

Sunnyside Lake

1814

1815

1815

Little Trappers Lake

Trappers Lake

Flat Tops Wilderness

1860

Bailey Lakes

Keener Lake

1859

1861

Derby Peak

Surprise Lake

Solitary Lake

1846

Stump Park

1803

Wall Lake

Deer Lake

Muskrat Lake

Mud Lake

Mirror Lake

North Fork

Parvin Lake

1802

1842

Middle Fork

1858

McMillan Lake

4WD

610

Cabin Creek

1818

1842

1842

Island Lake

1858

4WD

612

1817

Upper Island Lake

1857

2076

4WD

1836

1837

Derby Creek

610

1816

Mackinaw Lake

Crescent Lake

Emerald Lake

613

4WD

South Fork

Canard

4WD

Shingle Lake

2269

4WD

Deer Park

616

613

Shingle Peak

1817

Bull Lake

Shepard Lake

1816

Rim Lake

Crater Lake

Buck Lake

Star Lake

1817

White River

Fraser Creek

Turret Peak

1832

Turret Creek

2042

2060

Ute Trail

4WD

1856

Sweetwater Cr.

2067

2032

West Fork

East Fork

611

Little Mountain

Johnny Meyer Lake

1839

Ute Trail

Horse Lake

Sugarloaf Mtn.

1854

2067

Hack Lake

1855

1854

Cross Creek

2037

1867

1855

Sweetwater Lake

2032

150

2031

Darnell

Sweetwater Lake CG

2029

Lake Creek

618

Gruner Creek

Riland Creek

Sweetwater Creek

617

40

2036

1D

618

1833

Sams Spring

619

Cabin Creek Road 1 mile
Burns 6 miles

Cabin Creek Road 1 mile
Burns 7 miles

Gypsum - 9 miles

Trappers Lake Area

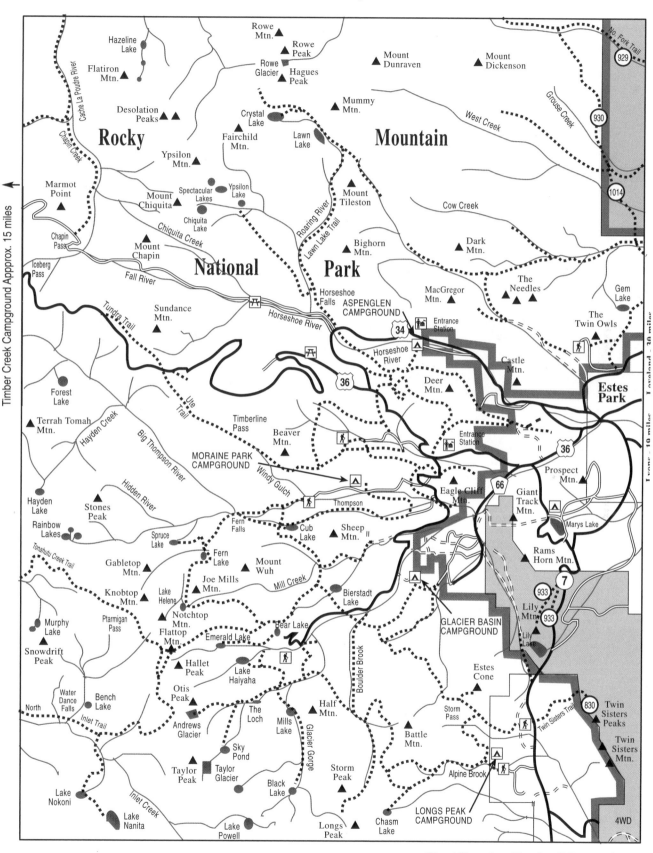

See text page 22

**East Portion Rocky Mountain
National Park**

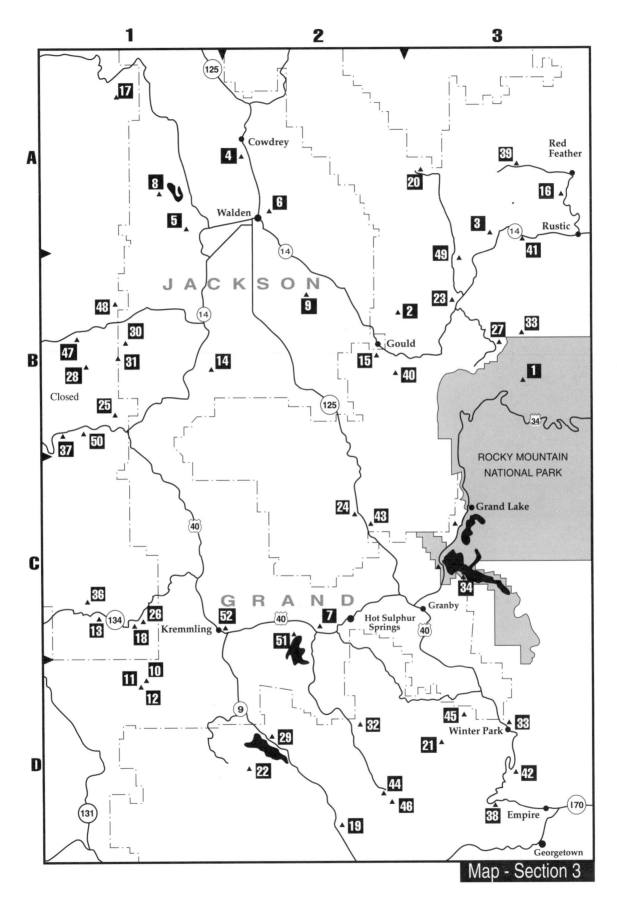

Map - Section 3

Section 3

Map No.	Campground Name	Map Loc.	Fee	No. of Units	RV's	Elev.	Toilets	Water	Miles from Estes Park
1	**Rocky Mountain National Park**	B-3	$	577	30'	8,600' +	Yes	Yes	National Parks Service

Rocky Mountain National Park is in north central Colorado. From the east it can be reached by automobile on US. 34, U.S. 36 and Colorado 7, and from the west by U.S. 40. The nearest major rail, air and bus terminals are at Denver, 65 miles from Estes Park, and at Cheyenne, 91 miles to the northeast.

The snow-mantled peaks of Rocky Mountain National Park rise above verdant subalpine valleys and glistening lakes. One third of the park is above tree line, and here alpine tundra predominates - a major reason these peaks and valleys have been set aside as a national park. This area was first traversed by French fur traders. In 1859 Joel Estes and his son, Milton, rode into the valley that bears their name. Few others settled in this rugged country and about 1909 Enos Mills, a naturalist, writer and conservationist began to campaign for preservation of this pristine area. Mill's campaign succeeded, and the area then became Rocky Mountain National Park in 1915. A feature of the park is the marked differences found with the changing elevation. At lower levels in the foothills and montane life zone, open stands of ponderosa pine and juniper grow on the slopes facing the sun; on cooler north slopes are Douglas-fir. Gracing the stream sides are blue spruces intermixed with dense stands of lodgepole pine. Here and there appear groves of aspen. Wildflowers dot meadows and glades. Above 9,000 feet forests of Englemann spruce and subalpine fir take over in the subalpine life zone. Openings in these cool, dark forests produce wildflower gardens of rare beauty and luxuriance, where the blue Colorado columbine reigns. At the upper edges of this zone, the trees are twisted, grotesque and hug the ground. Then the trees disappear and you are in the alpine tundra -a harsh, fragile world. Here, more than one-quarter of the plants you will see can also be found in the Arctic. From the valleys to its mountain-tops, Rocky Mountain National Park encompasses many worlds. We invite you to explore them.

Accommodations
There are no motels or hotels in the park.

Handicap
This backcountry camping area is specially designed for the disabled. It will accommodate ten campers and a maximum of five wheelchair users. Call (970) 586-1206

Camping
Camping limited park wide to 7 days, June through September; Longs Peak Campground (tents only) has a 3 day limit. The campgrounds fill early each day in the summer. There are no showers or recreation vehicle connections in any campground. Dump stations are at Moraine Park, Glacier Basin, and Timber Creek. Telephones are at Moraine Park, Glacier Basin, Timber Creek and Aspenglen. Wood fires are permitted only in fire grates in the campgrounds and picnic areas. Permits for fires outside these areas are required. Wood gathering is prohibited; firewood bundles are sold at the campgrounds. Pets are permitted in the campgrounds on a leash shorter than 6 feet. (2 meters) Complete services are available at Estes Park, east of the park, and at Grand Lake to the west. Reservations for Moraine Park and Glacier Basin family camp-

ing, and Glacier Basin Group Areas are available during the summer. Reservations may be made as early as 8 weeks in advance. For backcountry camping and bivouac climbing permits and information, call (970) 586-1206

Regulations: A permit is required for all overnight stays in the backcountry. The free permits may be obtained in advance or upon arrival at park headquarters, the West Unit Office, and at most ranger stations. Backcountry camping is limited to seven nights between May and September and 15 more nights during the remainder of the year. Backcountry camping is allowed in designated campsites only, or cross-country zones by permit only. No pets are permitted in the backcountry.

Fishing
In the mountain streams and lakes of Rocky Mountain National Park are four species of trout: German brown, rainbow, brook and cutthroat. These cold waters may not produce large fish, but you will enjoy the superb mountain scenery as you fish. Remember, you must have a valid Colorado fishing license. Use of live bait is prohibited except under certain special conditions. Review the special fishing regulations at park headquarters or at the nearest park ranger station before you fish. Fishing is not permitted in Bear Lake at any time. Other lakes and streams in the park are under restrictions to protect the Colorado River greenback cutthroat that is being reintroduced to its native habitat. Check with a ranger for details.

Climbing
For the climber, Rocky Mountain National Park offers a variety of challenging ascents throughout the year. A park concessionaire operates a technical climbing school and guide service that provides climbing and mountaineering instruction. For more information, contact park headquarters.
It is important to be familiar with the park's climbing regulations before you begin. These regulations have been established to provide as safe and satisfactory a situation for climbers as possible. Study them and check with a park ranger if you have any questions. Permits are not required for day hiking.

Technical climbs involving only day long excursions do not require registration either at the trailhead or in advance, but registration is always required for overnight bivouacs. It is your responsibility, however to leave details about your destination with someone who can report your absence if you happen to be overdue. For those who are not technical climbers but would like the experience of reaching a mountain top, Longs Peak is the answer. In July and August, and most of September, the Keyhole can be negotiated without technical climbing equipment. The North and East faces are technical climbing routes.

Hiking
Rocky Mountain is a park for hikers. More than 355 miles of trails provide access to the remote sections of the park so you can get away from the crowds and savor the streams, meadows, and mountains. For detailed information on elevations,

lakes, and hiking trails, purchase a U.S. Geological Survey topographic map or *The Best of Rocky Mountain National Park Trails Guide*. (Outdoor Books & Maps -- ISBN 0-930657-39-X). Because of the great numbers of people in the park during the summer, some trails are heavily used. If you wish to avoid this congestion, ask a ranger to suggest lightly used trails.
See map page 19.

Map No.	Campground Name	Map Loc.	Fee	No. of Units	RV's	Elev.	Toilets	Water	Miles from Estes Park
a	**Moraine Park ®**	B-3	$	247	Yes	8,150'	Yes	Yes	5.5

LOCATION: 5.5 miles from Estes Park. FACILITIES: Ranger Station, Dump Station, Public Telephone, Firewood, Ice, Bottled Water. Stay limit 7 days, no hook-ups or showers. ACTIVITIES: Campfire Talks, Horseback Riding, Hiking-Located east of Fern Lake and Cub Lake trailheads. Nature Trail, west of Moraine Park Museum.

Map No.	Campground Name	Map Loc.	Fee	No. of Units	RV's	Elev.	Toilets	Water	Miles from Estes Park
b	**Glacier Basin ®**	B-2	$	150	Yes	8,600'	Yes	Yes	9.0

LOCATION: 9.0 miles from Estes Park. FACILITIES: Ranger Station, Public Telephones, Firewood/Ice/Bottled Water. Stay limit 7 days, no hook-ups or showers. ACTIVITIES: Campfire Talks, Hiking-located northeast of Bierstadt, Spraugue Lake, Glacier Gorge Junction and Bear Lake Trailheads. Bear Lake is a self guide nature trail that is handicapped accessible.

Map No.	Campground Name	Map Loc.	Fee	No. of Units	RV's	Elev.	Toilets	Water	Miles from Estes Park
c	**Aspenglen**	B-2	$	54	Yes	8,230'	Yes	Yes	5.0

LOCATION: 5.0 mi from Estes Park. FACILITIES: Ranger Station, Public Telephone, Firewood/Ice/Bottled Water. Stay limit 7 days, no hook-ups or showers. ACTIVITIES: Campfire Talks, Hiking - located near several trails, Just south of Fall River Entrance Station.

Map No.	Campground Name	Map Loc.	Fee	No. of Units	RV's	Elev.	Toilets	Water	Miles from Estes Park
d	**Timber Creek**	B-2	$	100	Yes	8,900'	Yes	Yes	36.5

LOCATION: 36.5 mi from Estes Park. FACILITIES: Ranger Station, Dump Station, Public Telephone, Firewood, Ice, Bottled Water. Stay limit 7 days, no hook-ups or showers. ACTIVITIES: Hiking - Near Timber Lake, Colorado River, Red Mountain Trails. 1/2 mi N of Bowen/Baker Trailhead. 7 miles N of Grand Lake.

Map No.	Campground Name	Map Loc.	Fee	No. of Units	RV's	Elev.	Toilets	Water	Miles from Estes Park
e	**Longs Peak**	B-2	$	26	No	9,400'	Yes	Yes	11.0

LOCATION: 11.0 mi from Estes Park. FACILITIES: Ranger Station, Firewood/Ice/Bottled Water. Stay limit 3 days, no hook-ups or showers. ACTIVITIES: Campfire Talks, Hiking - Near Longs Peak Trailhead.

Map No.	Campground Name	Map Loc.	Fee	No. of Units	RV's	Elev.	Toilets	Water	Miles from Estes Park
f	**Glacier Basin Group ®**	B-2	$	15	No	8,600'	Yes	Yes	9.0

LOCATION: 9.0 mi from Estes Park. FACILITIES: Ranger Station, Public Telephone, Firewood/Ice/Bottled Water. Stay limit 7 days, no hook-ups or showers. RESERVATION PERIOD: 6/2-9/4.

GENERAL INFORMATION:
® = Reservations required during summer months. First-come, first-served if not on reservation system.
Individual sites = 6 people/1 vehicle. Group sites size = 10-50 people.

Section 3

Map No.	Campground Name	Map Loc.	Fee	No. of Units	Max. Length	Elev.	Toilets	Water	Agency
2	**Colorado State Forest ®**	B-2	$	105	35'	8-10,000'	Yes	Yes	Colorado Division of Parks

The Colorado State Forest is located 20 miles east of Walden on Highway 14. Within the boundaries of the Colorado State Forest lies 70,000 acres of the great outdoors as it was meant to he. The State Forest is high country, ranging in elevation form 8,500 to 12,500 feet, visitors may find they need time to acclimate. Sunburn is possible in the high, thin, cool air and until mid-summer mosquito repellent is necessary. The park stretches along the west side of the Medicine Bow Mountains and into the north end of the Never Summer Range. From Ft. Collins, visitors can take Highway 14 over Cameron Pass, a 75 mile drive. From Denver, the route leads over Berthoud and Willow Creek Passes to Walden, a 150 mile trip.

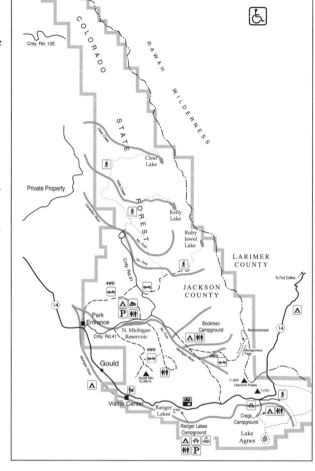

Camping
Ranger Lakes, The Crags, North Michigan Reservoir and the Bochman campgrounds have 105 campsites which can accommodate tents, trailers or pickup campers. Backcountry camping is allowed at various locations throughout the area and at Ruby Jewel, Kelly, Clear and American lakes. Minimum impact camping techniques are recommended. **No camping is allowed at Lake Agnes.** Campground users must have both a camping permit and a vehicle pass and must camp only in designated campsites. Before camping in the backcountry, campers should check with a ranger or at the park office for information. A dump station is located in the Ranger Lakes parking lot.

Fishing
Brook, brown, native, rainbow and golden trout are catchable. In North Michigan Reservoir and alpine lakes, only artificial fly and lure fishing is permitted.

Other Activities
Boating, Hiking, Horseback Riding, Trail bikes,4-Wheeling and Mountain Biki, backpacking.

Rustic Primitive cabins are available on a rental basis at No. Michigan Reservoir and at Lake Agnes Trailhead. Call 1-800 (678-2267) to reserve a cabin.

Daily Fee/Annual Pass
For more information Contact: Colorado State Forest , Star Route Box 91, Walden, CO 80408, (970) 723-8366.

Map No.	Campground Name	Map Loc.	Fee	No. of Units	Max. Length	Elev.	Toilets	Water	Agency
3	**Bliss State Wildlife Area**	A-3	0	Dispersed	Open	7,800'	Yes	No	Colorado Division of Wildlife

LOCATION: 5 mi N of LaPorte on Hwy 287, 41 mi W on Hwy 14. (352 acres.) FACILITIES: None. ACTIVITIES: Hunting, Fishing, Wildlife observation. OPEN FOR USE: Year Round. CONTACT: Colorado Division of Wildlife NE Region (970) 472-4300. NOTE: *Near Poudre River.* 7.5' TOPOGRAPHIC MAP: Boston Peak.

Map No.	Campground Name	Map Loc.	Fee	No. of Units	Max. Length	Elev.	Toilets	Water	Agency
4	**Cowdrey Lake State Wildlife Area**	A-2	0	Dispersed	18'	7,900'	Yes	No	Colorado Division of Wildlife

LOCATION: 2 mi S of Cowdrey on Hwy 125 or 7-8 mi N of Walden, W side of road. (280 acres land/80 acres water.) FACILITIES: Boat ramp, Dispersed sites, Pets OK. ACTIVITIES: Hunting, Fishing, Camping, Wildlife Observation. OPEN FOR USE: Year Round. CONTACT: Colorado Division of Wildlife (970) 472-4300. 7.5' TOPOGRAPHIC MAP: Cowdrey.

Map No.	Campground Name	Map Loc.	Fee	No. of Units	Max. Length	Elev.	Toilets	Water	Agency
5	**Delany Butte State Wildlife Area**	A-1	0	Dispersed	18'	8,300'	Yes	No	Colorado Division of Wildlife

LOCATION:1/2 mi W of Walden on Hwy 14 to County Rd 12, 5.3 mi W to County Rd 18, 4-5 mi W on Cty Rd 18, 1 mi N on Cty Rd 5. (2,620 acres.) FACILITIES: Boat ramp, Shade Shelters, Primitive Sites, (3 lakes). ACTIVITIES: Hunting, Fishing, Wildlife Observation. OPEN FOR USE: Year Round. CONTACT: Colorado Division of Wildlife NE Region (970) 472-4300. *Artificial flies and lures only.*

Map No.	Campground Name	Map Loc.	Fee	No. of Units	Max. Length	Elev.	Toilets	Water	Agency
6	**Diamond "J" State Wildlife Area**	A-2	0	20	22'	8,100'	Yes	No	Colorado Division of Wildlife

LOCATION: Parking areas are found 1, 2, and 4 mi N of Walden on Hwy 125. FACILITIES: Restrooms. (3,129 land acres/10 miles river.) ACTIVITIES: Hunting, Fishing, Picnic, Wildlife Observation. OPEN FOR USE: Mid-June thru mid-Nov. CONTACT: Colorado Division of Wildlife NE Region (970) 484-2836 (CALL FIRST). NOTE: Operated by City of Walden (970) 723-4344 PO Box 489, Walden, CO. 7.5' TOPOGRAPHIC MAP: Cowdrey.

Map No.	Campground Name	Map Loc.	Fee	No. of Units	Max. Length	Elev.	Toilets	Water	Agency
7	**Hot Sulphur Springs State Wildlife Area**	C-2	0	Dispersed	Open	7,500'	Yes	No	Colorado Division of Wildlife

LOCATION: 3 mi W of Hot Sulphur Springs on Hwy 40 to Cty Rd 50, at E end of bridge 2 mi S. FACILITIES: None. ACTIVITIES: Hunting, Fishing, Hiking, Snowmobiling, Wildlife Observation. OPEN FOR USE: Year Round. CONTACT: (970) 472-4300, Colorado Division of Wildlife NE Region. NOTE: On Colorado River 1.5 miles of open river. Camping in Beaver Creek and Lone Buck Units. 7.5' TOPOGRAPHIC MAP: Hot Sulphur Springs.

Map No.	Campground Name	Map Loc.	Fee	No. of Units	Max. Length	Elev.	Toilets	Water	Agency
8	**Lake John State Wildlife area**	A-1	$	---	18'	7,800'	Yes	Yes	Colorado Division of Wildlife

LOCATION: 1/2 mi W of Walden on Hwy 14, 8 mi W on Cty Rd 12, 7 mi N on Cty Rd. 7. (565 acres water/282 acres land.)FACILITIES: Boat ramp, Shade Shelters, Pets OK. ACTIVITIES: Hunting, Fishing, Picnic, Wildlife Observation. OPEN FOR USE: Year Round. CONTACT: Colorado Division of Wildlife NE Region (970) 472-4300. NOTE: Privately operated campground on north side of lake. 7.5' TOPOGRAPHIC MAP: Lake John.

Map No.	Campground Name	Map Loc.	Fee	No. of Units	Max. Length	Elev.	Toilets	Water	Agency
9	**Owl Mountain State Wildlife Area**	B-2	0	Dispersed	Open	8,200'	Yes	No	Colorado Division of Wildlife

LOCATION:13 mi SE of Walden on Hwy 14, 6 mi SW on Cty Rd 25. (920 acres.) FACILITIES: None. ACTIVITIES: Wildlife Observation, Hunting, Trapping. OPEN FOR USE: Year Round. CONTACT: Colorado Division of Wildlife NE Region (CALL FIRST) (970) 472-4300. 7.5' TOPOGRAPHIC MAP: Owl Ridge.

Map No.	Campground Name	Map Loc.	Fee	No. of Units	Max. Length	Elev.	Toilets	Water	Agency
10	**Pumphouse**	D-1	0	14	30'	7,000'	Yes	Yes	Bureau of Land Management

LOCATION:1 mi S from Kremmling on Hwy 9, SW on Trough Rd for approx. 15 mi, follow signs to river. FACILITIES: Tables, Disabled Accessible Toilets, Fire Rings. ACTIVITIES: River Running, Mtn. Biking, Hiking, Fishing. OPEN FOR USE: April 1 thru Oct.30. CONTACT: Little Snake Resource Area (970) 826-5000. *NOTE: River access for rafting Colorado River. Capacity 84 people.* 7.5' TOPOGRAPHIC MAP: Radium.

Section 3

Map No.	Campground Name	Map Loc.	Fee	No. of Units	Max. Length	Elev.	Toilets	Water	Agency
11	**Radium State Wildlife Area**	D-1	0	Dispersed	Open	7,000'	Yes	No	Colorado Division of Wildlife

LOCATION: 2-3 mi S of Kremmling on Hwy 9 to Cty Rd 1 (aka Trough Rd) to State Bridge, 12 mi SW to property. (4,426 acres.) FACILITIES: None. ACTIVITIES: Hunting, Fishing, Rock Climbing, Snowmobiling, Wildlife Observation. OPEN FOR USE: Year Round. CONTACT: Colo. Div. of Wildlife, NW Division (970) 255-6100.
NOTE: On Colorado River. 7.5' TOPOGRAPHIC MAP: Radium (CALL FIRST).

Map No.	Campground Name	Map Loc.	Fee	No. of Units	Max. Length	Elev.	Toilets	Water	Agency
12	**Radium (Riverine)**	D-1	0	2	30'	7,000'	Yes	Yes	Bureau of Land Management

LOCATION: 2 mi S of Kremmling on Hwy 9 to Trough Rd, approx. 20 mi S to campground. FACILITIES: Tables, Disabled Accessible Toilets, Fire Rings. ACTIVITIES: River Running, Mtn Biking, Hiking, Fishing. OPEN FOR USE: April 1 thru Oct. 30. CONTACT: Little Snake Resource Area (970) 826-5000. NOTE: Handicap Accessible; River access for rafting Colorado River. Capacity 40 people. 7.5' TOPOGRAPHIC MAP: Radium. ♿

Map No.	Campground Name	Map Loc.	Fee	No. of Units	Max. Length	Elev.	Toilets	Water	Agency
13	**Rock Creek State Wildlife Area**	C-1	0	Dispersed	Open	9,200'	Yes	No	Colorado Division of Wildlife

LOCATION: 6 mi. N of Kremmling on Hwy 40, 12 mi. W over Gore Pass on FDR 205, 2-3 mi. SW to property. FACILITIES: None. ACTIVITIES: Hunting, Fishing, Hiking, Wildlife Observation. OPEN FOR USE: Year Round. CONTACT: Colo. Div of Wildlife, NW Region (970) 255-6100. 7.5' TOPOGRAPHIC MAP: Lynx Pass.

Map No.	Campground Name	Map Loc.	Fee	No. of Units	Max. Length	Elev.	Toilets	Water	Agency
14	**Seymore Lake State Wildlife Area**	B-1	0	Dispersed	18'	8,625'	Yes	No	Colorado Division of Wildlife

LOCATION: 14 mi. SW of Walden on Hwy 14, 1 mi. S on Cty Rd 28, 3 mi. S on Cty Rd 11, 1/2 mi. W on Cty Rd 288 FACILITIES: Boat Ramp, Pets OK. ACTIVITIES: Fishing, 4-Wheel Drive, Hiking. OPEN FOR USE: Year Round. CONTACT: Colo Div of Wildlife, NE Region (970) 472-4300. NOTE: 80 acre Lake. 7.5' TOPOGRAPHIC MAP: Spicer Peak.

Map No.	Campground Name	Map Loc.	Fee	No. of Units	Max. Length	Elev.	Toilets	Water	Agency
15	**Aspen**	B-2	$	7	20'	8,900'	Yes	Yes	Routt National Forest

LOCATION: 21 mi. SE of Walden on Hwy 14 to Gould, 1 mi. SW on FDR 740, W 100 yards on FDR 741. FACILITIES: Tables, Grills, Pets OK. ACTIVITIES: Fishing. OPEN FOR USE: Mid May through mid Nov. CONTACT: Parks Ranger District - Walden (970) 723-8204. *NOTE: On South Fork Michigan River - One Mile from Colorado State Forest.*
7.5' TOPOGRAPHIC MAP: Gould.

Map No.	Campground Name	Map Loc.	Fee	No. of Units	Max. Length	Elev.	Toilets	Water	Agency
16	**Bellaire Lake**	A-3	$	26	60'	8,600'	Yes	Yes	Arapaho/Roosevelt National Forest

LOCATION: 1 mi. S of Red Feather on Cty Rd 74E, 3 mi. S on Cty Rd 162, 1 mi. W on FDR 163. FACILITIES: Tables, Grills, Pets OK, Electricity @ #1-22, Handicapped Accessible. ACTIVITIES: Hunting, Fishing, Hiking, Wildlife Observation. OPEN FOR USE: May through mid-Nov. CONTACT: Canyon Lakes Ranger District (970) 498-2770. NOTE: Molly Lake Trailhead. 7.5' TOPOGRAPHIC MAP: Red Feather Lakes. ♿

Map No.	Campground Name	Map Loc.	Fee	No. of Units	Max. Length	Elev.	Toilets	Water	Agency
17	**Big Creek Lake ®**	A-1	$	54	45'	8,997'	Yes	Yes	Routt National Forest

LOCATION: 9 mi. N of Walden on Hwy 127 to Cowdrey, 18 mi. NW on Cty Rd 6, 5-6 mi. SW on FDR 600. FACILITIES: Tables, Boat ramp, Trailhead, Pets OK. ACTIVITIES: Fishing, Hiking (Mt. Zirkel Wilderness). OPEN FOR USE: Mid-June through mid-Sept. CONTACT: Parks Ranger District - Walden (970) 723-8204. NOTE: 350 and 110 acre lakes - 5 miles open stream. 7.5' TOPOGRAPHIC MAP: Pearl.

Map No.	Campground Name	Map Loc.	Fee	No. of Units	Max. Length	Elev.	Toilets	Water	Agency
18	**Blacktail Creek**	C-1	$	8	40'	9,100'	Yes	Yes	Routt National Forest

LOCATION: 1/2 mi. S of Toponas on Hwy 131, 13 mi. E on Hwy 134. FACILITIES: Tables, Pets OK. ACTIVITIES: Fishing, Hiking. OPEN FOR USE: Mid-May through Oct. CONTACT: Yampa Ranger District (970) 638-4516. NOTE: Difficult fishing on Blacktail Creek. 7.5' TOPOGRAPHIC MAP: Gore Pass.

Map No.	Campground Name	Map Loc.	Fee	No. of Units	Max. Length	Elev.	Toilets	Water	Agency
19	**Blue River**	D-2	$	24	25'	8,400'	Yes	Yes	White River National Forest

LOCATION: 8-9 mi. NW of Dillon on Hwy 9. FACILITIES: Tables, Trailhead, Pets OK. ACTIVITIES: Fishing, Hiking. OPEN FOR USE: May through Sept. CONTACT: (970) 468-5400 Dillon Ranger District. NOTE: This section of Blue River is Gold Medal water - flies and lures only. 7.5' TOPOGRAPHIC MAP: Willow Lakes.

Map No.	Campground Name	Map Loc.	Fee	No. of Units	Max. Length	Elev.	Toilets	Water	Agency
20	**Browns Park**	A-3	$	28	30'	8,400'	Yes	No	Arapaho/Roosevelt National Forest

LOCATION: 4 mi. N of La Porte on Hwy 287, 55 mi. W on Hwy 14, 21 mi. N on Cty Rd 103. FACILITIES: Tables, Trailhead (Link McIntyre), Pets OK. ACTIVITIES: Fishing, Hiking (Near Rawah Wilderness) Link FDT 963. OPEN FOR USE: Mid-May through mid-Nov. CONTACT: Canyon Lakes Ranger District (970) 498-2770. 7.5' TOPOGRAPHIC MAP: Glendevy. ♿

Map No.	Campground Name	Map Loc.	Fee	No. of Units	Max. Length	Elev.	Toilets	Water	Agency
21	**Byers Creek**	D-3	$	6	32'	9,360'	Yes	Yes	Arapaho/Roosevelt National Forest

LOCATION: 6-7 mi. SW of Fraser on FDR 160 (St Louis Creek Rd). FACILITIES: Tables, Grills. ACTIVITIES: Fishing, Hiking, Mtn Biking, Pets OK. OPEN FOR USE: July through late Sept. CONTACT: Sulphur Ranger District (970) 887-4100. NOTE: Mtn bike trails near campground. 7.5' TOPOGRAPHIC MAPS: Byers Peak, Bottle Pass.

Map No.	Campground Name	Map Loc.	Fee	No. of Units	Max. Length	Elev.	Toilets	Water	Agency
22	**Cataract Creek**	D-2	$	4	21'	8,600'	Yes	Yes	White River National Forest

LOCATION:1-2 mi. SW of Green Mtn Reservoir on Cty Rd 1725. FACILITIES: Tables, Grills. ACTIVITIES: Fishing, Hiking, Pets OK. OPEN FOR USE: May through Sept. CONTACT: Dillon Ranger District (970) 468-5400. NOTE: Trailhead to Eagles Nest Wilderness. 7.5' TOPOGRAPHIC MAP: Mount Powell.

Map No.	Campground Name	Map Loc.	Fee	No. of Units	Max. Length	Elev.	Toilets	Water	Agency
23	**Chambers Lake ®**	B-3	$	52	30'	9,200'	Yes	Yes	Arapaho/Roosevelt National Forest

LOCATION: 4 mi. N of La Porte on Hwy 287, 56 mi. W on Hwy 14. FACILITIES: Tables, Boat ramp, Handicapped Accessible, Pets OK. ACTIVITIES: Fishing, Hiking, Rawah Wilderness Trailhead. OPEN FOR USE: June through Sept. CONTACT: Canyon Lakes Ranger District (970) 498-2770. NOTE: Reservations; 350 acre lake. Blue Lake TH, FDT 959, FDT 981. 7.5' TOPOGRAPHIC MAP: Chambers Lake. ♿

Map No.	Campground Name	Map Loc.	Fee	No. of Units	Max. Length	Elev.	Toilets	Water	Agency
24	**Denver Creek**	C-2	$	22	25'	8,800'	Yes	Yes	Arapaho/Roosevelt National Forest

LOCATION: 3 mi. NW of Granby on Hwy 40, 12 mi. NW on Hwy 125. FACILITIES: Tables. ACTIVITIES: Fishing, Hiking. OPEN FOR USE: June through Sept. CONTACT: Sulphur Ranger District (970) 887-4100. NOTE: Near Willow Creek. 7.5' TOPOGRAPHIC MAP: Radial Mountain.

Map No.	Campground Name	Map Loc.	Fee	No. of Units	Max. Length	Elev.	Toilets	Water	Agency
25	**Dumont Lake**	B-1	$	22	30'	9,508'	Yes	Yes	Routt National Forest

LOCATION: 22 mi. SE of Steamboat Springs on Hwy 40, 1-2 mi. NE on FDR 315. FACILITIES: Tables, Grills, Boat ramp, Pets OK. ACTIVITIES: Fishing. OPEN FOR USE: July through Oct. CONTACT: Hahns Peak/ Bears Ears Ranger District (970) 879-1870. NOTE: Several miles of 4-wheel drive roads near camp. 7.5' TOPOGRAPHIC MAP: Mount Werner. ♿

Map No.	Campground Name	Map Loc.	Fee	No. of Units	Max. Length	Elev.	Toilets	Water	Agency
26	**Gore Pass**	C-1	$	12	40'	9,500'	Yes	Yes	Routt National Forest

LOCATION: 1/2 mi. S of Toponas on Hwy 131, 15-16 mi. E on Hwy 134. FACILITIES: Tables, Fireplace, Pets OK. ACTIVITIES: Fishing, Hiking. OPEN FOR USE: June through Oct. CONTACT: Yampa Ranger District (970) 638-4516. NOTE: No firewood - Difficult fishing on Blacktail Creek. 7.5' TOPOGRAPHIC MAP: Gore Pass.

Map No.	Campground Name	Map Loc.	Fee	No. of Units	Max. Length	Elev.	Toilets	Water	Agency
27	**Grandview**	B-3	$	8	Tents Only	10,220'	Yes	Yes	Arapaho/Roosevelt National Forest

LOCATION: 4 mi. N of La Porte on Hwy 287, 61 mi. W on Hwy 14, 11 mi. SE on FDR 156. FACILITIES: Tables, Tent Sites, Boat Ramp, Pets OK. ACTIVITIES: Fishing, Trailhead (Neota Wilderness). OPEN FOR USE: Mid-June through Sept CONTACT: Canyon Lakes Ranger District (970) 498-2770. NOTE: Handicap Accessible. On 240 acre Long Draw Reservoir. 7.5' TOPOGRAPHIC MAP: Chambers Lake. ♿

Map No.	Campground Name	Map Loc.	Fee	No. of Units	Max. Length	Elev.	Toilets	Water	Agency
28	**Granite**	B-1	$	8	22'	9,900'	Yes	No	Routt National Forest

LOCATION: N of Steamboat Springs on Butcherknife Road 1.5 mi to FDR 60, E approx 12 mi to Buffalo Pass and Summit Lake, S on FDR 310 5 mi to Fish Creek Reservoir. FACILITIES: Boat ramp, tables, grills. ACTIVITIES: Fishing. OPEN FOR USE: July through October. CONTACT: Hahns Peak/Bears Ears Ranger District. (970) 879-1870. Located near Fish Creek Reservoir. 4 walk-in sites and 4 drive-in sites. 7.5' TOPOGRAPHIC MAP: Mt. Werner. ♿

Map No.	Campground Name	Map Loc.	Fee	No. of Units	Max. Length	Elev.	Toilets	Water	Agency
29	**Green Mountain Reservoir**	D-2				8,000'			White River National Forest
a.	Cow Creek		0	Dispersed	36		Yes	No	
b.	Davis Spring		0	7	15'		Yes	No	
c.	Elliot Creek		0	64	22'		Yes	No	
d.	McDonald Flats		$	13	21'		Yes	Yes	
e.	Prairie Point		$	44	20'		Yes	Yes	
f.	Willows		0	35	22'		Yes	No	

LOCATION: 20 mi N of Silverthorne on Hwy 9 - Services available in Heeney located west of reservoir. ACTIVITIES: Fishing, Boating, Sailing. OPEN FOR USE: June through Sept. CONTACT: Dillon Ranger District (970) 468-5400. NOTE: Swimming at Cow Creek swim beach. 7.5' TOPOGRAPHIC MAPS: Mount Powell, Squaw Creek, Battle Mountain, King Creek. See map page 35.

Map No.	Campground Name	Map Loc.	Fee	No. of Units	Max. Length	Elev.	Toilets	Water	Agency
30	**Grizzly Creek**	B-1	$	12	20'	8,500'	Yes	Yes	Routt National Forest

LOCATION: 13 mi. SW of Walden on Hwy 14, 10-11 mi. W on Cty Rd 24, 1/2 mi. W on FDR 615. FACILITIES: Tables, Grills, Trailhead (Mt. Zirkel Wilderness), Pets OK. ACTIVITIES: Fishing, Hiking. OPEN FOR USE: Mid-June through early Sept. CONTACT: Parks Ranger District - Walden (970) 723-8204. 7.5' TOPOGRAPHIC MAP: Teal Lake. *Note: Water may not be available.*

Map No.	Campground Name	Map Loc.	Fee	No. of Units	Max. Length	Elev.	Toilets	Water	Agency
31	**Hidden Lakes**	B-1	$	9	20'	8,900'	Yes	Yes	Routt National Forest

LOCATION:13 mi. SW of Walden on Hwy 14, 10-11 mi. W on Cty Rd 24, 2 mi. W on FDR 60, 4 mi. S on FDR 20. FACILITIES: Tables, Grills, Pets OK. ACTIVITIES: Hunting, Fishing, Hiking. OPEN FOR USE: Mid-June through mid-Sept. CONTACT: Parks Ranger District/ Walden (970) 723-8204. NOTE: Near 10 acre lake. 7.5' TOPOGRAPHIC MAP: Teal Lake.

Map No.	Campground Name	Map Loc.	Fee	No. of Units	Max. Length	Elev.	Toilets	Water	Agency
32	**Horseshoe**	D-2	$	7	23'	8,540'	Yes	Yes	Arapaho/Roosevelt National Forest

LOCATION: 16 mi. NW of Dillon on Hwy 9, 10 mi. NE on FDR 15 (Ute Pass Rd) to Henderson, 3-4 mi. NW on FDR 138, or 11 mi. S of Williams Fork Res, near Kremmling. FACILITIES: Tables, Grills. ACTIVITIES: Hunting, Fishing, Hiking. OPEN FOR USE: Mid-May through Sept. CONTACT: Sulphur Ranger District (970) 887-4100. NOTE: On Williams Fork. 7.5' TOPOGRAPHIC MAP: Sylvan Reservoir.

Map No.	Campground Name	Map Loc.	Fee	No. of Units	Max. Length	Elev.	Toilets	Water	Agency
33	**Idlewild**	D-3	$	24	32'	9,000'	Yes	Yes	Arapaho/Roosevelt National Forest

LOCATION: 1 mi. S of Winter Park on Hwy 40. FACILITIES: Tables, Pets OK. ACTIVITIES: Fishing, Hiking. OPEN FOR USE: June through mid-Sept. CONTACT: Sulphur Ranger District (970) 887-4100. NOTE: Near Winter Park Resort; Handicap Accessible. 7.5' TOPOGRAPHIC MAP: East Portal.

Section 3

Arapaho National Recreation Area

Map No.	Campground Name	Map Loc.	Fee	No. of Units	Max. Length	Elev.	Toilets	Water	Agency
34	**Lake Granby**	C-3	$			8,400'	Yes	Yes	Arapaho/Roosevelt National Forest
a.	Arapaho Bay ®			84	35'				
b.	Cutthroat Bay ®			Group	---				
c.	Stillwater ®			129	45'	+$5.00 for hook-ups			♿
d.	Sunset Point			25	50'				♿

LOCATION: 10 mi.. NE of Granby on Hwy 34, (Stillwater) 9 mi. E on Cty Rd 6 (Arapaho Bay). FACILITIES: Tables, Boat ramp. ACTIVITIES: Fishing, Hiking. OPEN FOR USE: Late May through early Sept. CONTACT: Sulphur Ranger District (970) 887-4100. NOTE: Reservations; Arapaho Bay and Stillwater - Handicap Accessible; Barrier Free Access at Arapaho Bay and Stillwater Campground. Dump Stations at Stillwater and Green Ridge Campgrounds; Area Map available at Forest Service Office, Arapaho National Recreation Area; A map of the area will assist in locating the campgrounds; Camping facilities are usually open around May 20, and remain open with full service until shortly after Labor Day. (Subject to weather) Boat-In camping along the northeast shore of Lake Granby. *See map page 31.*

Map No.	Campground Name	Map Loc.	Fee	No. of Units	Max. Length	Elev.	Toilets	Water	Agency
	Shadow Mtn Reservoir Green Ridge®	C-3	$	77	35'	8,360'	Yes	Yes	Arapaho/Roosevelt National Forest

LOCATION: 13-14 mi. NE of Granby on Hwy 34, 3 mi. SE on Cty Rd 66. Located on south end of reservoir. FACILITIES: Boat ramp, Dump Stations, Pets OK. ACTIVITIES: Fishing, Hiking, Boating. OPEN FOR USE: Late May through early Sept. CONTACT: Sulphur Ranger District (970) 887-4100. NOTE: Handicap Accessible; Green Ridge - Reservations. 7.5' TOPOGRAPHIC MAP: Shadow Mountain. ♿

Map No.	Campground Name	Map Loc.	Fee	No. of Units	Max. Length	Elev.	Toilets	Water	Agency
	Willow Creek Reservoir	C-3	$	35	25'	8,130'	Yes	Yes	Arapaho/Roosevelt National Forest

LOCATION: 6-7 mi. NE of Granby on Hwy 34, 3-4 mi. W on Cty Rd 90. (260 acre lake.)FACILITIES: Tables, Boat ramp. ACTIVITIES: Fishing. OPEN FOR USE: Late May through early Sept. CONTACT: Sulphur Ranger District (970) 887-4100. *Note: Wakeless boating*. 7.5' TOPOGRAPHIC MAP: Trail Mtn. *Construction 2001 - Call First.* ♿

End Arapaho National Recreation Area Campground Information

Map No.	Campground Name	Map Loc.	Fee	No. of Units	Max. Length	Elev.	Toilets	Water	Agency
35	**Long Draw**	B-3	$	25	30'	10,030'	Yes	Yes	Arapaho/Roosevelt National Forest

LOCATION: 4 mi. N of LaPorte on Hwy 287, 61 mi. W on Hwy 14, 9 mi. SE on FDR 156. FACILITIES: Tables, Grills. ACTIVITIES: Fishing, Hiking. OPEN FOR USE: Mid-June through Sept. CONTACT: Canyon Lakes Ranger District (970) 498-2770. NOTE: Handicap Accessible. Near Long Draw Reservoir, boat ramp at reservoir. Trailhead (Corral Creek). 7.5' TOPOGRAPHIC MAP: Fall River Pass. ♿

Map No.	Campground Name	Map Loc.	Fee	No. of Units	Max. Length	Elev.	Toilets	Water	Agency
36	**Lynx Pass**	C-1	$	11	40'	8,900'	Yes	Yes	Routt National Forest

LOCATION: 10 mi. SE of Yampa on Hwy 131, 8 mi. NE on Hwy 134, 3 mi. N on FDR 270. FACILITIES: Tables, Grills. ACTIVITIES: Hunting, Hiking, Fishing. OPEN FOR USE: June through Oct. CONTACT: Yampa Ranger District (970) 638-4516. NOTE: Near Trailhead. 7.5' TOPOGRAPHIC MAP: Lynx Pass.

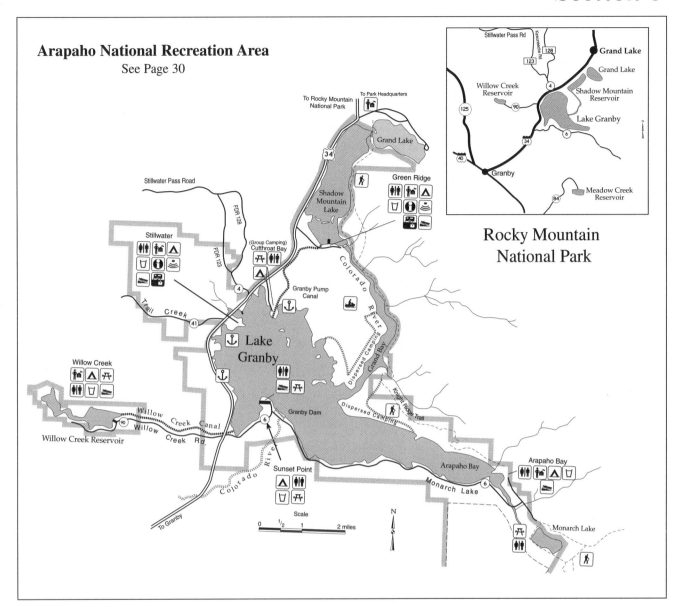

Arapaho National Recreation Area
See Page 30

Rocky Mountain National Park

Map No.	Campground Name	Map Loc.	Fee	No. of Units	Max. Length	Elev.	Toilets	Water	Agency
37	**Meadows**	B-1	$	30	30'	9,300'	Yes	Yes	Routt National Forest

LOCATION: 15 mi. SE of Steamboat on Hwy 40. FACILITIES: Tables, Pets OK. ACTIVITIES: Fishing, Wildlife Observation, Traveler stop over. OPEN FOR USE: July thru Oct. CONTACT: Hahns Peak/ Bears Ears Ranger District (970) 879-1870. 7.5' TOPOGRAPHIC MAP: Walton Peak.

Map No.	Campground Name	Map Loc.	Fee	No. of Units	Max. Length	Elev.	Toilets	Water	Agency
38	**Mizpah**	D-3	$	10	20'	9,600'	Yes	Yes	Arapaho/Roosevelt National Forest

LOCATION: 6 mi. W of Empire on Hwy 40. FACILITIES: Tables, Grills. ACTIVITIES: Fishing, Wildlife Observation, Traveler Stop-Over. OPEN FOR USE: Late May through mid-Oct. CONTACT: (303) 567-3000 Clear Creek Ranger District. NOTE: Near south side of Berthoud Pass. 7.5' TOPOGRAPHIC MAP: Berthoud Pass.

Map No.	Campground Name	Map Loc.	Fee	No. of Units	Max. Length	Elev.	Toilets	Water	Agency
39	**North Fork Poudre**	A-3	$	9	30'	9,200'	Yes	Yes	Arapaho/Roosevelt National Forest

LOCATION: 1 mi. S of Red Feather on Cty Rd 74E, 7 mi. W on Cty Rd 162. FACILITIES: Tables. Pets OK . ACTIVITIES: Fishing. OPEN FOR USE: June through Oct. CONTACT: Canyon Lakes Ranger District (970) 498-2770. NOTE: Trailhead Killpecker FDT 956. 7.5' TOPOGRAPHIC MAP: South Bald Mountain.

Map No.	Campground Name	Map Loc.	Fee	No. of Units	Max. Length	Elev.	Toilets	Water	Agency
40	**Pines**	B-2	$	11	20'	9,200'	Yes	Yes	Routt National Forest

LOCATION: 21 mi. SE of Walden on Hwy 14 to Gould, 4 mi. SE on FDR 740. FACILITIES: Tables, Grills, Pets OK. ACTIVITIES: Fishing. OPEN FOR USE: Mid- May through Oct. CONTACT: Parks Ranger District (970) 723-8204. NOTE: On South Fork Michigan River. 7.5' TOPOGRAPHIC MAP: Jack Creek Ranch.

Map No.	Campground Name	Map Loc.	Fee	No. of Units	Max. Length	Elev.	Toilets	Water	Agency
41	**Poudre River & Joe Wright Creek**	A-3	$				Yes	Yes	Arapaho/Roosevelt National Forest
a.	Big Bend (Near Bliss SWA)			6	20'	7,700'	Near Roaring Creek Trailhead #952		
b.	Sleeping Elephant			15	20'	7,850'			
c.	Big South			4	25'	8,440'			
d.	Aspen Glen			8	30'	8,660'			

LOCATION: Four campgrounds located on Cache le Poudre River west from Rustic to Chambers Lake on Hwy 14. FACILITIES: Tables, Grills. ACTIVITIES: Fishing, Hiking. OPEN FOR USE: May to Nov. CONTACT: Canyon Lakes Ranger District. (970) 498-2770. 7.5' TOPOGRAPHIC MAPS: Kinninnik, Boston Peak, Chambers Lake. See map page 33.

Map No.	Campground Name	Map Loc.	Fee	No. of Units	Max. Length	Elev.	Toilets	Water	Agency
42	**Robbers Roost**	D-3	$	11	45'	9,826'	Yes	Yes	Arapaho/Roosevelt National Forest

LOCATION: 5 mi. S of Winter Park on Hwy 40. FACILITIES: Tables, Pets OK. ACTIVITIES: Fishing. OPEN FOR USE: Late June through Sept. CONTACT: Sulphur Ranger District (970) 887-4100. NOTE: Near Eva Creek. 7.5' TOPOGRAPHIC MAP: Berthoud Pass.

Map No.	Campground Name	Map Loc.	Fee	No. of Units	Max. Length	Elev.	Toilets	Water	Agency
43	**Sawmill Gulch**	C-2	$	6	32'	8,780'	Yes	Yes	Arapaho/Roosevelt National Forest

LOCATION: 3 mi. NW of Granby on Hwy 40, 10 mi. NW on Hwy 125. FACILITIES: Tables, Pets OK. ACTIVITIES: Fishing, Hiking. OPEN FOR USE: June through Sept. CONTACT: Sulphur Ranger District (970) 887-4100. NOTE: Near Willow Creek. 7.5' TOPOGRAPHIC MAPS: Cabin Creek.

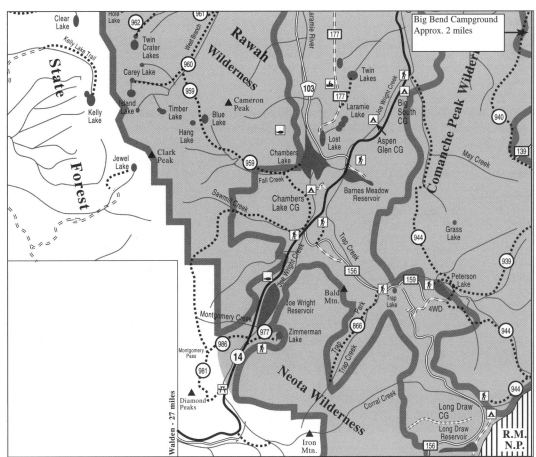

**Poudre River
West of Rustic**

(Text page 32)

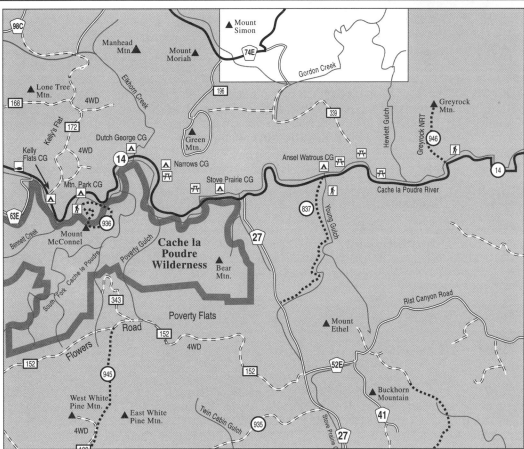

**Poudre River West
of Fort Collins**

(Text page 44)

Map No.	Campground Name	Map Loc.	Fee	No. of Units	Max. Length	Elev.	Toilets	Water	Agency
44	**South Fork**	D-2	$	21	23'	8,940'	Yes	Yes	Arapaho/Roosevelt National Forest

LOCATION: 16 mi. NW of Dillon on Hwy 9, 10 mi. NE on FDR 15 (Ute Pass Road), 4 mi. SE on FDR 138. ACTIVITIES: Fishing, Hiking Trailhead. OPEN FOR USE: Mid-May through Sept. CONTACT: Sulphur Ranger District (970) 887-4100. NOTE: Near Williams Fork. 7.5' TOPOGRAPHIC MAP: Ute Peak.

Map No.	Campground Name	Map Loc.	Fee	No. of Units	Max. Length	Elev.	Toilets	Water	Agency
45	**St. Louis Creek**	D-3	$	16	32'	8,900'	Yes	Yes	Arapaho/Roosevelt National Forest

LOCATION: 3 mi. S of Fraser on FDR 160 (St. Louis Creek Rd). FACILITIES: Tables, Trails, Pets OK. ACTIVITIES: Fishing, Hiking. OPEN FOR USE: Late June through early Sept. CONTACT: Sulphur Ranger District (970) 887-4100. NOTE: Near St. Louis Creek. 7.5' TOPOGRAPHIC MAP: Fraser. ♿

Map No.	Campground Name	Map Loc.	Fee	No. of Units	Max. Length	Elev.	Toilets	Water	Agency
46	**Sugarloaf**	D-2	$	11	23'	8,970'	Yes	Yes	Arapaho/Roosevelt National Forest

LOCATION: 16 mi. NW of Dillon on Hwy 9, 10 mi. NE on FDR 15 (Ute Pass Rd), 4 mi. SE on FDR 138. ACTIVITIES: Fishing, Hiking Trailhead. OPEN FOR USE: Mid-May through Sept . CONTACT: Sulphur Ranger District (970) 887-4100. NOTE: Near Williams Fork. 7.5' TOPOGRAPHIC MAP: Ute Peak. ♿

Map No.	Campground Name	Map Loc.	Fee	No. of Units	Max. Length	Elev.	Toilets	Water	Agency
47	**Summit Lake**	B-1	$	16	18'	10,300'	Yes	Yes	Routt National Forest

LOCATION: 2 mi. N of Steamboat Springs on Strawberry Pk Rd, 2 mi. NE on Cty Rd 36, 11-12 mi. E on FDR 60. FACILITIES: Tables, Grills, Pets OK. ACTIVITIES: Fishing, Hiking - Located near Mt. Zirkel Wilderness Trail FDT 1011, Wyoming FDT 1101. OPEN FOR USE: Mid-July through mid-Sept. CONTACT: Hahns Peak/Bears Ears Ranger District (970) 879-1870. 7.5' TOPOGRAPHIC MAP: Buffalo Pass. ♿

Map No.	Campground Name	Map Loc.	Fee	No. of Units	Max. Length	Elev.	Toilets	Water	Agency
48	**Teal Lake**	B-1	$	17	25'	8,812'	Yes	Yes	Routt National Forest

LOCATION: 11 W of Hebron on Cty 24, N 2.5 mi. on FDR 615 to Teal Lake. FACILITIES: Tables, Grills, Pets OK. ACTIVITIES: Fishing on 16 acre Teal Lake, Hiking near Mt Zirkel Wilderness, Trail #1132. OPEN FOR USE: May through Sept. CONTACT: Parks Ranger District (970) 723-8204. 7.5' TOPOGRAPHIC MAP: Teal Lake. *Teal Lake Group ®.*

Map No.	Campground Name	Map Loc.	Fee	No. of Units	Max. Length	Elev.	Toilets	Water	Agency
49	**Tunnel**	B-3	$	49	40'	8,600'	Yes	Yes	Arapaho/Roosevelt National Forest

LOCATION: 4 mi. N of La Porte on Hwy 287, 55 mi. W on Hwy 14, 6 mi. N on Cty Rd 103. FACILITIES: Tables, Grills, Pets OK. ACTIVITIES: Fishing, Hiking, Trailhead Rawah Wilderness. OPEN FOR USE: Mid-May through mid-Oct CONTACT: Canyon Lakes Ranger District (970) 498-2770. NOTE: Handicap Accessible. 4 mi. N of Chambers Lake on Laramie River. Near TH, FDT 968. 7.5' TOPOGRAPHIC MAP: Boston Peak. ♿

Map No.	Campground Name	Map Loc.	Fee	No. of Units	Max. Length	Elev.	Toilets	Water	Agency
50	**Walton Creek**	B-1	$	16	22'	9,400'	Yes	Yes	Routt National Forest

LOCATION: 17 mi. SE of Steamboat Springs on Hwy 40. FACILITIES: Tables, Pets OK. ACTIVITIES: Fishing, Travelers Stop-Over. OPEN FOR USE: June through Oct. CONTACT: Hahns Peak/Bears Ears Ranger District (970) 879-1870. 7.5' TOPOGRAPHIC MAP: Mount Werner.

Map No.	Campground Name	Map Loc.	Fee	No. of Units	Max. Length	Elev.	Toilets	Water	Agency
51	**Williams Fork Reservoir**	C-2	0	36	32'	7,800'	Yes	Yes	Denver Water Department

LOCATION: 4 mi. S of Parshall on Hwy 3. FACILITIES: Dump Station, Tables, Boat Ramp. ACTIVITIES: Fishing. OPEN FOR USE: Late May through early Sept. CONTACT: Denver Water Department (303) 628-6526. NOTE: Rated excellent fishing. 7.5' TOPOGRAPHIC MAP: Parshall. *Stay limited to a 14 days.*

Map No.	Campground Name	Map Loc.	Fee	No. of Units	Max. Length	Elev.	Toilets	Water	Agency
52	**Wolford Mountain Reservoir**	C-1	$	48	32'	7,500'	Yes	Yes	Colorado River Conservation Dist.

LOCATION: 5 mi. N of Kremmling on Hwy 40. FACILITIES: Grates, Shelters, Water, Electricity, Dump Station, Tables, Boat ramp. ACTIVITIES: Fishing. OPEN FOR USE: Late May through early Sept. CONTACT: Wolford Mountain Project (800) 416-6992. NOTE: 1,450 acre reservoir has two group sites by reservation only. Day use are with shelter, picnic tables and charcoal grills. 7.5' TOPOGRAPHIC MAP: Kremmling.

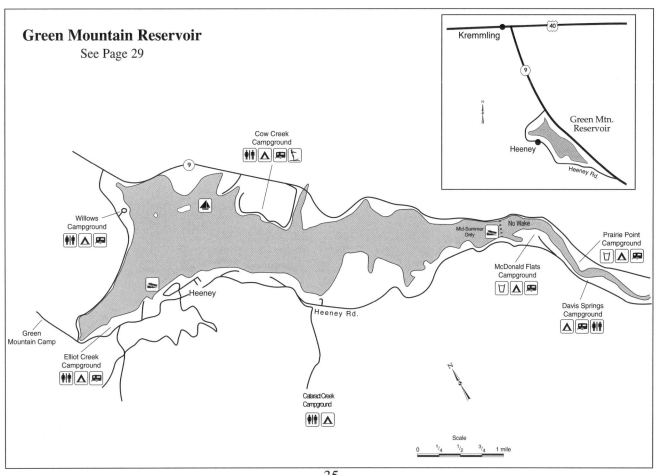

Green Mountain Reservoir

See Page 29

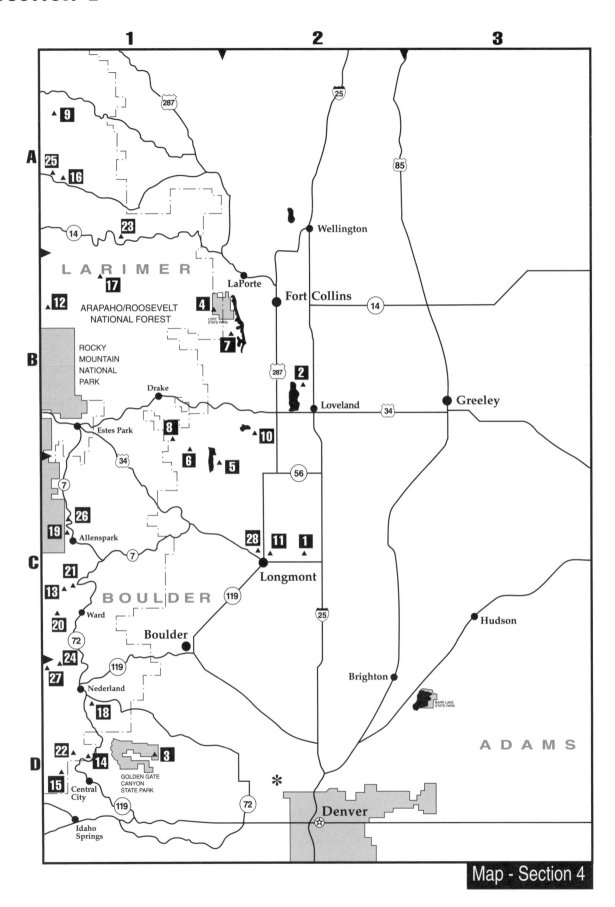

Map - Section 4

Contents Section 4

Map No.	Name	Map Loc.	Fee	No. of Units	Max. Length	Elev.	Toilets	Water	Agency
1	**Barbour Ponds State Park ®**	C-2	$	60	30'	4,830'	Yes	Yes	Colorado State Parks

Barbour Ponds State Park is located 2 miles west of 1-25 on Hwy 119, in the shadow of Longs Peak, only 30 miles from Denver. Although small, with only 50 land acres and 80 water acres, the park offers full size recreational enjoyment. The setting is scenic and convenient, including large cottonwood trees for shade and a great view of Longs Peak. The park's four quiet ponds offer some of the best warm water fishing in northern Colorado. The ponds are stocked with rainbow trout in the spring and fall, creating a great fishery for all ages during those long seasons.

Camping

Barbour Ponds offers 60 campsites located in its east and west campground near waterside, and near the north end of the park, and a group site that can accommodate 12 units. Please camp only in designated numbered sites and display your camping permit in the marker at your campsite. A dump station is located alongside the park entrance road.

Barrier Free Access

Because the area around the ponds is relatively flat, Barbour Ponds is accessible for the physically challenged, especially with some assistance. Concrete ramps are provided to access the two toilets in the campgrounds and the toilet at the entrance.

Fishing

The ponds contain bluegill, bass, channel catfish, and crappie. Rainbow trout are stocked every spring and fall. This program provides great fishing beginning in late March. Fall stocking begins in late September and creates great fishing all fall and good ice fishing.

See map page 45.

Daily Fee/Annual Pass
For more information contact:
Barbour Ponds State Park
4995 Weld Cty Rd 24 1/2
Longmont, CO 80501
(303) 678-9402

Section 4

Map No.	Name	Map Loc.	Fee	No. of Units	Max. Length	Elev.	Toilets	Water	Agency
2	**Boyd Lake State Park ®**	B-2	$	148	35'	4,958'	Yes	Yes	Colorado State Parks

Boyd Lake State Park is a water sports haven for northern Colorado. The park attracts visitors who enjoy boating, water skiing, swimming, fishing and windsurfing. The park also features camping and picnicking. Boating is the primary activity on the two-mile-long lake.

A 6 lane paved boat ramp with docks is located north of the swim beach at the inlet area and a 2 lane paved ramp is located north of the group picnic area.

The spacious and comfortable 70-degree water of Boyd Lake attracts water skiers of all abilities. The entire lake is open to boating and sailing. The Boyd Lake swim beach, a gentle sloping cove of clean, fine sand, provides cool relief on Colorado's beautiful summer days. A pavilion at the beach supplies showers, restrooms, a first-aid station and a food concession. Inner tubes, air mattresses and similar devices may be used in the buoyed-off swim area. Picnic tables are conveniently located just a Frisbee throw from the beach.

Camping
There are 148 paved, pull-through campsites with picnic tables, fire pits, restrooms and dump station. The sites are located on a grassy knoll dotted with trees near the lake. The sites can accommodate tents, pick-up campers, trailers and motor homes. Three restrooms with showers, playground equipment and horseshoe pits are scattered throughout the campground.

Information: Park office (970) 669-1739; Handicapped accessible visitors center, restrooms, showers, swimming, trails, fishing and camping; some facilities available with assistance.

Daily Fee/Annual Pass
Information Contact:
Boyd Lake State Park
3720 N. County Road 11C
Loveland CO 80538
(970) 669-1739

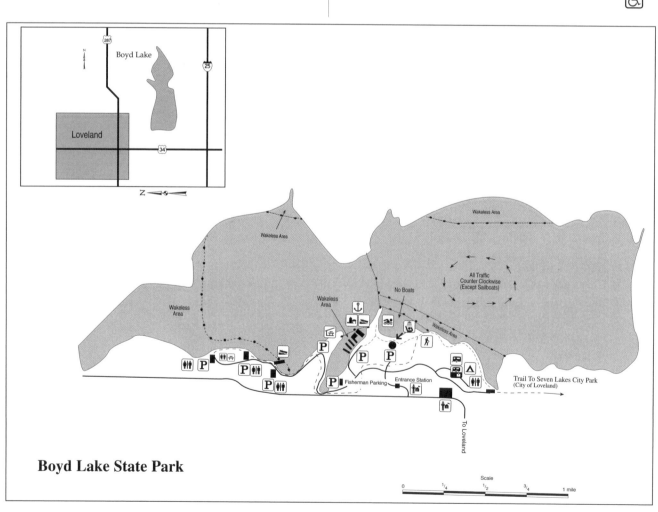

Boyd Lake State Park

Map No.	Name	Map Loc.	Fee	No. of Units	Max. Length	Elev.	Toilets	Water	Agency
3	**Golden Gate Canyon State Park ®**	D-1	$	168	35'	9,100'	Yes	Yes	Colorado State Parks

To reach Golden Gate Canyon State Park, take Highway 93 north from Golden about one mile to Golden Gate Canyon road. Turn left and continue for 15 miles to the park. Green mountain meadows, lush aspen groves and pine covered hills greet you at Golden Gate Canyon State Park, 16 miles northwest of Golden.

With over 10,500 acres of beauty ranging in elevation from 7,600 to 10,400 feet Golden Gate offers a variety of outdoor recreation opportunities within an hours drive of the Denver area.

Camping
For summer camping information call (303)642-3856. The 106 site Reverend's Ridge Campground in the northwest corner of the park accommodates trailers, pick-up campers and tents and offers flush toilets, hot showers and laundry facilities. The campground is designed in a series of 10 loops to minimize traffic. Restrooms are centrally located throughout campgrounds. During the summer months, campfire programs are presented in an outdoor amphitheater. There is a holding tank dump station at Reverend's Ridge Campground. Aspen Meadow campground in the north central area of the park provides 35 campsites for tents only. Facilities include water pumps, vault toilets and fire rings. The area has two loops and offers more privacy than Reverend's Ridge. Rimrock Loop at Aspen Meadow has camping sites and parking designed for horseback riders.

Hiking
Nearly 60 miles of hiking trails in the park offer pleasures and challenges for everyone. The difficulty of the trail is indicated by the background shape and color of the marker.

Fishing
Fishing is permitted in any stream or pond in the park except the Visitor Center Show Pond.

Other Activities
Mountain Biking, Hiking, Horseback Riding, Picnicking, and Photography.

Daily Fee/Annual Pass
For more information contact:
Golden Gate Canyon State Park
3873 Highway 46
Golden CO 80403 (303) 582-3707

Map No.	Name	Map Loc.	Fee	No. of Units	Max. Length	Elev.	Toilets	Water	Agency
4	**Lory State Park ®**	B-1	$	6	Tent Only	7,015'	Yes	Yes	Colorado State Parks

Hiking, picnicking, horseback riding, sight seeing, nature study, and just plain relaxing. Lory State Park is west of Horsetooth Reservoir only 20 minutes from Ft. Collins, this foothills playground is an easy get-away for the day, or even for an hour.

This four season park is noted for its rock formations and for terrain and vegetation that change with the altitude. Park boundaries preserve 2,400 acres of the transition ecology of the Rocky Mountain foothills. While in the grassy plains portion of the park, visitors see the red sandstone hogbacks typical of the front range. Named for an early resident of the area, the rocks 6,780 elevation offers a spectacular view of the Ft. Collins area.

Backcountry Camping
Lory State Park offers overnight backcountry camping at designated sites by permit only. Permits are available at the park entrance station. Backpack stoves are recommended, as no open fires are permitted. Water is available at the entrance station only. No motorized or vehicular overnight camping is permitted at Lory. Tent camping is not allowed in the lower sections of the park.

Hiking
Lory is a great park for hikers! Varying from leisurely to challenging, the park's trail's offer approximately 30 miles of fun. Some of these trails were once logging or ranch roads. Trail grades rarely exceed 12 percent with occasional abrupt elevation change. Many of the trails are also suitable for horseback riding, jogging, and mountain bike use. Each trail is named and marked. Safe drinking water or restrooms facilities are not available on the trails. An adequate water supply should be carried, and may be obtained near the park entrance station.

Other Activities
Horseback Riding, Nature Study, Picnicking, and Photography.

Daily Fee/Annual Pass
For more information contact:
Lory State Park
708 Lodgepole Drive
Bellvue, CO 80512 (970) 493-1623

Section 4

Map No.	Campground Name	Map Loc.	Fee	No. of Units	Max. Length	Elev.	Toilets	Water	Agency
5	**Carter Lake**	C-1	$	190	35'	5,760'	Yes	Yes	Larimer County Parks & Open Land

LOCATION: Located in the foothills west of Loveland. FACILITIES: Dump Station ACTIVITIES: Fishing, sailing, camping, water-skiing. OPEN FOR USE: Year round. NOTE: Carter Lake Marina (970) 667-1062 offers restaurant service, fishing, camping supplies, firewood, boat mooring, and boat rentals. *See map page 41.*

Map No.	Campground Name	Map Loc.	Fee	No. of Units	Max. Length	Elev.	Toilets	Water	Agency
6	**Flatiron Reservoir**	C-1	$	42	35'	5,470'	Yes	Yes	Larimer County Parks & Open Land

LOCATION: NW of Carter Lake. ACTIVITIES: Fishing, camping. OPEN FOR USE: Year round.
CONTACT: Larimer County Parks & Open Land Dept.
NOTE: No boating or swimming is allowed. A group picnic area may be reserved by contacting a Park Ranger.

Map No.	Campground Name	Map Loc.	Fee	No. of Units	Max. Length	Elev.	Toilets	Water	Agency
7	**Horsetooth Reservoir**	B-2	$	129	35'	5,430'	Yes	Yes	Larimer County Parks & Open Land

LOCATION: Foothills west of Fort Collins. FACILITIES: Dump Station, Restaurant, Firewood. Marina has fishing and camping supplies, boat moorings, gasoline, and boat rentals. ACTIVITIES: Fishing, Boating, Waterskiing, Camping OPEN FOR USE: Year Round. CONTACT: Larimer County Parks & Open Land Dept. (970) 679-4570 NOTE: The Inlet Bay Marina's phone is (970) 223-0140. *See map page 41.*

Map No.	Campground Name	Map Loc.	Fee	No. of Units	Max. Length	Elev.	Toilets	Water	Agency
8	**Pinewood Lake**	B-1	$	16	35'	6,580'	Yes	Yes	Larimer County Parks & Open Land

LOCATION: W of Carter Lake. FACILITIES: Metal Grates for fires. ACTIVITIES: Boating, Mountain Biking, Horseback Riding, Hiking, Sailing. OPEN FOR USE: Year Round. CONTACT: Larimer County Parks & Open Land Dept. (970) 679-4570.

Camping
Camping facilities for motor homes, vehicles and tents are provided at Carter Lake. Camping is allowed only in designated areas at all four lakes. Backcountry camping is allowed at Horsetooth Reservoir and Horsetooth Mountain Park. All campsites are on a first come first served basis. Reserving campsites is not allowed. Camping for more than 14 days within a 30 day period in the Larimer Park system is not allowed.

Campfires
Campfires are allowed in all Larimer County parks in the metal grates provided. Campfires are not allowed outside metal grates except below the high water line at the reservoirs. Please destroy fire rings when you leave. Campfires must not be unattended at anytime. For projection of the resources collection of firewood including cutting trees is prohibited.

Boating
Boating is offered at Carter Lake, Horsetooth Reservoir and Pinewood Lake.

Other Activities
Mountain Biking, Horseback Riding, Hiking and Sailing.

Daily Fee/ Annual Pass
For more information contact: Larimer County Parks & Open Land Dept., 1800 S. County Rd. 31
Loveland, CO 80537. (970) 679-4570

Map No.	Campground Name	Map Loc.	Fee	No. of Units	Max. Length	Elev.	Toilets	Water	Agency
9	**Cherokee Park State Wildlife Area**	A-1	0	Dispersed	Open	7,700'	Yes	No	Colorado Division of Wildlife

LOCATION: 20 mi. N of Ft. Collins on Hwy 287, 8 mi. W on Red Feather Lakes Rd 80C. FACILITIES: Toilets. ACTIVITIES: Hunting, Fishing, Hiking, Wildlife Observation. OPEN FOR USE: June through August. CONTACT: Colorado Division of Wildlife NE Region (970) 472-4300. NOTE: 3 units - Lower Unit open to fishing.
7.5' TOPOGRAPHIC MAPS: Livermore Mountain, Haystack Mountain.

Map No.	Campground Name	Map Loc.	Fee	No. of Units	Max. Length	Elev.	Toilets	Water	Agency
10	**Lon Hagler State Wildlife Area**	B-2	$		Open	5,400'	Yes	No	Colorado Division of Wildlife

LOCATION: From Hwy 287, W 3 mi. of Champion on Cty Rd 14 W, 1 mi. N on Cty Rd 21 S, W to site. FACILITIES: Boat ramp, Toilets. ACTIVITIES: Fishing, Hiking, Archery, Wildlife Observation. OPEN FOR USE: Year Round. CONTACT: Colorado Division of Wildlife NE Region (970) 472-4300. NOTE: 50 acre reservoir.
7.5' TOPOGRAPHIC MAP: Carter Lake. *Designated camping.*

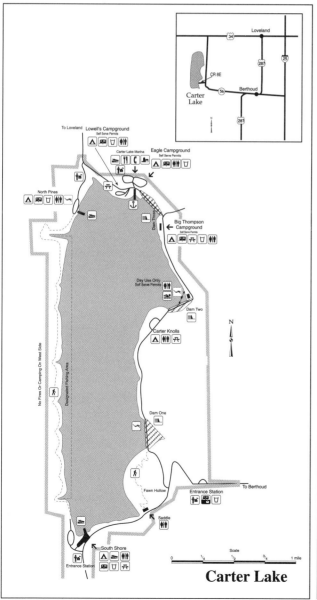

Carter Lake

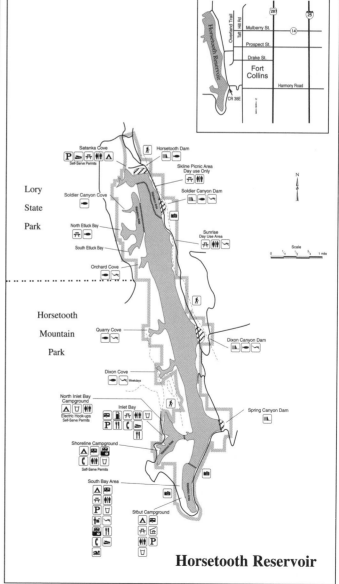

Horsetooth Reservoir

Map No.	Campground Name	Map Loc.	Fee	No. of Units	Max. Length	Elev.	Toilets	Water	Agency
11	**Union Reservoir ®**	C-2	$	42	50'	4,956'	Yes	Yes	City of Longmont

LOCATION: Entrance 1 mi. N of Hwy 119 on County Line Rd, E of Longmont. FACILITIES: Tables, Grills, Boat ramp. ACTIVITIES: Fishing, Sailing, Swimming, Wildlife Observation. OPEN FOR USE: March through Sept. CONTACT: Reservations --Union Reservoir Park Office (303) 772-1265. NOTE: Handicap Accessible. 800 acre lake allows no-wake boating. Fourteen tent sites. 7.5' TOPOGRAPHIC MAP: Longmont.

Map No.	Campground Name	Map Loc.	Fee	No. of Units	Max. Length	Elev.	Toilets	Water	Agency
12	**Tom Bennett**	B-1	$	12	20'	9,000'	Yes	No	Arapaho/ Roosevelt National Forest

LOCATION: West of Kelly Flats CG turn south from Hwy 14 on Cty Rd 63E (131). Continue to Cty Rd 44H. W on Cty Rd 44H approx.3.5 miles to Campground. Campground is near CSU Pingree Park Campus. FACILITIES: Grills, Firepits, Tables. OPEN FOR USE: May through Sept.. CONTACT: Canyon Lakes Ranger District. (970) 498-2770. NOTE: Campground located near several Trailheads. Beaver Creek TH (942), Emmaline Lake TH (854), Stormy Peaks (980). Trails lead into Comanche Peak Wilderness. 7.5' Topographic Map: Pingree Park.

Map No.	Campground Name	Map Loc.	Fee	No. of Units	Max. Length	Elev.	Toilets	Water	Agency
13	**Camp Dick ®**	C-1	$	41	55'	8,650'	Yes	Yes	Arapaho/ Roosevelt National Forest

LOCATION: N of Ward on Hwy 72 approx. 7 mi, W on FDR 114 1 mi. FACILITIES: Tables, Grills. OPEN FOR USE: Late may through mid-Oct. CONTACT: Boulder Ranger District (303) 444-6600. NOTE: Near Buchanan Pass Trailhead, FDT 910. 7.5' TOPOGRAPHIC MAP: Allens Park.

Map No.	Campground Name	Map Loc.	Fee	No. of Units	Max. Length	Elev.	Toilets	Water	Agency
14	**Cold Springs ®**	D-1	$	38	50'	9,200'	Yes	Yes	Arapaho/ Roosevelt National Forest

LOCATION: 4-5 mi. N of Black Hawk on Hwy 119. FACILITIES: Tables, Pets OK. ACTIVITIES: Fishing, Hiking, 4-Wheeling. OPEN FOR USE: Late May through mid-Oct. CONTACT: Clear Creek Ranger District (303) 567-3000. NOTE: Reservations, Handicap Accessible, On Peak to Peak Hwy, 4 miles from Casinos 7.5' TOPOGRAPHIC MAP: Black Hawk.

Map No.	Campground Name	Map Loc.	Fee	No. of Units	Max. Length	Elev.	Toilets	Water	Agency
15	**Columbine ®**	D-1	$	47	20'	9,200'	Yes	Yes	Arapaho/ Roosevelt National Forest

LOCATION: 2-3 mi. NW of Central City on Cty Rd 279. FACILITIES: Tables, Pets OK. ACTIVITIES: Fishing, Hiking, 4-Wheel Drive Roads. OPEN FOR USE: Late May through mid-Oct. CONTACT: Clear Creek Ranger District (303) 567-3000. NOTE: Two miles from Gambling Casinos. 7.5' TOPOGRAPHIC MAP: Central City.

Map No.	Campground Name	Map Loc.	Fee	No. of Units	Max. Length	Elev.	Toilets	Water	Agency
16	**Dowdy Lake ®**	A-1	$	62	40'	8,100'	Yes	Yes	Arapaho/ Roosevelt National Forest

LOCATION: 1 mi. E of Red Feather on Cty Rd 4, 1 mi. E on FDR 218. FACILITIES: Tables, Grills, Trails, Boat ramp, Pets OK. ACTIVITIES: Fishing, Hiking, Boating. OPEN FOR USE: May through Sept. CONTACT: Canyon Lakes Ranger District (970) 498-2770. NOTE: Reservations, Handicap Accessible, Located on Dowdy Lake. 7.5' TOPOGRAPHIC MAP: Red Feather Lakes.

Map No.	Campground Name	Map Loc.	Fee	No. of Units	Max. Length	Elev.	Toilets	Water	Agency
17	**Jacks Gulch**	B-1	$	70	50'	8,100'	Yes	Yes	Arapaho/ Roosevelt National Forest

LOCATION: 6 mi. E of Rustic on Hwy 14, S on Cty Rd 63E (131) approx. 5 mi. south. FACILITIES: Tables, Pets OK. ACTIVITIES: Fishing, Hiking. OPEN FOR USE: June through mid-Sept. CONTACT: Canyon Lakes Ranger District (970) 498-2770. NOTE: Near Bear Creek Trailhead to Comanche Wilderness. 7.5' TOPOGRAPHIC MAPS: Pingree Park. *Jacks Gulch Group ®.*

Map No.	Campground Name	Map Loc.	Fee	No. of Units	Max. Length	Elev.	Toilets	Water	Agency
18	**Kelly Dahl ®**	D-1	$	46	40'	8,600'	Yes	Yes	Arapaho/ Roosevelt National Forest

LOCATION: 3 mi. S of Nederland on Hwy 119. FACILITIES: Tables, Pets OK. ACTIVITIES: Fishing, Hiking. OPEN FOR USE: May through Oct. CONTACT: Boulder Ranger District (303) 444-6600. NOTE: Handicap Accessible. Reservations. 7.5' TOPOGRAPHIC MAP: Tungsten.

Map No.	Campground Name	Map Loc.	Fee	No. of Units	Max. Length	Elev.	Toilets	Water	Agency
19	**Olive Ridge ®**	C-1	$	56	30'	8,350'	Yes	Yes	Arapaho/ Roosevelt National Forest

LOCATION: 15 mi. S of Estes Park on Hwy 7. FACILITIES: Tables, Trails, Pets OK. ACTIVITIES: Fishing, Hiking. OPEN FOR USE: May through Oct. CONTACT: Boulder Ranger District (303) 444-6600. NOTE: Reservations; Handicap Accessible. Near Rocky Mountain National Park and Indian Peaks Wilderness. 7.5' TOPOGRAPHIC MAP: Allens Park.

Map No.	Campground Name	Map Loc.	Fee	No. of Units	Max. Length	Elev.	Toilets	Water	Agency
20	**Pawnee ®**	C-1	$	55	45'	10,350'	Yes	Yes	Arapaho/ Roosevelt National Forest

LOCATION: 6 mi. W of Ward on FDR 112. FACILITIES: Tables, Trailhead, Pets OK. ACTIVITIES: Fishing, Hiking. OPEN FOR USE: July through mid-Oct. CONTACT: Boulder Ranger District (303) 444-6600. NOTE: Reservations, Near Brainard Lake - Indian Peaks Wilderness. 7.5' TOPOGRAPHIC MAP: Ward.

Map No.	Campground Name	Map Loc.	Fee	No. of Units	Max. Length	Elev.	Toilets	Water	Agency
21	**Peaceful Valley ®**	C-1	$	17	55'	8,500'	Yes	Yes	Arapaho/ Roosevelt National Forest

LOCATION: N of Ward on Hwy 72 approx. 7 mi, W on FDR 114 .25 mi. FACILITIES: Tables, Grills. OPEN FOR USE: Late May through mid-Oct. CONTACT: Boulder Ranger District (303) 444-6600. NOTE: Near Buchanan Pass Trailhead, FDT 910. 7.5' TOPOGRAPHIC MAP: Allens Park.

Map No.	Campground Name	Map Loc.	Fee	No. of Units	Max. Length	Elev.	Toilets	Water	Agency
22	**Pickle Gulch Group ®**	D-1	$	Group	Group	9,100'	Yes	Yes	Arapaho/ Roosevelt National Forest

LOCATION: 3 mi. N of Black Hawk on Hwy 119, 1 mi. W on access Rd. FACILITIES: Tables, Pets OK. ACTIVITIES: Fishing, Hiking. OPEN FOR USE: Late May through mid-Oct. CONTACT: Clear Creek Ranger District (303) 567-3000. NOTE: Handicap Accessible, Reservations. 7.5' TOPOGRAPHIC MAP: Central City.

Map No.	Campground Name	Map Loc.	Fee	No. of Units	Max. Length	Elev.	Toilets	Water	Agency
23	**Poudre River Fort Collins to Rustic**	A-1	$				Yes	Yes	Arapaho/ Roosevelt National Forest
a.	Ansel Watrous			19	30'	5,800'	*Construction 2001- Call first.*		
b.	Stove Prairie			9	30'	6,000'			
c.	Narrows			15	30'	6,500'			
d,	Dutch George Flats			20	33'	6,500'			
e.	Mountain Park ®			55	50'	6,650'			
f.	Kelly Flats			29	50/75'	6,750'			

LOCATION: 4 mi. NW of LaPorte on Hwy 287, W on Hwy 14 to Rustic. FACILITIES: Tables, Grills, Pets OK. ACTIVITIES: Fishing, Hiking, Mountain Biking, Wildlife Observation. OPEN FOR USE: Year Round except for Mountain Park which is open Memorial Day though Labor Day. CONTACT: Canyon Lakes Ranger District (970) 498-2770. NOTE: Mountain Park - Reservations. All Handicap Accessible except Narrows. On Poudre River near trailheads to Cache La Poudre Wilderness. 7.5' TOPOGRAPHIC MAPS: Big Meadows, Poudre Park. See map page 33. ♿

Map No.	Campground Name	Map Loc.	Fee	No. of Units	Max. Length	Elev.	Toilets	Water	Agency
24	**Rainbow Lakes**	D-1	$	16	20'	10,000'	Yes	Yes	Arapaho/ Roosevelt National Forest

LOCATION: 6-7 mi. N of Nederland on Hwy 72, 5 mi. W on Cty Rd 116. FACILITIES: Tables, Pets OK. ACTIVITIES: Fishing, Hiking. OPEN FOR USE: Late June through mid-Oct. CONTACT: Boulder Ranger District (303) 444-6600. NOTE: Near trail to Arapaho Glacier Trail and Indian Peaks Wilderness. 7.5' TOPOGRAPHIC MAP: Monarch.

Map No.	Campground Name	Map Loc.	Fee	No. of Units	Max. Length	Elev.	Toilets	Water	Agency
25	**West Lake ®**	A-1	$	29	50'	8,200'	Yes	Yes	Arapaho/ Roosevelt National Forest

LOCATION:1 mi. S of Red Feather on Cty Rd 74E. FACILITIES: Grills, Tables, Trails, Boat Ramp, Pets OK. ACTIVITIES: Fishing, Hiking. OPEN FOR USE: May through Sept. CONTACT: Canyon Lakes Ranger District (970) 498-2770. 7.5' TOPOGRAPHIC MAP: Red Feather Lakes. *Construction 2001 - Call first.* ♿

Map No.	Campground Name	Map Loc.	Fee	No. of Units	Max. Length	Elev.	Toilets	Water	Agency
26	**Meeker Park**	C-1	$	29	25'	8,600'	Yes	No	Arapaho/Roosevelt National Forest

LOCATION: East of Meeker Park on Colorado Highway 7. FACILITIES: Grills, Tables, Pets OK. ACTIVITIES: Fishing, Hiking. OPEN FOR USE: May thru mid-Oct. CONTACT: Boulder Ranger District (303) 444-6600.. NOTE: Adjacent to Rocky Mtn. National Park. 7.5' TOPOGRAPHIC MAP: Allens Park.

Map No.	Campground Name	Map Loc.	Fee	No. of Units	Max. Length	Elev.	Toilets	Water	Agency
27	**Buckingham**	D-1	$	10	35'	10,061'	Yes	Yes	Boulder County

LOCATION:Ten miles NW of Nederland at end of Cty Rd 111. FACILITIES: Grills, Tables, Pets OK. ACTIVITIES: Fishing, Hiking. OPEN FOR USE: July thru mid-Oct. CONTACT: Boulder County Mountain Parks (303) 441-3440. NOTE: Near Diamond Lake and Trailhead to Indian Peaks Wilderness. 7.5' TOPOGRAPHIC MAP: Monarch Lake.

Map No.	Campground Name	Map Loc.	Fee	No. of Units	Max. Length	Elev.	Toilets	Water	Agency
28	**Fairgrounds**	C-2	$	92	52'	5,000'	Yes	Yes	Boulder County

LOCATION: SW Longmont at intersection of Hover & Nelson at Boulder County Fairgrounds. FACILITIES: Grills, Tables, Wheelchair accessible, Pets OK. ACTIVITIES: Near shopping mall and County fairgrounds. OPEN FOR USE: Year Round. CONTACT: Boulder County Parks & Open Space. (303) 441-3440 7.5' TOPOGRAPHIC MAP: City of Longmont.

Map Symbol Explanation

P Parking Area	🏠 Forest Service Facility	(285) U.S. Highway	National Forest Area
🪑 Picnic Area	🎣 Fishing Area	(126) State Highway	Water
🚶 Trailhead	🚐 RV Dump Station	(9) County Highway	•••• Trail
⛷ Downhill Ski Area	🚻 Restrooms	(200) Trail Number	River or Stream
⛵ Boat Launch	♿ Handicap Accessible	358 Forest Service Road	Primary Road - Paved
🚲 Bicycle Trail	🦌 Hunting	▲ Mountain/Peak	Improved Road - Unpaved
🛺 4WD Road	⛺ Campground	Colorado Trail	Unimproved Road - 4WD
🏍 Motorcycle Trail	Towns & Locals	CDT Continental Divide Trail	Forest/Wilderness Boundary

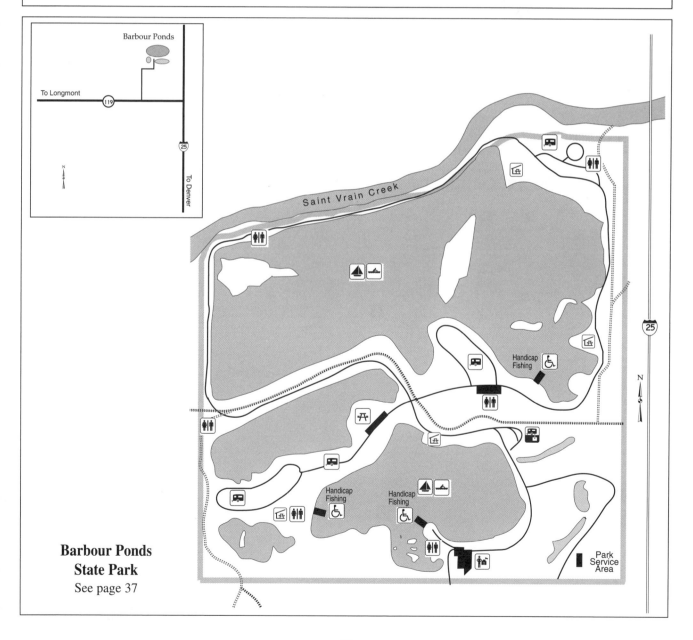

Barbour Ponds

To Longmont — (119)

(25) To Denver

Saint Vrain Creek

Handicap Fishing

Handicap Fishing

Handicap Fishing

(25)

N

Park Service Area

**Barbour Ponds
State Park**
See page 37

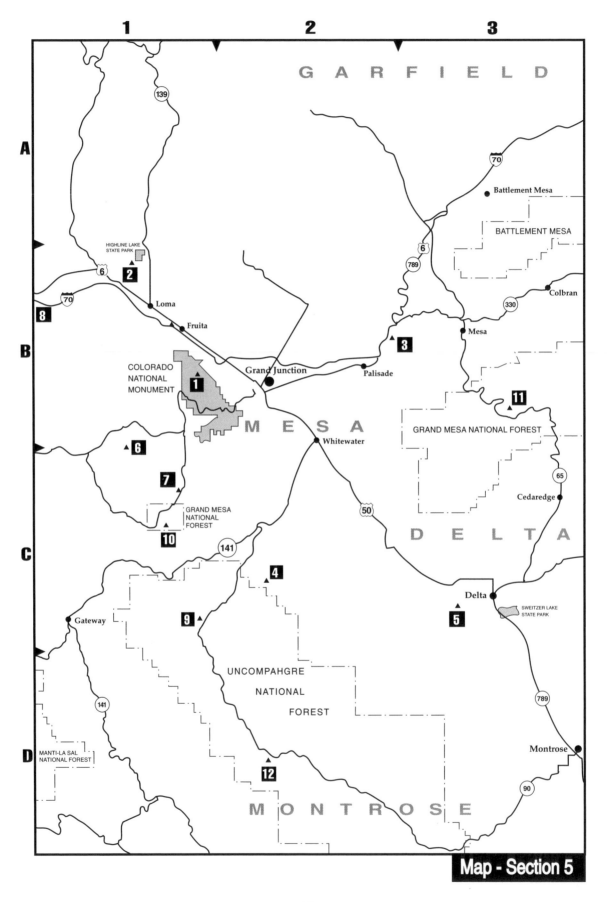

Map - Section 5

Grand Mesa Plateau

Grand Mesa is located between the towns of Mesa and Cedaredge on Colorado 65. It was named by Spanish explorers, "Mesa Grande", which means large table. While not officially recognized as such the Mesa is regionally known as the World's Largest Flat Top Mountain.

The Grand Mesa is, in fact, a very large, flat topped mountain of volcanic origin whose summit area covers some 800 square miles. The Grand Mesa averages 10,000 feet in elevation and towers 6,000 feet above the surrounding Colorado and Gunnison River valleys.

In addition to its geological notoriety, the Grand Mesa is well known for its numerous natural lakes. In all, some 300 lake and reservoirs lie on the benches and top of the Grand Mesa. Of these, roughly a third provide the aquatic habitat needed to sustain trout populations on a year-round basis.

Volcanic activity produced lava flows forming the massive Y- shaped basalt cap with the tail to the east. Pleistocene glaciers caused a weathering process known as "slumping" whereby lava blocks from the margin of the Grand Mesa's cap slid down the mountain side to produce broad landslide benches. It is these slump benches, primarily along the tail of the Y-shaped cap, which have been dammed to create reservoirs. The reservoirs on these benches of the Grand Mesa hold and grow the trout eagerly sought by anglers.

The Grand Mesa offers fishing opportunities for seven species of trout including rainbow, Colorado River cutthroat, Snake River cutthroat, brown and brook trout, as well as splake (hybrid) between lake and brook trout), and Arctic grayling.

Almost all of the lakes and streams lie between 8,000 and 11,000 feet in elevation. Keep in mind your physical abilities at these elevations. This altitude combined with strenuous activity can aggravate or trigger health problems.

The climate at these elevations can change drastically as storms come and go. Near freezing temperatures, even in the middle of the summer, can result following a small thunderstorm in Colorado's high country. Be prepared by taking a jacket along, even if you are only going to fish the other side of the lake.

Nowhere else in Colorado boasts so many diverse trout fishing options situated so close together. These options include various combinations of trout species in the different lakes, along with access ranging from roads suitable for four-wheel drive or motor homes to trails accessible by foot and horseback only. All of these opportunities are located within an hour drive of the conveniences offered by the larger towns of Grand Junction and Delta and all the smaller towns in between.

From "Fishing The Grand Mesa"
Colorado Division Of Wildlife

Map No.	Campground Name	Map Loc.	Fee	No. of Units	Max. Length	Elev.	Toilets	Water	Agency
1	**Colorado National Monument**	B-1	$	80	35'	5,800'	Yes	Yes	National Parks Service

Entrance located 4 miles west of Grand Junction on Colorado 340. Colorado National Monument preserves one of the grand landscapes of the American West. Bold, big, and brilliantly colored, this plateau-and-canyon country, with its towering masses of naturally sculpted rock, embraces 32 square miles of rugged, up-and-down terrain. This is a special place, where you can contemplate glorious views that stretch to distant horizons; where you can discover solitude deep in a remote canyon; where you can delight in wild country where desert bighorns roam and golden eagles soar. In the spirit of those with the foresight to create Colorado National Monument in 1911, and the many since who have sought to protect it, please treat the park with respect so you and others can share in its grandeur tomorrow.

Atop The Plateau
The high country of Colorado National Monument rises more than 2,000 feet above the Grand Valley of the Colorado River. Situated at the edge of the Uncompahgre Uplift, the park is part of the greater Colorado Plateau, which also embraces such geologic wonders as the Grand Canyon, Bryce Canyon, and Arches. It is a semi-desert land of pinyon pines and Utah junipers, ravens and jays, desert bighorns and coyotes. Magnificent views from highland trails and the Rim Rock Drive, which winds along the plateau, stretch from the colorful sheer-walled canyons and fascinating rock sculptures to the distant Colorado River valley, the purple-gray Book Cliffs, and the huge flat-topped mountain called Grand Mesa.

Backcountry Canyons
In the deep canyons of Colorado National Monument, where vertical cliff walls and great natural rock sculptures tower overhead, the grand scale of the scenery is overpowering. Nowhere is this more true than in Monument and Wedding Canyons, where the giant rock forms of Independence Monument, the Pipe Organ, the Kissing Couple, Sentinel Spire, and the Praying Hands rise from the canyon floor like skyscrapers-in-stone.

But the canyons are places, too, where the cascading song of the canyon wren echoes; where small life-sustaining pools linger after summer rains; where cottonwood trees turn golden in autumn. The canyons can be explored along backcountry trails, on foot, or on horseback. On a slow and quiet journey, you might encounter mule deer, desert cottontails, antelope, ground squirrels, chipmunks, lizards, or canyon birds such as pinyon jays, white-throated swifts, and rock wrens. Mountain lions, midget faded rattlesnakes, and other rare or secretive members of the canyon community are seen less often.

Masterpieces of Erosion
From 450 foot high Independence Monument, the largest freestanding rock formation in the park, to the smallest detail carved in stone, the grand sculptor in Colorado National Monument has been erosion. Time-and lots of it has been a loyal ally, for it has taken millions of years to carve the many massive rock spires, huge domes, balanced rocks, arches, windows, stone pedestals, and sheer-walled canyons that make up the scenic splendor of the park. The erosive forces of water, wind and frost work very slowly. Differences in the characteristics of the many layers of sandstone, shale, and other sedimentary rocks of the area help determine what form the rocks will take. The harder rock layers are more resistant to erosion. One such layer-the Kayenta Formation forms the protective caprock of Independence Monument and other hold, angular rock forms. Once it has been eroded rounded shapes like those of the Coke Ovens are formed from the less resistant underlying layers. Fractures in the rock also influence erosive forces. The remarkable colors-vivid reds, purples, oranges, and browns-are created by iron and other minerals in the rock.

Camping
Saddlehorn Campground is situated near the visitor center in a pinyon-juniper scrub forest. Campsites are available first-come, first-served. Each site offers a table, charcoal grill, and access to drinking water and restrooms. A fee is charged. Backcountry camping is free and is permitted anyplace more than 1/4 mile from roads and 100 yards from trails. Other federal, state, and commercial campgrounds are located near the park. Water is available in the slimmer months only.

Barrier Free Access
Some park overlooks, backcountry areas, and other park sites and facilities are handicap-accessible; check at the visitor center for information.

Park Trails
Exploring by trail is a good way to see Colorado National Monument in any season. Choose short trails to spectacular overlooks or backcountry trails into canyons or across mesa's. Plateau trails are level or gradually sloping; other trails may have short stretches requiring steep ascent or descent. Take your time, interests, hiking experience, and physical fitness into account. Carry plenty of water and wear hiking boots or other footgear appropriate for rocky or sandy surfaces. Pace yourself if you begin to tire and watch the weather. If you hike the backcountry or off-trail, carry a topographic map and notify a ranger or a friend of your plans. Mountain bikes, other off-road vehicles, and pets are prohibited on trails or anywhere in the backcountry. Horse use is allowed on all backcountry trails except Serpents Trail. Some trails may be too steep or narrow for riding or leading animals readily - or at all.

Information:
For information write Colorado National Monument, Fruita, CO 81521
(970) 858-3617.

Map No.	Campground Name	Map Loc.	Fee	No. of Units	Max. Length	Elev.	Toilets	Water	Agency
2	**Highline State Park ®**	B-1	$	25	35'	4,697'	Yes	Yes	Colorado State Parks

Highline State Park, located 7 miles northwest of Loma near Highway 139, is the center for water sports and recreation in the Grand Valley. Its warm waters provide comfortable settings for water skiing, swimming, fishing and picnicking. Highline Lake, completed in 1969 has 16 surface-acres for water recreation. Mack Mesa Lake provides good fishing and solitude, away from motorized boats. In winter, large numbers of migratory birds use the park as a rest stop. Whether you visit Highline to rest or to play, its wildlife and recreational opportunities will entertain you.

Camping
Highline State Recreation Area offers 25 grassy campsites that can accommodate both tents and RV's. A holding tank dump station is located in the campground. Campers must have both a camping permit and a parks pass, both available at the park entrance.

Wildlife
More than 150 species of birds have been observed at Highline State Recreation Area, and migrating ducks and geese winter at Highline Lake. Birds such as the great blue heron, white pelican, snowy egret, whopping crane, golden eagle and bald eagle are seen in the park.

Accessibility
A fishing jetty with wheelchair stops is located on the southwest side of Mack Mesa Lake, and is designed specifically to accommodate persons with disabilities.

Fishing
Mack Mesa Lake is noted for its fine early season trout fishing. Only hand or electric powered boats are allowed. Highline Lake has good warm water fishing, especially for catfish and crappie.

Other Activities
Boating, Hiking, Group Picnicking, and Swimming.

Daily Fee/Annual Pass
For more information contact:
Highline State Park
1800 11.8 Road
Loma, CO 81524 (97O) 858-7208

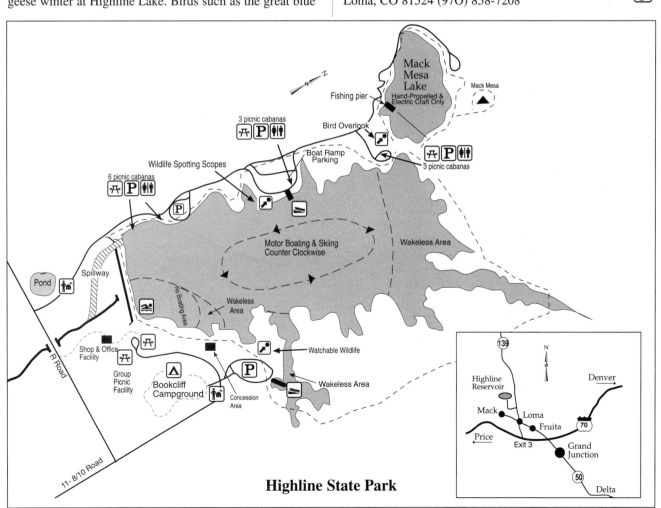

Highline State Park

Section 5

Map No.	Campground Name	Map Loc.	Fee	No. of Units	Max. Length	Elev.	Toilets	Water	Agency
3	**Colorado River State Park ®**	B-2	$	53	35'	5,000'	Yes	Yes	Colorado State Parks

Colorado River State Park follows the Colorado River for miles through Grand Junction and the Grand Valley at Colorado's western border. The park will link together all the various trails in the area along the river corridor from Island Acres on the east to the Loma boat launch to the west. Along this trail system there are a number of small park picnic sites and fishing areas managed by the Colorado State Parks.

Camping
Island Acres is the only area of Colorado River State Park that offers camping. Located 15 miles east of Grand Junction on Interstate 70 there are 34 campsites that can accommodate either tents or campers. Campground users must display a valid camping permit in the provided campsite marker. Camping is permitted in designated sites only. A dump station is located near the park entrance.

Facilities for the Disabled
Island Acres provides accessible parking areas, restrooms and campsites. The park's concrete fishing pier is safe, secure and wheelchair accessible.

Wildlife
The best time for viewing wildlife is in early evening. The careful observer may see mule deer, skunks, cottontail rabbits, weasels, ducks, Canadian geese, hawks, bald eagles blue herons and bull snakes all of which are common in the park and the surrounding area.

Fishing
Good rainbow trout fishing is available March through May, and September through October. Catfish, bluegill, carp, and an occasional bass may be caught year round.

Other Activities
Picnicking, Boating, Swimming and Hiking.

Daily Fee/Annual Pass
For more information contact:
Colorado River State Park
PO Box 700
Clifton, CO 81520
(970) 434-3388

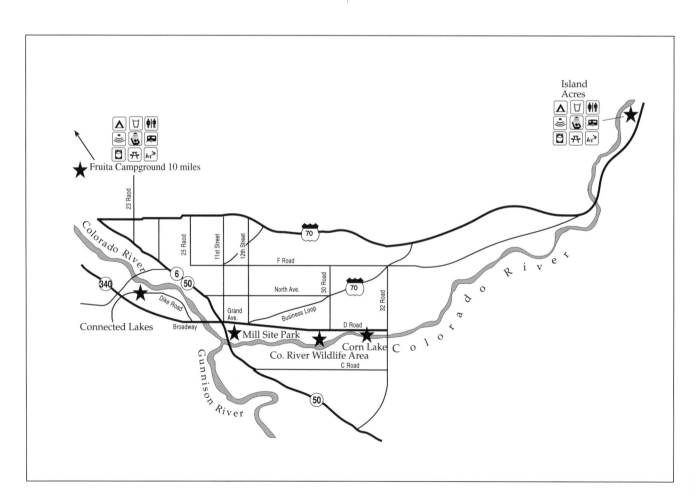

Map No.	Campground Name	Map Loc.	Fee	No. of Units	Max. Length	Elev.	Toilets	Water	Agency
4	**Big Dominguez**	C-2	0	9	18'	7,500'	Yes	Yes	Bureau of Land Management

LOCATION: 9 mi. SE of Grand Junction on Hwy 50 to Whitewater, 14 mi. SW on Hwy 141, Left at FDR 402, follow signs approx. 8 miles. FACILITIES: None. ACTIVITIES: Fishing, Hiking. OPEN FOR USE: Late May through Oct. CONTACT: Grand Junction Resource Area (970) 244-3000. NOTE: Camp is beside Big Dominguez Creek. A service map is advised 7.5' TOPOGRAPHIC MAP: Jacks Canyon.

Map No.	Campground Name	Map Loc.	Fee	No. of Units	Max. Length	Elev.	Toilets	Water	Agency
5	**Escalante State Wildlife Area**	C-3	0	Dispersed	Open	5,000'	Yes	No	Colorado Division of Wildlife

LOCATION: 12 NW of Delta, on Hwy 50, to Escalante Rd. (Rest Area), 3 miles S to River, 3/4 mi. up stream on S side Gunnison River (Primitive Road). FACILITIES: None. ACTIVITIES: Fishing, Hunting, Hiking, interpretative program, historical area. OPEN FOR USE: Late May through Oct. CONTACT: Colorado Division of Wildlife NW Region (970) 255-6100. *NOTE: Located near Gunnison River.* 7.5' TOPOGRAPHIC MAP: Mack.

Map No.	Campground Name	Map Loc.	Fee	No. of Units	Max. Length	Elev.	Toilets	Water	Agency
6	**Miracle Rock**	C-1	0	4	30'	7,000'	Yes	No	Bureau of Land Management

LOCATION: W on Hwy 340 from Grand Junction, left at National Monument 12.5 mi. S to Glade Park Store sign, S on Cty Rd. 16.5 8 miles. FACILITIES: None. ACTIVITIES: Fishing, Hiking. OPEN FOR USE: May through Oct. CONTACT: Grand Junction Resource Area (970) 244-3000. NOTE: Located on Little Dolores River. (CALL FIRST). 7.5' TOPOGRAPHIC MAP: Payne Wash.

Map No.	Campground Name	Map Loc.	Fee	No. of Units	Max. Length	Elev.	Toilets	Water	Agency
7	**Mud Springs**	C-1	0	12	30'	8,000'	Yes	Yes	Bureau of Land Management

LOCATION: From Grand Junction W on Hwy 340, left to Colorado Monument for 7.5 mi. past E entrance. Left at Glade Park sign for 5.0 mi., S on FDR 165 6.6 mi. FACILITIES: None. ACTIVITIES: 4-Wheeling Drive, Hiking. OPEN FOR USE: May through Oct. CONTACT: Grand Junction Resource Area (970) 244-3000 (CALL FIRST). 7.5' TOPOGRAPHIC MAP: Glade Park.

Map No.	Campground Name	Map Loc.	Fee	No. of Units	Max. Length	Elev.	Toilets	Water	Agency
8	**Rabbit Valley**	B-1	0	8	30'	4,500'	Yes	Yes	Bureau of Land Management

LOCATION: E of Utah State line 2 mi. (Exit 2), S 1 mi. to area. FACILITIES: Toilets,Picnic tables. ACTIVITIES: OHV riding, Horseback Riding, Hiking. OPEN FOR USE: Year Round. CONTACT: Grand Junction Resource Area (970) 244-3000. NOTE: OHV Staging area, hiking trailhead. Capacity 30 people. 7.5' TOPOGRAPHIC MAPS: Bitter Creek Well.

Map No.	Campground Name	Map Loc.	Fee	No. of Units	Max. Length	Elev.	Toilets	Water	Agency
9	**Divide Fork**	C-1	$	11	22'	9,200'	Yes	Yes	Uncompahgre National Forest

LOCATION: S of Grand Junction on Hwy 50 to Whitewater, 13 mi SW on Hwy 141, 15 mi SW on FDR 402. FACILITIES: Picnic tables. ACTIVITIES: Fishing, Hiking, FDT 622. OPEN FOR USE: Late May thru Oct. CONTACT: Grand Junction Ranger District (970) 242-8211. 7.5' TOPOGRAPHIC MAP: Casto Reservoir.

Map No.	Campground Name	Map Loc.	Fee	No. of Units	Max. Length	Elev.	Toilets	Water	Agency
10	**Hay Press**	C-1	0	11	16'	9,300'	Yes	Yes	Grand Mesa National Forest

LOCATION: 10 mi. SW of Grand Junction on Hwy 340, 20 mi. S on Cty Rd 400. FACILITIES: Picnic Tables. ACTIVITIES: Fishing, Hiking. OPEN FOR USE: Late May through Nov. CONTACT: Grand Junction Ranger District (970) 242-8211. *NOTE: Camp is along Little Fruita Reservoir No. 3 on Hay Press Creek.* 7.5' TOPOGRAPHIC MAP: Fish Creek.

Map No.	Campground Name	Map Loc.	Fee	No. of Units	Max. Length	Elev.	Toilets	Water	Agency
11	**Grand Mesa Plateau**	B-3	$						Grand Mesa National Forest
	Map 1 Page 53								
a.	Big Creek			11	30'	10,000'	Yes	No	Grand Junction RD
b.	Cobbett (Carp Lake)			20	30'	10,000'	Yes	Yes	Grand Junction RD
c.	Cottonwood Lake			42	30'	10,000'	Yes	Yes	Collbran RD
d.	Crag Crest			11	30'	10,100'	Yes	Yes	Grand Junction RD
e.	Eggleston + Group ®			6	30'	10,100'	Yes	Yes	Grand Junction RD
f.	Island Lake			41	45'	10,300'	Yes	Yes	Grand Junction RD
g.	Jumbo (FDT 502)			26	22'	9,800'	Yes	Yes	Collbran RD
h.	Kiser Creek			12	16'	10,100'	Yes	No	Grand Junction RD
i.	Little Bear			36	22'	10,200'	Yes	Yes	Grand Junction RD
j.	Spruce Grove			16	22'	9,900'	Yes	Yes	Collbran RD
k.	Ward Lake			27	20'	10,200'	Yes	Yes	Grand Junction RD
	Map 2 Page 54								
l.	Twin Lake			13	22'	10,300'	Yes	No	Grand Junction RD
m.	Weir & Johnson (FDT 717)			12	22'	10,500'	Yes	No	Grand Junction RD

LOCATION: From Cedaredge on the south, or Mesa on the north, Hwy 65 Approx. 16 mi. either direction. FACILITIES: Most campgrounds are fully developed. Boat ramps are at the following locations; Big Creek Reservoir, Cottonwood Reservoir #1, Vega Reservoir, Alexander Lake, Eggleston Lake, Island Lake, Park Reservoir, Vela Reservoir, Youngs Creek Reservoir #3. ACTIVITIES: Fishing, Hiking. OPEN FOR USE: Late June through mid-Oct. CONTACT: Grand Junction Ranger District (970) 242-8211, Grand Junction Ranger District (970) 242-8211. NOTE: Fishing in many of the 300 stream fed lakes, hiking trails, wildlife viewing. Crag Crest National Recreation Trail a 10 mile long circular trail provides magnificent views of Battlement Mesa to the north, West Elk Mountains and San Juan Range to the south. 7.5' TOPOGRAPHIC MAPS: Mesa Lakes, Grand Mesa and Leon Peak.

♿ Little Bear Campground

Map No.	Campground Name	Map Loc.	Fee	No. of Units	Max. Length	Elev.	Toilets	Water	Agency
12	**Columbine**	D-2	$	6	30'	9,000'	Yes	No	Uncompahgre National Forest

LOCATION: Approx. 25 northeast of Nucla on FDR 503. Near Columbine Pass. FACILITIES: Picnic tables. fire grates, Pets OK. ACTIVITIES: Fishing, Hiking. OPEN FOR USE: Late May through Labor Day.. CONTACT: Ouray Ranger District (970) 240-5300 7.5' TOPOGRAPHIC MAP: Starvation Point.

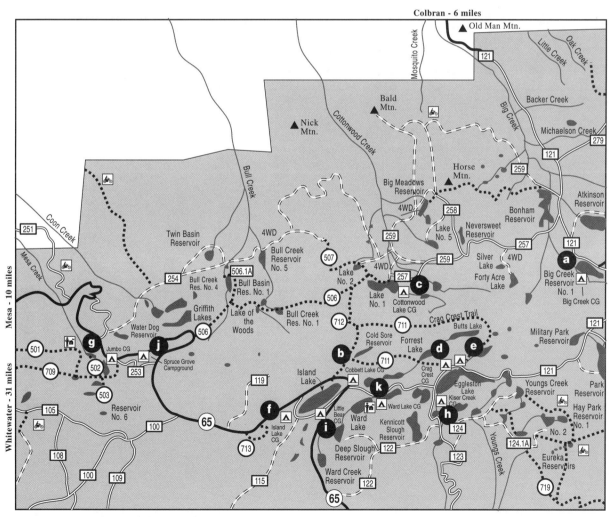

(W/2)   Grand Mesa Map 1

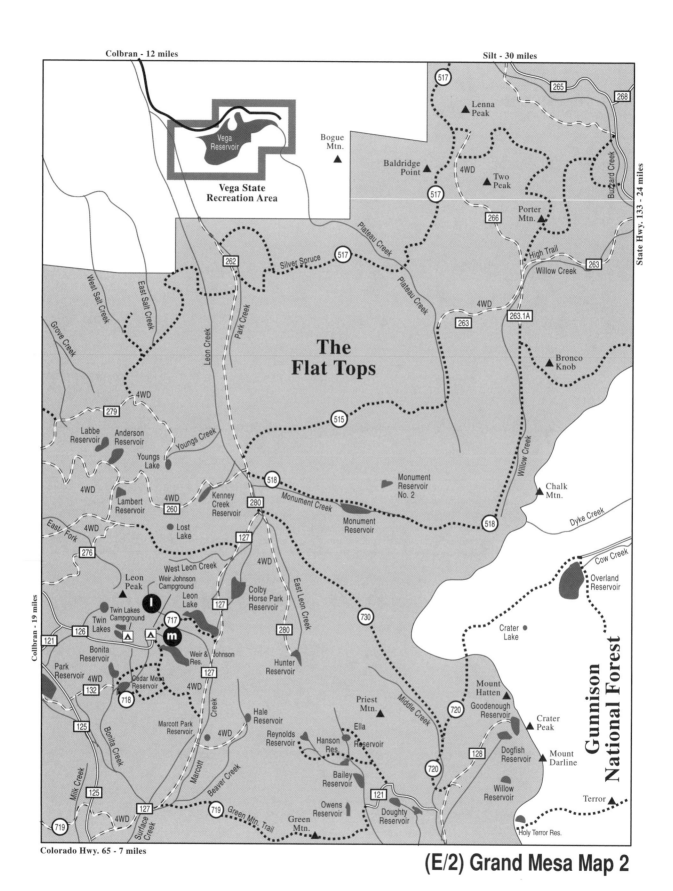

Colbran - 12 miles

Silt - 30 miles

Vega Reservoir

Vega State Recreation Area

Bogue Mtn.

Lenna Peak

Baldridge Point

Two Peak

Porter Mtn.

Buzzard Creek

State Hwy. 133 - 24 miles

Plateau Creek

Silver Spruce

High Trail

Willow Creek

West Salt Creek

East Salt Creek

Grove Creek

Leon Creek

Park Creek

The Flat Tops

4WD

Bronco Knob

Willow Creek

Youngs Creek

Labbe Reservoir

Anderson Reservoir

Youngs Lake

Kenney Creek Reservoir

Monument Reservoir No. 2

Chalk Mtn.

Dyke Creek

4WD

Lambert Reservoir

4WD

Lost Lake

Monument Creek

Monument Reservoir

East Fork

4WD

West Leon Creek

Weir Johnson Campground

Colby Horse Park Reservoir

East Leon Creek

Cow Creek

Overland Reservoir

Leon Peak

Leon Lake

Crater Lake

Gunnison National Forest

Twin Lakes Campground

Twin Lakes

Bonita Reservoir

Weir & Johnson Res.

Hunter Reservoir

Park Reservoir

4WD

Cedar Mesa Reservoir

4WD

Mount Hatten

Goodenough Reservoir

Crater Peak

Marcott Park Reservoir

4WD

Hale Reservoir

Priest Mtn.

Ella Reservoir

Dogfish Reservoir

Mount Darline

Bonita Creek

Reynolds Reservoir

Hanson Res.

Milk Creek

Marcott Creek

Beaver Creek

Bailey Reservoir

Willow Reservoir

Terror

Owens Reservoir

Doughty Reservoir

Surface Creek

Green Mtn. Trail

Green Mtn.

Holy Terror Res.

Colbran - 19 miles

Colorado Hwy. 65 - 7 miles

(E/2) Grand Mesa Map 2

STATE WILDLIFE AREA CAMPGROUNDS
Don Schuchardt

Colorado is home to tens of thousands of campers, and the demand for campsites to accommodate all of them are commensurate. Fortunately, Colorado is blessed with a multitude of campgrounds. Camping is found in National Forests, Parks, Monuments, and Recreation Areas, as well as Bureau of Land Management campsites. Many additional sites are found within our State Parks system. Surprisingly, there is even a number of small towns (municipalities) that permit overnight camping in small overnight rest areas. Pheasant hunters traveling eastern Colorado, Kansas, and Nebraska have enjoyed these for years. Some towns operate impressively large parks with campgrounds. An outstanding example is Lakewood's Bear Creek Lake Park.

Not to be overlooked are thousands of sites in privately operated campgrounds throughout the Centennial state. Even with such an impressive array of choices for RV campers, and tent campers, many are quickly filled during the summer, especially during the "Big 3" holidays. This is especially true of the "high profile" campgrounds such as those in our State Parks.

The Colorado State Park system has enjoyed a steady stream of revenue from the state lottery. This money has financed dramatic improvements in all of our state parks, and Colorado campers have been quick to recognize them. Although many State Park campgrounds still have open availability during the middle of the week, weekends usually require a reservation.

If your favorite campground is full (or too crowded to suit your tastes) don't despair. There is a category of campgrounds available that usually has unused campsites and does not require reservations and (with few exceptions) charges no fee. (Pinch yourself if you think you're dreaming!) They are operated by the state Division of Wildlife and are referred to as State Wildlife Areas (SWA). Fishermen and hunters have used these for years and, of course, many of these outdoors men are also campers.

Although the original purpose of adding campsites to SWA's was to provide overnight camping for the fisherman and hunters, they have since proven to be a boon to the general camping fraternity, including those who do not hunt or fish.

Virtually all of them are in a pleasant, natural (sometimes pristine) setting, away from the noise and traffic of urban areas. Some are in near-wilderness settings. Most provide a dramatic overlook from the front door of your tent or RV. It may be a lake, a stream, a mountain, or a high plains panorama. Most provide excellent opportunities for wildlife observation, bird watching, hiking, and (frequently) fishing and hunting.

A complete list of SWA's is found in the current Fishing Season Information pamphlet, printed by the Colorado Division of Wildlife, and available free at all stores that sell fishing licenses.

The current list comprises approximately 243 properties! However, camping is not permitted in all State Wildlife Areas. You will have to read your brochure carefully to determine which units prohibit camping. Better yet, your Complete Colorado Campground Guide has done the work for you, by listing those SWA's in which camping is legal. They are a cinch to locate because they are listed in the Alphabetical Campground Index located in the last pages of this guide. They're easy to spot because each one has the denotation SWA following the name in the information bar heading.

Another simple location system we've devised in this issue of the Complete Colorado Campground Guide is found in the Section pages. You'll notice that the last column in each campground entry is titled "Agency" This box identifies the government agency which manages this particular campground. If the campground is a SWA, the "agency" will show as Colorado Division of Wildlife.

Start on page 2 and pick the section of the state in which you wish to camp, then turn to the pages that contain that section. Now, start turning pages in that section while scanning the far right column of each page entitled "agency." Whenever you spot the letters DOW in the "Agency" box, you have located a State Wildlife Area that permits camping, along with a description. You will notice that some of these (usually larger) units have restrooms, drinking water, and even boat launching ramps. Most DOW areas have no fee and few have drinking water. The description will provide the information.

Don't confuse their level of luxury (or lack thereof) with Colorado's State Parks, some of which can truthfully be described as "luxury campground destination resorts," e.g. Ridgway State Park. On the other hand, some SWA campgrounds could qualify for the term "semi-primitive." This can work to your advantage (provided your RV has a toilet, and drinking water), in providing an additional measure of natural serenity, less traffic and noise, fewer people, and a high quality nature experience. The no-fee feature is an added bonus.

If you have not yet tried the SWA experience, do it this year. It might open up a refreshingly new dimension to your camping scene.

Don Schuchardt is a free-lance writer from Littleton and is a previous contributor to our publication. His articles also appear in the Beacon Review. He is well known among Colorado RV campers, having sold RV's for many years at Nolan's RV Center.

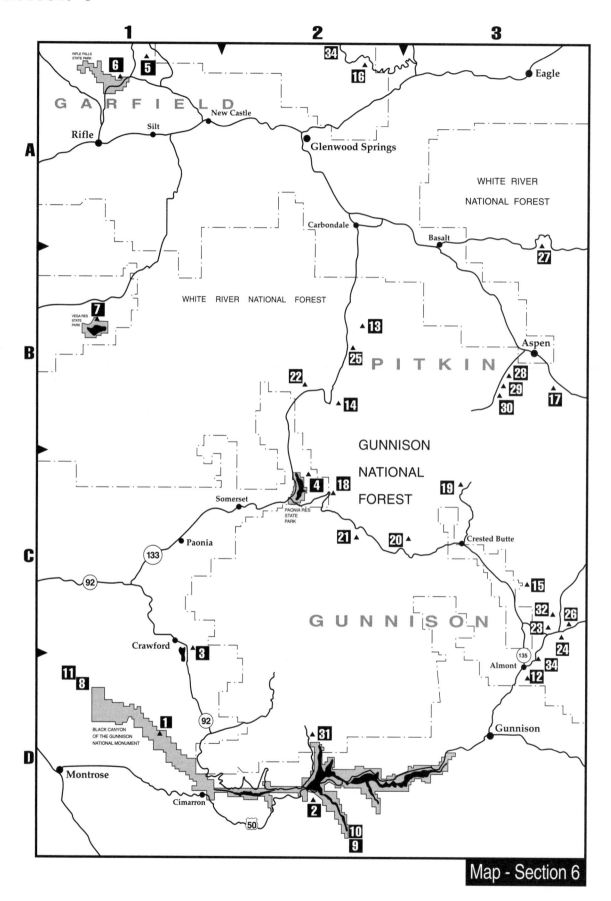

Map - Section 6

PhotDisc

Map No.	Name	Map Loc.	Fee	No. of Units	Max. Length	Elev.	Toilets	Water	Agency
1	**Black Canyon of the Gunnison**	D-1	$	115	35'	8,700'	Yes	Yes	National Parks Service

Black Canyon of the Gunnison National Park is located in west-central Colorado 15 miles east of Montrose via U.S. 50 and Colorado 347. No over-night lodging, other than camping, is available within the park.

Several western canyons exceed the Black Canyon in overall size. Wallace Hansen wrote after studying the geology of the region for a number of years. "Some are longer, some are deeper, some are narrower, and a few have walls as steep, but no other canyon in North America combines the depth, narrowness, sheerness, and somber countenance of the Black Canyon of the Gunnison." And its largely because of this unique combination of geologic features that the Black Canyon has been preserved in its wild state.

The Black Canyon, which has been carved by the Gunnison River as it hurries to join the Colorado, is 53 miles long, but only the deepest, most spectacular 12 miles of the gorge lie within Black Canyon of the Gunnison National Monument. Slanting rays of sunlight penetrate the deep and narrow canyon's dark gray walls of schist and gneiss that are shrouded in heavy shadows most of the day, hence, "Black Canyon:" East of the park the Gunnison River has been impounded and tamed behind three dams. In the Black Canyon, however, it remains one of the few unspoiled wild rivers in the country.

The canyon and its rims are home to a variety of wildlife, from the chipmunks and ground squirrels to weasels, badgers, marmots, and black bear. Infrequently, bobcat and cougars are sighted, and at night, coyotes may be heard. If you come across trees that have been gnawed on, you have found evidence that porcupines are thereabouts, for the bark of pinyon pine is a favored winter food of this quill covered rodent. The Gambel oak and service berry cover most of the Gunnison Uplift provide a good habitat for towhees, western tanagers, pinyon and scrub jays, and black billed magpies. The cliffs are home to white throated swifts, violet-green swallows, golden eagles, turkey vultures, and red-tailed hawks, who all take advantage of the updrafts for soaring. The canyon is also a shelter for the peregrine falcon.

Though a home to wildlife, the canyon has been a mighty barrier to human beings. Archaeology indicates that pre-historic man, and later the Utes, used only the canyon rims, never living in the gorge. The first white men to see the great chasm actually were members of the Hayden Expedition in 1873-74. It appears that the Spaniards, including the famed Dominguez-Escalante Expedition in 1776, all missed seeing the canyon as they came over the Uncompahgre Plateau and into the Uncompahgre Valley on various journeys of exploration. Even the group led by Capt John W. Gunnison, whose name has become permanently attached to the river, bypassed the gorge itself in the search for a river crossing. The Hayden Expedition and later surveying parties for the Denver & Rio Grande Railroad pronounced the Black Canyon "inaccessible."

By the last decade of the 19th century there was much interest in tapping the Gunnison River as a source of water for the Uncompahgre Valley. In 1900, five valley men made a heroic effort to float through the canyon with surveying equipment, but after a month's effort, they had to admit defeat. In 1901 William Torrence and Abraham Lincoln Fellows, learning a lesson from the previous trip, took a rubber mattress for a raft, arranged to be supplied at various points from the rim, and were able to make their way through the canyon- 33 miles in nine days. From the engineering log the two men kept, it was obvious that an irrigation tunnel was a feasible project. In January 1905 construction work began on the diversion tunnel. Progress was slow because of the many difficulties that the work crews encountered. Intense heat, violent cascades of water, and unstable rock formations were just a few of the problems the engineers had to deal with. When finished the tunnel measured 5.8 miles long and could carry enough water to irrigate a sizable farming community. Eight years after Torrence and Fellow's trip, on September 23, 1909, President William Howard Taft presided over the dedication ceremonies for the Gunnison Diversion Tunnel, a notable engineering achievement for this or any time.

The Visitor Center
Begin your stay in the park at the visitor center, where you can get information on current activities and the staff can answer your questions. Exhibits explain the history, flora and fauna, and geology.

Camping
The park has two campgrounds-one on each rim. North Rim (Campground Map #1) has 13 campsites, South Rim; (Campground Map #2) has 102 campsites, campsites are available on first-come, first-served basis. Water must be used sparingly because it has to be hauled by tank truck. Each campsite has its own fireplace or charcoal grill, and a table. Wood gathering is not permitted, nor is wood provided. Bring charcoal, or wood and water with you. There is a normal camping charge.

Information
For further information, write: Superintendent, 2233 East Main, Montrose, CO 81402; or call: (970) 641-2337

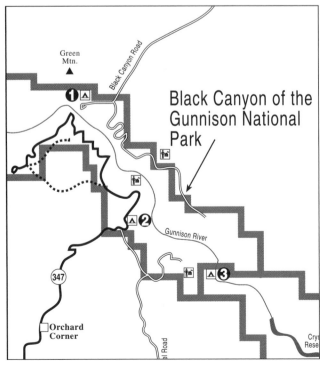

Map No.	Name	Map Loc.	Fee	No. of Units	Max. Length	Elev.	Toilets	Water	Agency
2	**Curecanti National Recreation Area**	D-2		365	35'	7,500'			National Parks Service

Curecanti National Recreation Area's stark landscape bears the imprint of attempts to alter these rugged mesa's and canyons for human purposes. The most recent major alteration was the construction of three dams on the Gunnison River, to provide irrigation and hydroelectric power. These Wayne N. Aspinal Unit dams of the Bureau of Reclamation Upper Colorado River Storage Project have transformed this semi-arid locale into a lake-based recreation mecca. The high, dry eroded vistas are now interrupted not only by the Gunnison Rivers narrow thread, but also by three lakes; Blue Mesa, Morrow Point, and Crystal. Blue Mesa serves as the main storage reservoir. Morrow Point Dam generates most of the power and Crystal Dam maintains an even flow through Black Canyon of the Gunnison. The old rock faces of the Black Canyon that holds the water of Morrow Point and Crystal lakes tell of changes which have occurred over 2 billion years. Surrounding mesa's are capped with cliffs and rocky spires telling of violent volcanic eruptions some 30 million years ago. These formed the West Elk Mountains to the north. Later episodes to the south, forming southwestern Colorado's scenic San Juan Mountains, spewed vast quantities of ash over this area. The ancestral Gunnison River readily cut down through this volcanic matter, but below lay ancient rock that is exposed in Black Canyon. This canyon lends the fjord-like character to Morrow Point Lake's steep, rock walls. Crystal Lake is also steep-walled. Blue Mesa's lake bed formed in less-resistant volcanic mud-flow materials. As these eroded beneath solidified volcanic layers, spires formed.

You can see a fine example of this formation when hiking the Dillon Pinnacles Trail. The most striking feature of the lower lakes is the spire like Curecanti Needle. It is best viewed from the tour boat on Morrow Point Lake. Curecanti's fish - brown, rainbow and Mackinaw trout and kokanee salmon - attract the greatest number of people to the park. Recreational opportunities abound; power boating, sailing, wind surfing, camping, hiking and hunting. Any season offers such rewarding sightseeing as the Morrow Point Dam power plant tour, Pioneer Point, the Cimarron Railroad Exhibit's historic narrow gauge and the Gunnison Diversion Tunnel. But for the most part, you have the rare opportunity to savor here the solitude and silence of canyons and mesa's.

Hiking

Curecanti's trail system offers varied hiking experiences. Bird watchers especially enjoy the .5 mile Never Sink Trail, with its lush, stream-side habitat that birds favor. The 2.5 mile Dillon Pinnacles Trail threads dry mesa country to the spectacular Dillon Pinnacles and on for an impressive view of Blue Mesa Lake. Curecanti Creek and Hermits Rest Trails lead to Morrow Point Lake from Colorado Highway 92.

Caution: The rapid vertical elevation change on these trails is about 1,000 feet. But these trails are ideal for short backpacking trips or long day hikes. Crystal Creek Trail, also strenuous, leads to an overlook of Crystal Lake, the canyon and surrounding San Juan and West Elk mountain ranges. Mesa Creek Trail follows Crystal Lake's rocky shore for 0.75 miles as a fishing access trail.

Pine Creek Trail leads down to Morrow Point Lake for the boat tour, shore fishing, boat launching or sightseeing along a limited section of the narrow gauge railroad bed. Hikers please note: Curecanti lies 7,500 feet above sea level. Easy trails may he strenuous if you are not used to the altitude.

Camping

Curecanti's major developed campgrounds are Elk Creek, Lake Fork, Stevens Creek, and Cimarron. Smaller areas along Blue Mesa at Dry Gulch, Red Creek, Ponderosa and Gatesview offer more seclusion. Camping is allowed in designated areas only. It is on first-come, first-served basis and is limited to 14 days. The East Elk Creek Group Campground requires reservations. Make them by calling (970) 641-2337. Each lake also offers water access camping sites for boaters.

Map No.	Name	Fee	Sites	Toilets	Water
3.	Cimarron	$	22	Yes	Yes
11.	Ponderosa	$	21	Yes	Yes
14.	Lake Fork	$	87	Yes	Yes
15.	Gateview	0	7	Yes	Yes
19.	Red Creek	$	7	Yes	Yes
21.	Dry Gulch	$	10	Yes	Yes
22.	East Elk Creek ®	$	Group	Yes	Yes
22a.	Elk Creek Visitors Center				
		$	179	Yes	Yes
26	Stevens Creek	$	54	Yes	Yes

Campground west of mapped area -- See map page 60

	East Portal	$	15	Yes	Yes

Location: Elk Creek; 16 mi W of Gunnison. Lake Fork; 27 mi W of Gunnison. Stevens Creek; 12 mi W of Gunnison. Cimarron; E of Montrose. Dry Gulch; Just N of Hwy 50, 17 mi W of Gunnison. Red Creek; Just N of Hwy 50, 19 mi W of Gunnison. Gateview; S end of Lake Fork arm of Blue Mesa Lake. Access from Hwy 149,7 mi W of Powderhorn. Proceed N 6 mi on an improved narrow gravel road. Ponderosa; NW end of Soap Creek arm of Blue Mesa Lake. Access Hwy 92, 1/2 mi W of Blue Mesa Dam. Proceed N 7 mi on Soap Creek gravel road. Note: 7 mi of Soap Creek Road are accessible to RV's & trailers during dry conditions. Rain can make the road hazardous. East Portal; 2 mi below Crystal Dam at the bottom of Black Canyon. Access Hwy 347, 6 mi N of junction Hwy 50. 5 mi down East Portal Road. Note: trailers, buses and RV's are not permitted on East Portal road because of steep grade and sharp, narrow curves.

For Information Contact:
Curecanti National Recreation Area
102 Elk Creek, Gunnison, CO 81230
(970) 641-2337

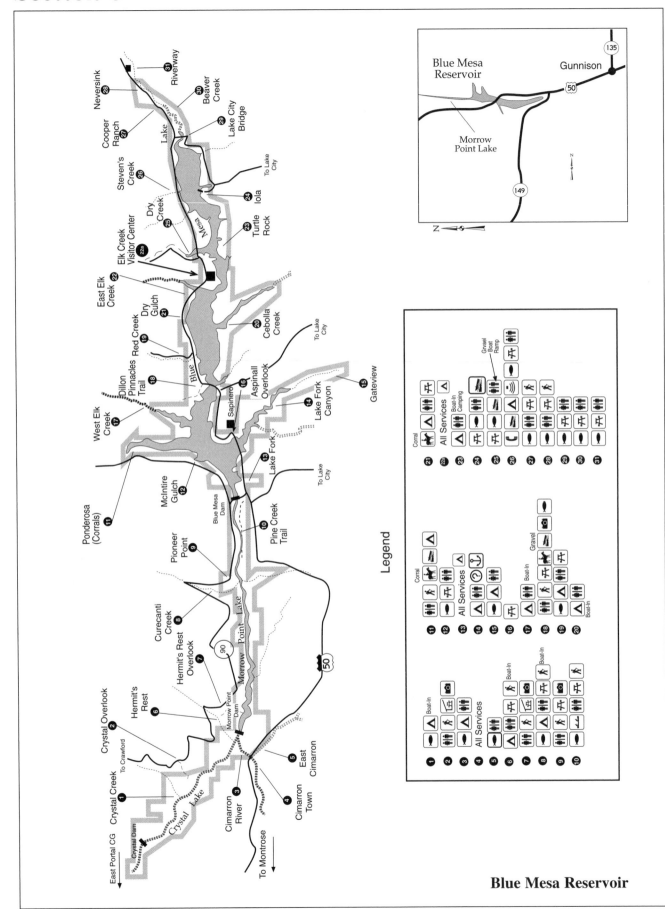

Blue Mesa Reservoir

Map No.	Name	Map Loc.	Fee	No. of Units	Max. Length	Elev.	Toilets	Water	Agency
3	**Crawford State Park ®**	C-1	$	66	35'	6,600'	Yes	Yes	Colorado State Parks

Crawford State Park, 1 mile south of Crawford on Colorado Hwy 92, offers its visitors camping, fishing, watersports, hunting and numerous other leisure time activities in scenic mountain terrain. The park's 6,600 ft. elevation guarantees visitors a mild climate at any season. The famous and spectacular Black Canyon of the Gunnison is only l4 miles from the park. Nearer landmarks visible from Crawford State Park are Needle Rock, Castle Rock and Cathedral Peak. Within the boundaries of Crawford State Park are 821 land acres and a 400 acre reservoir.

Camping
Crawford offers 66 modern campsites for your enjoyment. These can accommodate tents, trailers and campers. Tables, grills and use pads are available at each campsite. Water hydrants are found in both main campgrounds. A dump station is located in the center campground.

Wildlife
Beavers, chipmunks, rabbits and even mule deer live in or around the park and may frequently he seen at shoreline late in the evening. A variety of waterfowl, from western grebes to graceful Canada geese, may be seen at Crawford State Park, either stopping off during migrations or nesting.

Fishing
Crawford State Park is well known as a quality trout fishery. Rainbow, German brown trout and channel catfish are stocked in the reservoir. Several record yellow perch have also been caught here.

Activities
Swimming, Picnicking, Scuba Diving and Water-skiing.

Daily Fee(Annual Pass
For more information contact:
Crawford State Park
Box 147
Crawford, Colorado 81415
(970) 921-5721

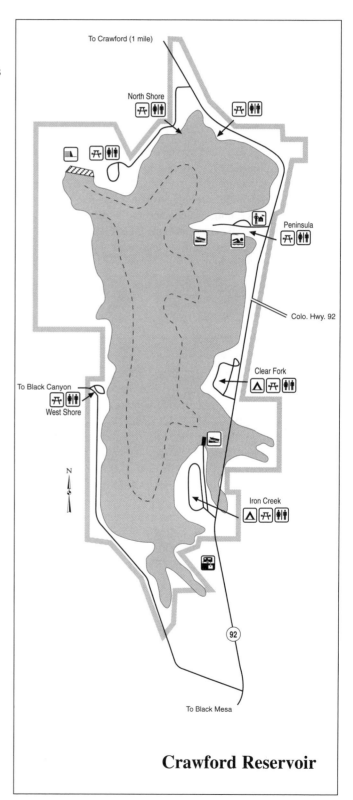

Crawford Reservoir

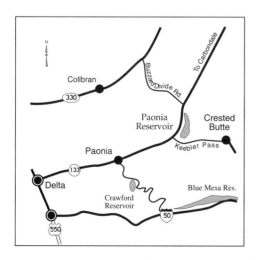

Map No.	Name	Map Loc.	Fee	No. of Units	Max. Length	Elev.	Toilets	Water	Agency
4	**Paonia State Park ®** **(Reservoir)**	C-2	$	15	30'	6,500'	Yes	No	Colorado State Parks

Scenic Paonia State Park located approximately 16 miles northeast of the town of Paonia on State Highway 133. From Glenwood Springs, nine south miles on Highway 82 to Carbondale, turn south on Highway 133 and travel 44 miles. The reservoir has 334 surface acres of water, and the dam was constructed in 1960. Paonia offers 16 campsites, vault toilets, and a concrete boat ramp. There is no drinking water available, so make sure you bring your own.

Camping
Paonia State Park has 15 campsites, located in two separate campgrounds. Spruce campground, located next to Highway 133, offers eight campsites in scenic settings with towering Blue Spruce trees and a babbling stream a few feet away. Hawsapple campground, situated across the river, is popular with water skiers. All campsites have a picnic table, a fire ring and vault toilets are nearby. Please note that no drinking water is available in the park

Fishing
Some northern pike and rainbow trout can he caught in the reservoir from late June until late August. The best fishing is fly fishing the confluence of the Muddy Creek and the Anthracite Creek below the dam.

Other Activities
Picnicking, and Water-skiing.

Daily Fee/Annual Pass
For more information contact:
Paonia State Park
c/o Crawford State Park
Box 147 Crawford, Colorado 81415
(970) 921-5721

Map No.	Name	Map Loc.	Fee	No. of Units	Max. Length	Elev.	Toilets	Water	Agency
5	**Rifle Falls** **State Park ®**	A-1	$	20	35'	6,800'	Yes	Yes	Colorado State Parks

Rifle Falls State Park, located approximately 16 miles north of Rifle on County Road 325, is one of the gem stones of Colorado's State Park system. The breathtaking waterfall, created by East Rifle Creek, has constant flow year-round. Dark caves lurk in the limestone cliff that runs along the falls, including a 90 foot hollow that demands a flashlight for visitor exploration. Squirrel Trail and Coyote Trail allow visitors to discover yet preserve the park for future visitors.

Rifle Falls shines with box-elders, narrow-leaf cottonwoods, hawthorns and choke-cherries. Scattered across the mountains are wild columbines, the state flower. The park office is located northwest of Rifle Gap Reservoir at Rifle Gap State Park.

Camping
Rifle Falls has 12 drive-in and 7 walk-in camping sites. The drive-in sites will accommodate tents, trailers, motor homes and pick-up campers. The walk-in sites are for tent camping only. Please camp in designated sites only. Display the camping permit in the plastic holder at the campsite. Campsites may he reserved in advance.

Wildlife
Beavers, chipmunks and mule deer live at or around Rifle Falls. Ducks and hummingbirds are also found here.

Nature Trail
A self-guided nature trail with interpretive view stations leads hikers above and over the triple waterfall.

Fishing
Rainbow and brown trout can he caught out of East Rifle Creek as it flows through Rifle Falls. Fish up to 19 inches have been taken, 10 to 12 inches is the average size. A holding-tank dump station is located at Rifle Gap State Park. Please use this facility.

Hunting
Big game hunting is excellent in the White River National Forest and on lands administered by US Bureau of land Management.

Other Activities
Picnicking and Hunting.

Daily Fee/Annual Pass
For more information contact:
Rifle Falls State Park
0050 County Road 219
Rifle, CO 81650 (970) 625-1607

Map No.	Name	Map Loc.	Fee	No. of Units	Max. Length	Elev.	Toilets	Water	Agency
6	**Rifle Gap State Park (Reservoir) ®**	A-1	$	47	35'	6,000'	Yes	Yes	Colorado State Parks

Lying at an elevation of 6,000 feet and located 7 miles north of Rifle on County Road 325, Rifle Gap State Park has something to offer every outdoor enthusiast. The clean, clear waters of this 350 acre reservoir afford some of the best scuba diving, boating, swimming, water-skiing and windsurfing in Colorado. Camping, hiking and picnicking opportunities at this 1,305 acre park also await the Rifle Gap visitor. The fun doesn't stop in the wintertime- there's ice fishing, cross-country skiing and snowmobiling for the cold weather buffs.

Camping
Rifle Gap State Park has 47 campsites that can accommodate tents, small trailers and pickup campers. There are some pull-through sites. A dump station is located at Cottonwood campground.

Wildlife
Many mammals, ranging from deer, elk, beaver, chipmunks and rabbits to bobcats and weasels, live around Rifle Gap. Blue heron, several kinds of hummingbirds and a wide variety of ducks and waterfowl are found here.

Water Sports
Swimming, scuba diving, waterskiing, sailing and wind surfing.

Other Activities:
Hunting, Ice fishing and Snowmobiling. Fishing; Rainbow and brown trout, walleye, smallmouth and largemouth bass are just some of the fish you are likely to catch at Rifle Gap Reservoir.

Daily Fee/Annual Pass
For more information contact: Rifle Gap State Park
0050 County Road 219, Rifle, CO 81650
(970) 625-1607

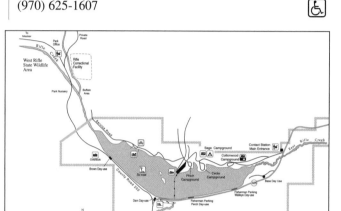

Map No.	Name	Map Loc.	Fee	No. of Units	Max. Length	Elev.	Toilets	Water	Agency
7	**Vega State Park ® (Reservoir)**	B-1	$	101	35'	7,985'	Yes	Yes	Colorado State Parks

High above the little mountain town of Collbran, Colorado, 12 miles east on Road 330, lies Vega State Park, 1,830 acres of scenic mountain splendor nestled near the Grand Mesa.

Visitors through out the year now enjoy Vega's sub-alpine beauty. Colorado wildflowers abound within the park as does so many kinds of wildlife. Visitors are encouraged to enjoy Vega's access to the Grand Mesa park trails; these trails are open to hikers, 4 wheelers, trail bikers and snowmobilers. There are historical sites to see including the area where the Dominguez-Escalante expedition camped in 1776 and the Vega cemetery.

Camping
Vega State Park offers 110 individual and group campsites for your enjoyment These can accommodate RV's, tents and campers. Sites are available on a first come, first served basis, or you can reserve the special site. A holding tank station is located in the Oak Point Campground.

Wildlife
Deer, elk, beaver and many kinds of waterfowl frequent Vega. Also found here are weasel, rabbits, chipmunks,

hawks, blue grouse and the elusive wild turkey. Coyotes and bobcat are known in the area.

Fishing
Vega reservoir is about two miles long when full. It is the largest body of water in the Grand Valley region. Because Vega is about 2,000 feet lower in elevation than Grand Mesa, it is the last to freeze in the fall and the first to thaw in the spring. Few lakes anywhere can surpass Vega reservoir as a trout fishery.

Other Activities
Water Sports, Nature Trail, and Picnicking.

Daily Fee/Annual Pass
For more information contact:
Vega State Park
Box 186
Collbran, CO 81624
(970) 487-3407

Map No.	Campground Name	Map Loc.	Fee	No. of Units	Max. Length	Elev.	Toilets	Water	Agency
8	**Chukar Trailhead**	D-1	0	4	18'	5,800'	Yes	No	Bureau of Land Management

LOCATION: 1 mi. S of Olathe on Hwy 50, E on Falcon Rd 3.6 mi., S on Rd 64, 2.5 mi. to Holly Rd, E on access Rd approx. 6 mi. FACILITIES: Tables, Grills. ACTIVITIES: Fishing, Hiking. OPEN FOR USE: April through Oct. CONTACT: Uncompahgre Resource Area (970) 240-5300. NOTE: Primary float boating ingress for Gunnison River, 1 mi. hiking trail to river. 4-Wheel drive and service map is advised. 7.5' TOPOGRAPHIC MAP: Red Rock Canyon.Capacity 25

Map No.	Campground Name	Map Loc.	Fee	No. of Units	Max. Length	Elev.	Toilets	Water	Agency
9	**The Gate (Riverine)**	D-2	$	8	21'	8,400'	Yes	No	Bureau of Land Management

LOCATION: 14 mi. N of Lake City on Hwy 149. FACILITIES: Tables. ACTIVITIES: Fishing, Rafting. OPEN FOR USE: May through Oct. CONTACT: Gunnison Resource Area (970) 641-0471. NOTE: Riverine campground and day use area. Capacity 30 people. 7.5' TOPOGRAPHIC MAP: Poison Draw.

Map No.	Campground Name	Map Loc.	Fee	No. of Units	Max. Length	Elev.	Toilets	Water	Agency
10	**Red Bridge (Riverine)**	D-2	$	5	21'	7,800'	Yes	No	Bureau of Land Management

LOCATION: 20 mi. N of Lake City on Hwy 149. FACILITIES: Fire Rings. ACTIVITIES: Fishing, Wildlife Viewing, Rafting. OPEN FOR USE: May through Oct. CONTACT: Gunnison Resource Area (970) 641-0471. NOTE: Riverine campground, capacity 30 people. 7.5' TOPOGRAPHIC MAP: Gateview.

Map No.	Campground Name	Map Loc.	Fee	No. of Units	Max. Length	Elev.	Toilets	Water	Agency
11	**Ute Trailhead**	D-1	0	2	NA	6,600'	Yes	No	Bureau of Land Management

LOCATION: From Olathe on David Rd E 2 mi. to Rd 62.00, N 4 mi. to Peach Valley Rd, N 0.4 mi., E 2.5 mi. to Trailhead. FACILITIES: Picnic Tables. ACTIVITIES: Fishing, Hiking. OPEN FOR USE: Early June through mid-Oct. CONTACT: Uncompahgre Resource Area (970) 240-5300. NOTE: 4.5 mi. constructed trail to river. Gradual slope all the way. 4-wheel drive and service map recommended. Capacity 12 people. 7.5' TOPOGRAPHIC MAP: Black Ridge. Capacity 12 people.

Map No.	Campground Name	Map Loc.	Fee	No. of Units	Max. Length	Elev.	Toilets	Water	Agency
12	**Almont**	D-3	$	10	28'	8,000'	Yes	Yes	Gunnison National Forest

LOCATION: 11 mi. N of Gunnison on Hwy 135 to Almont. FACILITIES: Picnic Tables. ACTIVITIES: Fishing, Hiking. OPEN FOR USE: Late May through mid-Oct. CONTACT: Gunnison Ranger District (970) 641-0471. NOTE: Camp located on Gunnison River. 7.5' TOPOGRAPHIC MAP: Almont.

Map No.	Campground Name	Map Loc.	Fee	No. of Units	Max. Length	Elev.	Toilets	Water	Agency
13	**Avalanche**	B-2	$	13	25'	7,400'	Yes	Yes	White River National Forest

LOCATION: 0.5 mi. S of Carbondale on Hwy 133, 2.6 mi. E on FDR 310. FACILITIES: Picnic Tables, Pets OK. ACTIVITIES: Fishing, Hiking. OPEN FOR USE: Late May through early Nov. CONTACT: Sopris Ranger District (970) 963-2266 NOTE: Camp is along Avalanche Creek close to Maroon Bells Snowmass Wilderness, Avalanche TH, FDT 1959. 7.5' TOPOGRAPHIC MAP: Redstone.

Map No.	Campground Name	Map Loc.	Fee	No. of Units	Max. Length	Elev.	Toilets	Water	Agency
14	**Bogan Flats ®**	B-2	$	37	40'	7,600'	Yes	Yes	White River National Forest

LOCATION: S of Glenwood Springs on Hwy 82 to Carbondale, 20.5 mi. S on Hwy 133, 1.5 mi. S on Cty Rd 314. FACILITIES: Picnic Tables, Pets OK. Adjacent to Bogan Flats Group Campground. ACTIVITIES: Fishing, Hiking. OPEN FOR USE: Late May through late Sept. CONTACT: Sopris Ranger District (970) 963-2266. NOTE: Reservations; Camp is beside Crystal River and is near Maroon Bells Snowmass Wilderness and Raggeds Wilderness.7.5' TOPOGRAPHIC MAP: Chair Mountain.

Map No.	Campground Name	Map Loc.	Fee	No. of Units	Max. Length	Elev.	Toilets	Water	Agency
15	**Cement Creek**	C-3	$	13	28'	9,000'	Yes	Yes	Gunnison National Forest

LOCATION: 20.5 mi. N of Gunnison on Hwy 135, 4 mi. NE on FDR 740. FACILITIES: Picnic Tables. ACTIVITIES: Fishing, Hiking. OPEN FOR USE: Mid-May through late Oct. CONTACT: Gunnison Ranger District (970) 641-0471 NOTE: Campground near Cement Creek and Walrad Gulch Trailhead. 7.5' TOPOGRAPHIC MAP: Cement Mountain.

Map No.	Campground Name	Map Loc.	Fee	No. of Units	Max. Length	Elev.	Toilets	Water	Agency
16	**Coffee Pot Spring**	A-2	$	15	20'	10,160	Yes	Yes	White River National Forest

LOCATION: From Dotsero N @ exit 133, 6 mi. N on Sweetwater Rd, 21 mi. NW on FDR 600. FACILITIES: Picnic Tables, Grills. ACTIVITIES: Hunting, Hiking. OPEN FOR USE: Mid-June through mid-Nov. CONTACT: Eagle Ranger District (970) 328-6388. NOTE: Campground is at Coffee Pot Springs, Lots of 4-Wheel drive roads nearby. 7.5' TOPOGRAPHIC MAP: Broken Rib Creek.

Map No.	Campground Name	Map Loc.	Fee	No. of Units	Max. Length	Elev.	Toilets	Water	Agency
17	**Difficult ®**	B-3	$	47	40'	8,200'	Yes	Yes	White River National Forest

LOCATION: 4.3 mi. SE of Aspen on Hwy 82, 0.6 mi. SE on FDR 108. FACILITIES: Picnic Tables, Firewood, Pets OK. ACTIVITIES: Fishing, Hiking. OPEN FOR USE: Late May through late Sept. CONTACT: Aspen Ranger District (970) 925-3445. NOTE: Reservations; Camp is at the confluence of Roaring Fork River and Difficult Creek and is adjacent to the Collegiate Peaks Wilderness. Difficult Crk TH, FDT 2196. 7.5' TOPOGRAPHIC MAP: Aspen. ♿

Map No.	Campground Name	Map Loc.	Fee	No. of Units	Max. Length	Elev.	Toilets	Water	Agency
18	**Erickson Springs**	C-2	$	18	35'	6,800'	Yes	Yes	Gunnison National Forest

LOCATION: 20 mi. NE on Hwy 50 from Delta on Hwy 92, 23.6 mi. NE on Hwy 133, 7 mi. E on Cty Rd 12. FACILITIES: Picnic Tables, Hand Pumped Water. ACTIVITIES: Fishing, Hiking. OPEN FOR USE: Mid-May through mid-Nov. CONTACT: Paonia Ranger District (970) 527-4131. NOTE: Camp is along Anthracite Creek, near trails to Raggeds Wilderness. Near Paonia Reservoir and Paonia State Park. 7.5' TOPOGRAPHIC MAP: Paonia Reservoir.

Map No.	Campground Name	Map Loc.	Fee	No. of Units	Max. Length	Elev.	Toilets	Water	Agency
19	**Gothic**	C-3	$	4	Short	9,600'	Yes	No	Gunnison National Forest

LOCATION: 28 mi. N of Gunnison on Hwy 135 to Crested Butte, 7.3 N on Cty Rd 3, 2 mi. N on FDR 317. FACILITIES: Picnic Tables, Pets OK. ACTIVITIES: Fishing, Hiking. OPEN FOR USE: Early June through Sept. CONTACT: Gunnison Ranger District. (970) 641-0471. NOTE: Camp is on East River near Gothic Natural Area, FDT 403. 7.5' TOPOGRAPHIC MAP: Oh-Be-Joyful, Gothic.

Map No.	Campground Name	Map Loc.	Fee	No. of Units	Max. Length	Elev.	Toilets	Water	Agency
20	**Lake Irwin ®**	C-3	$	32	35'	10,200'	Yes	Yes	Gunnison National Forest

LOCATION: 28 mi. N of Gunnison on Hwy 135 to Crested Butte, 7.2 mi W on Cty Rd 12, 2.6 mi N on FDR 826. FACILITIES: Picnic Tables. ACTIVITIES: Fishing, Hiking. OPEN FOR USE: June 25 through late Oct. CONTACT: Gunnison Ranger District (970) 641-0471. NOTE: Reservations. Campground near Lake Irwin, at the foot of Ruby Mountain Range, access to Raggeds Wilderness. 7.5' TOPOGRAPHIC MAP: Oh-Be-Joyful.

Map No.	Campground Name	Map Loc.	Fee	No. of Units	Max. Length	Elev.	Toilets	Water	Agency
21	**Lost Lake**	C-2	$	11	21'	9,600'	Yes	No	Gunnison National Forest

LOCATION: 28 mi. N of Gunnison on Hwy 135 to Crested Butte, 15 mi. W on Cty Rd 12, 2 mi. S on FDR 706. FACILITIES: Picnic Tables. ACTIVITIES: Fishing, Hiking. OPEN FOR USE: Mid-June through mid-Oct. CONTACT: Paonia Ranger District (970) 527-4131. NOTE: Campground is near Lost Lake and access to West Elk Wilderness, FDT 843. 7.5' TOPOGRAPHIC MAP: Anthracite Range.

Map No.	Campground Name	Map Loc.	Fee	No. of Units	Max. Length	Elev.	Toilets	Water	Agency
22	**McClure**	B-2	$	19	35'	8,200'	Yes	Yes	Gunnison National Forest

LOCATION: 12 mi S of Glenwood Springs on Hwy 82 to Carbondale, S on Hwy 133 29 mi. FACILITIES: Picnic Tables, Pets OK. ACTIVITIES: Fishing, Hiking. OPEN FOR USE: June through mid-Nov. CONTACT: Paonia Ranger District (970) 527-4131. NOTE: Camp is along Lee Creek close to McClure Pass. 7.5' TOPOGRAPHIC MAP: Placita.

Map No.	Campground Name	Map Loc.	Fee	No. of Units	Max. Length	Elev.	Toilets	Water	Agency
23	**North Bank**	C-3	$	17	35'	8,600'	Yes	Yes	Gunnison National Forest

LOCATION: 11 mi. N of Gunnison on Hwy 135 to Almont, 7.8 mi. NE on FDR 742. FACILITIES: Picnic Tables. ACTIVITIES: Fishing, Hiking. OPEN FOR USE: Late May through Sept. CONTACT: Gunnison Ranger District (970) 641-0471. NOTE: Campground is near Taylor River and several other campgrounds. 7.5' TOPOGRAPHIC MAP: Almont.

Map No.	Campground Name	Map Loc.	Fee	No. of Units	Max. Length	Elev.	Toilets	Water	Agency
24	**One Mile ®**	C-3	$	25	35'	8,600'	Yes	Yes	Gunnison National Forest

LOCATION: 11 mi. N of Gunnison on Hwy 135 to Almont, 7.9 mi. NE on FDR 742. FACILITIES: Picnic Tables, electric hook-ups all sites. ACTIVITIES: Fishing, Hiking. OPEN FOR USE: Late May through late Sept. CONTACT: Gunnison Ranger District (970) 641-0471. NOTE: Reservations; Campground is near Taylor River. 7.5' TOPOGRAPHIC MAP: Almont.

Map No.	Campground Name	Map Loc.	Fee	No. of Units	Max. Length	Elev.	Toilets	Water	Agency
25	**Redstone ®**	B-2	$	20	40'	7,200'	Yes	Yes	White River National Forest

LOCATION: 12 mi. S of Glenwood Springs on Hwy 82 to Carbondale, 13 mi. S on Hwy 133. FACILITIES: Picnic Tables, Showers, Pets OK. ACTIVITIES: Fishing, Hiking. OPEN FOR USE: Late May through late Sept. CONTACT: Sopris Ranger District (970) 963-2266. NOTE: Handicap Accessible. Campground is on the Crystal River, 1 mi N of Redstone. 7.5' TOPOGRAPHIC MAP: Redstone.

Map No.	Campground Name	Map Loc.	Fee	No. of Units	Max. Length	Elev.	Toilets	Water	Agency
26	**Rosy Lane ®**	C-3	$	20	35'	8,600'	Yes	Yes	Gunnison National Forest

LOCATION: 11 mi. N of Gunnison on Hwy 135 to Almont, 8.0 mi. NE on FDR 742. FACILITIES: Picnic Tables, Pets OK. ACTIVITIES: Fishing, Hiking. OPEN FOR USE: Late May through mid-Oct. CONTACT: Gunnison Ranger District (970) 641-0471. NOTE: Reservations, Camp is along Taylor River. 7.5' TOPOGRAPHIC MAPS: Almont,Crystal Creek.

Map No.	Campground Name	Map Loc.	Fee	No. of Units	Max. Length	Elev.	Toilets	Water	Agency
27	**Ruedi Reservoir**	A-3	$			7,800'	Yes	Yes	White River National Forest
a.	Dearhamer			13	35'				
b.	Little Mattie			20	40'				
c.	Little Maud			22	40'				
d.	Mollie B ® (FDT 1912, Ruedi)			26	40				
e.	Ruedi Marina			5	--				

LOCATION: 24 mi SE of Glenwood Springs on Hwy 82 to Basalt. 16 mi. E on Cty Rd 105. FACILITIES: Full service Campgrounds with supplies in nearby Meredith. ACTIVITIES: Fishing, Hiking, Sailboarding, Sailing. OPEN FOR USE: June through Oct. CONTACT: Sopris Ranger District (970) 963-2266. 7'5' TOPOGRAPHIC MAP: Ruedi Reservoir.

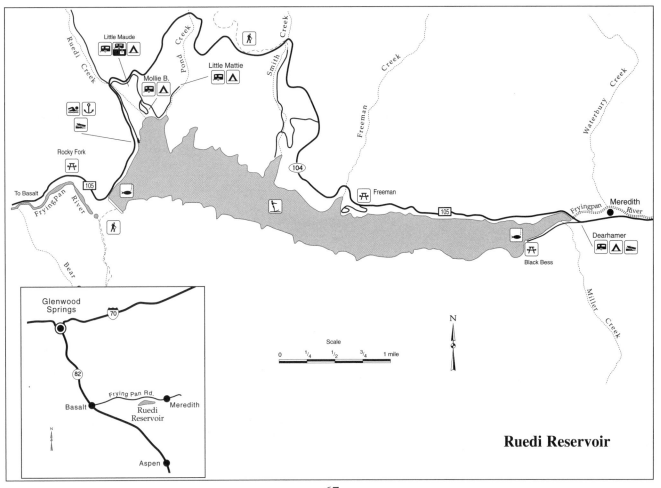

Ruedi Reservoir

Map No.	Campground Name	Map Loc.	Fee	No. of Units	Max. Length	Elev.	Toilets	Water	Agency
28 29 30	**Maroon Creek Valley**	B-3	$				Yes	Yes	White River National Forest
28	Silver Bar ®			4	30'	8,460'			
29	Silver Bell ®			5	30'	8,490'			
30	Silver Queen ® (FDT 1982, Maroon Cr)			6	30'	8,680'			

LOCATION: 1.4 mi. W of Aspen on Hwy 82, 5.9 mi. SW on FDR 125. FACILITIES: Picnic Tables, Firewood, Pets OK. ACTIVITIES: Fishing, Hiking. OPEN FOR USE: Mid-June through late Sept. CONTACT: Aspen Ranger District (970) 925-3445. NOTE: Reservations; There are 14 campsites in the Maroon Creek Valley. Campsites are assigned at Maroon Bells entrance station. A 3 day stay is required. From 8:30 am to 5 pm Maroon Creek Road is closed beyond T-Lazy Ranch to all but overnight campers with permits, handicapped individuals and RFTA buses. Buses depart from Aspen on the 1/2 hour 9 through 4:35 pm daily - Discounted Parking available for Maroon Bells Tour Riders - There is also a combination Maroon Bells Bus Tour/ Silver Queen Gondola ride. 7.5' TOPOGRAPHIC MAP: Highland Peak.

Map No.	Campground Name	Map Loc.	Fee	No. of Units	Max. Length	Elev.	Toilets	Water	Agency
31	**Soap Creek**	D-2	$	21	35'	7,700'	Yes	Yes	Gunnison National Forest

LOCATION: 6.1 mi. W of Gunnison on Hwy 50, 0.6 mi. NW on Hwy 92, 7.2 mi. N on FDR 721, 0.5 mi NE on FDR 824. FACILITIES: Picnic Tables, Pets OK. ACTIVITIES: Fishing, Hiking. OPEN FOR USE: Early June through late Sept. CONTACT:Gunnison Ranger District (970) 641-0471. NOTE: Trailhead to West Elk Wilderness on Soap Creek. 7.5' TOPOGRAPHIC MAP: Little Soap Park. Horse corral and bins.

Map No.	Campground Name	Map Loc.	Fee	No. of Units	Max. Length	Elev.	Toilets	Water	Agency
32	**Spring Creek**	C-3	$	12	35'	10,900'	Yes	Yes	Gunnison National Forest

LOCATION: 11 mi. N of Gunnison on Hwy 135 to Almont, 7.2 mi. NE on FDR 742, 2 mi. N on FDR 744. FACILITIES: Picnic Tables. ACTIVITIES: Fishing, Hiking. OPEN FOR USE: Early June through mid-Oct. CONTACT: Gunnison Ranger District (970) 641-0471. NOTE: Camp is along Spring Creek. 7.5' TOPOGRAPHIC MAPS: Almont, Cement Mountain.

Map No.	Campground Name	Map Loc.	Fee	No. of Units	Max. Length	Elev.	Toilets	Water	Agency
33	**Taylor Canyon Tent**	D-3	$	7	Tent	8,600'	Yes	No	Gunnison National Forest

LOCATION: 11 mi. N of Gunnison on Hwy 135 to Almont, 7.8 mi. NE on FDR 742. FACILITIES: Picnic Tables, Pets OK. ACTIVITIES: Fishing, Hiking. OPEN FOR USE: Late May through late Sept. CONTACT: Gunnison Ranger District (970) 641-0471. NOTE: Near Taylor River. 7.5' TOPOGRAPHIC MAP: Almont.

Map No.	Campground Name	Map Loc.	Fee	No. of Units	Max. Length	Elev.	Toilets	Water	Agency
34	**White Owl**	A-2	0	5	20'	9,500'	Yes	No	White River National Forest

LOCATION: From Dotsero N @ Exit 133 6 mi to Sweetwater Rd, W approx. 30 mi. to White Owl Lake Rd, S 0.5 mi. FACILITIES: Picnic Tables, Grills, Pets OK. ACTIVITIES: Fishing, Hiking. OPEN FOR USE: Mid-June through mid-Nov. CONTACT: Eagle Ranger District (970) 328-6388. NOTE: Near White Owl Lake. 7.5' TOPOGRAPHIC MAP: Carbonate.

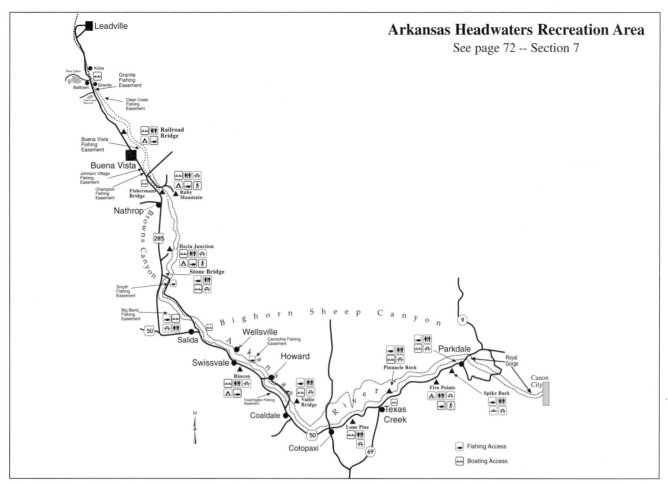

Arkansas Headwaters Recreation Area
See page 72 -- Section 7

Leadville

Kobe

Twin Lakes

Balltown
Granite
Granite Fishing Easement

Clear Creek Reservoir
Clear Creek Fishing Easement

Railroad Bridge

Buena Vista Fishing Easement

Buena Vista

Johnson Village Fishing Easement

Champion Fishing Easement

Fisherman's Bridge

Ruby Mountain

Nathrop

Browns Canyon

285

Hecla Junction

Stone Bridge

Smyth Fishing Easement

Big Bend Fishing Easement

50

Salida

Wellsville

Carrochia Fishing Easement

Bighorn Sheep Canyon

Arkansas River

Howard

Swissvale

Rincon

Treat/Ogden Fishing Easement

Vallie Bridge

Coaldale

Pinnacle Rock

Five Points

Parkdale

Royal Gorge

Canon City

Spike Buck

Texas Creek

Lone Pine

50

Cotopaxi

69

9

⬛ Fishing Access

⬛ Boating Access

N

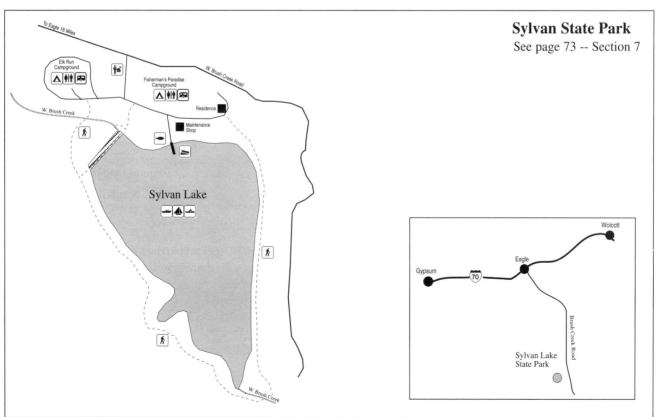

Sylvan State Park
See page 73 -- Section 7

To Eagle 16 Miles

Elk Run Campground

W. Brush Creek Road

Fisherman's Paradise Campground

Residence

W. Brush Creek

Maintenance Shop

Sylvan Lake

W. Brush Creek

Wolcott

Gypsum

Eagle

70

Brush Creek Road

Sylvan Lake State Park

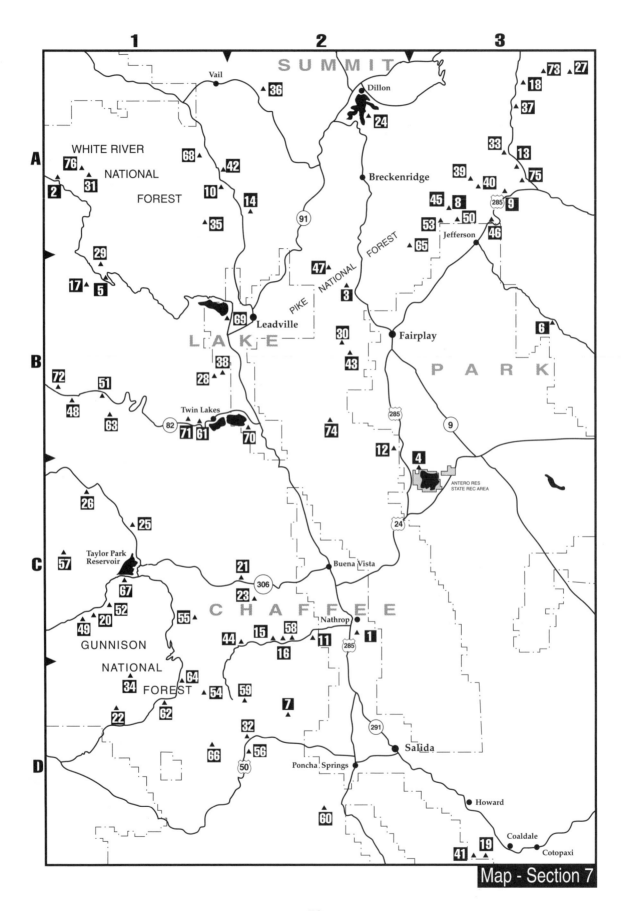

Map - Section 7

Map No.	Name	Map Loc.	Fee	No. of Units	Max. Length	Elev.	Toilets	Water	Agency
1	**Arkansas Headwaters Recreation Area ®**	C-2	$	81	30'	4-9,000'	Yes	No	Colorado State Parks
a.	Railroad Bridge			14		7,500'			
b.	Ruby Mountain			20		7,500'			
c.	Hecla Junction			22		7,500'			
d.	Rincon			5		7,400'			
e.	Five Points			20		6,000'			

The upper Arkansas River Valley is a treasure of geology, history, wildlife, scenery and just plain good times. Whether you want to explore a ghost town, run a rapid, hook a trout, watch a bighorn sheep or stare into the depths of the Royal Gorge, chances for adventure are all around you. The valley is also home to several thriving communities. The rich human history of the area adds another fascinating dimension for visitors to the area.

What follows is a brief tour of the towns and country within the boundaries of the Arkansas Headwaters Recreation Area.

LEADVILLE TO BUENA VISTA

The river below Leadville formed when ancient glacial dams broke, scattering huge boulders across the river bottom. At first, this upper stretch flows fairly quietly between banks that are sometimes open, sometimes forested with Douglas-fir and Englemann spruce. Below Granite, the river changes dramatically as it flows into a narrow canyon that is home to Pine Creek rapids (Class V-VI). Below Pine Creek, the Arkansas offers kayakers and rafters technically challenging (Class III-V) water all the way to Buena Vista. The Arkansas flows by Buena Vista where a community park on the edge of town provides river access. The town also offers lodging, dining and camping. To the west, the 14,000 foot Collegiate Peaks, Oxford, Harvard, Yale and Princeton- rise. A scenic overlook with a spectacular view of the mountains and valley lies a mile east of John Village on US. 24/285.

Please note: The segment is bordered by large areas of private land, with few public access points. Railroad Bridge, at the tail end of the "Numbers" rapids, and Buena Vista's River Park are the main ones. Check the Arkansas Headwaters Office in Salida for more information.

BUENA VISTA TO SALIDA

This stretches outstanding feature is Brown's Canyon, a pink granite gorge of whitewater rapids. The lower elevation and lower annual rainfall here mean a difference in vegetation - pinon pine and juniper woodlands scattered with Ponderosa pines.

The busiest stretch of the river, Brown's Canyon is a wild ride at high water... pour overs, standing waves, sharp turns, and narrow chutes, at any water level it is a beautiful and challenging river trip. This stretch also offers fine fishing, as well as camping and picnicking. Ruby Mountain, the canyon's northern gateway, provides access to the 6,660-acre Browns Canyon Wilderness Study Area. Here, visitors can hike, backpack, camp and view wildlife. Below Browns Canyon, the valley widens again and the river calms though spectacular views remain. This stretch, called the Big Bend, offers prime trout fishing and numerous Colorado Division of Wildlife easements provide fishermen with river access on private land. Please observe posted rules when using fishing easements.

SALIDA TO VALUE BRIDGE

Just below Salida the river flows into Bighorn Sheep Canyon, a granite canyon dotted with stands of pinon pine, juniper and oak brush. Drier conditions mean cactus thrives here. Each spring, cholla cactus burst with brilliant pink flowers throughout the canyon.

Anglers especially enjoy this segment - it offers deep pools, rock banks and gravel bars. In addition to Public land access along the river, Division of Wildlife fishing easements provide river access.

Boaters will find intermediate rapids in this segment.

VALLIE BRIDGE TO PARKDALE

A few miles below Vallie Bridge, the river enters the segment known historically as the "Grand Canyon of the Arkansas". Towering cliffs form a spectacular backdrop to the river. Here, public land predominates along the river. This is a prime area for wildlife viewing. Bighorn sheep come down the steep slopes to drink from the river. Watch for motorists slowing to take a look. The river drops sharply in this segment. Rapids with names like Maytag, Lose-Your-Lunch, Three Rocks and Shark's Tooth make this prime territory for whitewater boating.

Anglers can take advantage of trout habitat improvements between Coaldale and Parkdale. Here, groupings of large rocks placed in the river provide resting areas where trout take shelter from the fast currents. Public river access is available at several pull-offs and recreation sites. Lone Pine Recreation Site offers a fishing trail accessible to physically challenged individuals. Pinnacle Rock, the most popular boating access to the lower canyon, is also a good place to view bighorn sheep. Stop at Five Points Recreation Site to visit the Watchable Wildlife Exhibit and to watch boaters run Five Points rapids.

PARKDALE TO CANON CITY

Near Parkdale, the river travels through an open area bordered by cottonwood and willow, South Webster Park. From this peaceful spot, the river plunges into the Royal Gorge, the Arkansas' most famous achievement. Over millions of years, the river carved through the hard rock of the Royal Gorge Plateau forming the 1,000 foot plus walls of the gorge.

Parkdale Recreation Site provides public access to the river and the last boating access before the river enters the Royal Gorge. Boaters who want to view the gorge from the bottom up should take note: Within the gorge, the river gives you a wild ride, with Class V (extremely difficult) rapids. East of Parkdale on US. 50 is the primary road access to the Royal Gorge Park and Bridge, a fee is charged for admission. After eight miles, the river emerges from the Royal Gorge and flows through Canon City.

CANON CITY TO PUEBLO RESERVOIR

Below Canon City, the Arkansas changes into a quiet, meandering Great Plains river. A wide ribbon of cottonwood, willow and water-loving plants along its bank creates a "riparian zone" that is extremely important to wildlife. This stretch offers find wildlife viewing and fishing.

The slower pace of the river also makes for excellent canoeing, but caution and skill are necessary to avoid low dams and overhanging and fallen trees. Most of the river here is bordered by private land. Please respect landowners and do not trespass. The Arkansas Headwaters Recreation Area ends at Lake Pueblo State Park.
See map page 69.

Information:
Colorado State Parks
PO Box 126
Salida, CO
(719) 539-7289

Map No.	Campground Name	Map Loc.	Fee	No. of Units	Max. Length	Elev.	Toilets	Water	Agency
2	**Sylvan Lake State Park ®**	A-1	$	50	35'	8,500'	Yes	Yes	Colorado State Parks

Sylvan Lake State Park is one of the most beautiful getaways in the state. Located 16 miles south of Eagle on West Brush Creek Road, Sylvan Lake Park is one of western Colorado's best kept secrets. Nestled in the heart of the majestic Rocky Mountains, it is surrounded by the White River National Forest. The visitor enjoys a spectacular 360 degree panoramic view of the alpine scenery from this 8,500 foot high park.

Not only is the park one of the most scenic getaways, it has some of the best year-round trout fishing anywhere. Anglers can snare brook and rainbow trout at this 40 acre lake. Sylvan Lake is also a haven for campers, boaters, picnickers, photographers, and hikers as well as a base camp for hunters during Colorado's big game hunting season.

Camping
Sylvan Lake Park has 50 campsites for your enjoyment, 30 at Elk Run Campground and 20 at Fishermen's Paradise Campground. The sites can accommodate tents, trailers and campers and there are some larger pull-through sites. Campers must have a permit.

Wildlife
Wildlife watchers can spot mule deer, rabbits, chipmunks, beavers, elk, hummingbirds and waterfowl throughout the park.

Fishing
Sylvan Lake is stocked with brook and rainbow trout by the Colorado Division of Wildlife.

Water Recreation
Only non-motorized boats and electric motors are allowed on the lake.

Other Activities
Ice fishing, cross-country skiing and snowmobiling.

See map page 69.

Daily Fee/Annual Pass
For more information contact:
Sylvan Lake State Park
Rifle Gap State Park
0050 Road 219
Rifle, CO 81650 (970) 625-1607

Map No.	Campground Name	Map Loc.	Fee	No. of Units	Max. Length	Elev.	Toilets	Water	Agency
3	**Alma State Wildlife Area**	B-2	0	Dispersed	Open	10,000'	Yes	No	Colorado Division of Wildlife

LOCATION: 1.5 mi N of Alma on Hwy 9, 1/4 mi NW on Cty Rd 4. FACILITIES: Picnic Tables. ACTIVITIES: Fishing, Hiking. OPEN FOR USE: May through Sept. CONTACT: Colorado Division of Wildlife SE Region (719) 227-5200. NOTE: Near Bristle Cone Pine Scenic Area (CALL FIRST). 7.5' TOPOGRAPHIC MAP: Alma.

Map No.	Campground Name	Map Loc.	Fee	No. of Units	Max. Length	Elev.	Toilets	Water	Agency
4	**Antero State Wildlife Area**	C-3	0	Dispersed	Open	9,000'	No	No	Colorado Division of Wildlife

LOCATION: 5 mi SW of Hartzel on Hwy 24 to Reservoir. FACILITIES: Boat Ramp, Picnic Tables. ACTIVITIES: Fishing, Hiking. OPEN FOR USE: May through Sept. CONTACT: Denver Water Dept. or Colorado Division of Wildlife SE Region (719) 227-5200. NOTE: 1000 acre reservoir (Full) is considered one of the best cold water fisheries in Colorado (CALL FIRST). 7.5' TOPOGRAPHIC MAP: Antero Reservoir.

Map No.	Campground Name	Map Loc.	Fee	No. of Units	Max. Length	Elev.	Toilets	Water	Agency
5	**Coke Oven State Wildlife Area**	B-1	0	Dispersed	Open	8,800'	Yes	No	Colorado Division of Wildlife

LOCATION: 30 mi E of Basalt on FDR 105 (Fryingpan River Rd). FACILITIES: Picnic Tables. ACTIVITIES: Fishing, Hiking. OPEN FOR USE: May through Sept. CONTACT: Division of Wildlife NW Region (970) 255-6100. NOTE: On Cellar Creek near Frying Pan River (CALL FIRST). 7.5' TOPOGRAPHIC MAP: Nast.

Map No.	Campground Name	Map Loc.	Fee	No. of Units	Max. Length	Elev.	Toilets	Water	Agency
6	**Tarryall Reservoir State Wildlife Area**	B-3	0	Dispersed	Open	9,500'	Yes	No	Colorado Division of Wildlife

LOCATION: 15 mi SE of Jefferson on Cty Rd 77. From Lake George go NW of Hwy 24 14 mi on Cty Rd 77. (886 acres.)FACILITIES: Picnic Tables, Boat Ramp. ACTIVITIES: Fishing, Hiking, Hunting. OPEN FOR USE: May through Sept. CONTACT: Colorado Division of Wildlife SE Region (719) 227-5200. NOTE: Campground is located on 175 acre Tarryall Reservoir. 7.5' TOPOGRAPHIC MAP: Farnum Peak.

Map No.	Campground Name	Map Loc.	Fee	No. of Units	Max. Length	Elev.	Toilets	Water	Agency
7	**Angel of Shavano**	D-2	$	20	45'	9,200'	Yes	Yes	San Isabel National Forest

LOCATION: 10 mi W of Salida on Hwy 50, 5 mi N on Cty Rd 240. FACILITIES: Picnic Tables, Pets OK. ACTIVITIES: Fishing, Hiking. OPEN FOR USE: May through early Oct. CONTACT: Salida Ranger District (719) 539-3591. NOTE: Adjacent to Angel of Shavano Group Campground. Camp on the North Fork of the South Arkansas River. Colo.Trail, FDT 1776 nearby. 7.5' TOPOGRAPHIC MAP: Maysville.

Map No.	Campground Name	Map Loc.	Fee	No. of Units	Max. Length	Elev.	Toilets	Water	Agency
8	**Aspen ®**	A-3	$	12	25'	9,900'	Yes	Yes	Pike National Forest

LOCATION: 2 mi NW of Jefferson on Cty Rd 35, 1 mi N on Cty Rd 37, 1.8 mi NW on FDR 401. FACILITIES: Picnic Tables, Boat Ramp, Pets OK. ACTIVITIES: Fishing, Hiking. OPEN FOR USE: Mid-May through late Sept. CONTACT: South Park Ranger District (719) 836-2031. NOTE: Reservations. Colo.Trail, FDT 1776 nearby. Camp is set on Jefferson Creek, 2 miles S of Jefferson Lake. Parking Fee. 7.5' TOPOGRAPHIC MAP: Jefferson. Note: $3.00 parking fee.

Map No.	Campground Name	Map Loc.	Fee	No. of Units	Max. Length	Elev.	Toilets	Water	Agency
9	**Timberline Group ®**	A-3	$		Open	10,900'	Yes	Yes	Pike National Forest

LOCATION: 6 mi N of Jefferson on Highway 285. FACILITIES: Picnic Tables, Fire rings. ACTIVITIES: Hiking, picnicking. FOR USE: May through early Oct. CONTACT: South Platte Ranger District (303) 275-5610. 7.5' TOPOGRAPHIC MAP: Jefferson.

Map No.	Campground Name	Map Loc.	Fee	No. of Units	Max. Length	Elev.	Toilets	Water	Agency
10	**Blodgett**	A-1	$	6	30'	8,900'	Yes	Yes	White River National Forest

LOCATION: 3 mi S of Redcliffe on Hwy 24, 1/2 mi SW on FDR 703. FACILITIES: Picnic Tables, Pets OK. ACTIVITIES: Fishing, Hiking. OPEN FOR USE: June through early Sept. CONTACT: Holy Cross Ranger District (970) 827-5715. NOTE: On Homestake Creek near trailhead to Holy Cross Wilderness. 7.5' TOPOGRAPHIC MAP: Pando.

Map No.	Campground Name	Map Loc.	Fee	No. of Units	Max. Length	Elev.	Toilets	Water	Agency
11	**Bootleg**	C-2	$	6	---	8,400'	Yes	Yes	San Isabel National Forest

LOCATION: From Nathrop 1/2 mi S on Hwy 285, 6 mi W on Cty Rd 162. FACILITIES: Picnic Tables. ACTIVITIES: Fishing, Hiking. OPEN FOR USE: Late May through mid-Oct. CONTACT: Salida Ranger District (719) 539-3591. NOTE: Campground is set near Chalk Creek, along Spring Creek Reservoir. Colo.Tr. FDT 1776 nearby. 7.5' TOPOGRAPHIC MAP: Mount Antero.

Map No.	Campground Name	Map Loc.	Fee	No. of Units	Max. Length	Elev.	Toilets	Water	Agency
12	**Buffalo Springs ®**	B-2	$	17	25'	9,000'	Yes	Yes	Pike National Forest

LOCATION: 6.5 mi N of Antero Junction on Hwy 285, 1/2 mi W on FDR 431. FACILITIES: Picnic Tables, Pets OK. ACTIVITIES: Fishing, Hiking. OPEN FOR USE: Late May through early Sept. CONTACT: South Park Ranger District (719) 836-2031. NOTE: Approx. 10 miles to Antero Reservoir. 7.5' TOPOGRAPHIC MAP: Garo.

Map No.	Campground Name	Map Loc.	Fee	No. of Units	Max. Length	Elev.	Toilets	Water	Agency
13	**Burning Bear**	A-3	$	13	20'	9,500'	Yes	Yes	Pike National Forest

LOCATION: 5.2 mi NW of Grant on Cty Rd 62. FACILITIES: Picnic Tables, Pets OK. ACTIVITIES: Fishing, Hiking. OPEN FOR USE: May through mid-Oct. CONTACT: South Platte Ranger District (303) 275-5610. NOTE: Near the confluence of Bear Creek and Scott Gomer Creek, near trailhead to Mount Evans Wilderness.Abyss Lake, FDT 602. 7.5' TOPOGRAPHIC MAP: Mount Evans.

Map No.	Campground Name	Map Loc.	Fee	No. of Units	Max. Length	Elev.	Toilets	Water	Agency
14	**Camp Hale Memorial**	A-2	$	21	60'	9,200'	Yes	Yes	White River National Forest

LOCATION: 7 mi N of Leadville on Hwy 24, 1/4 mi E on FDR 729, 1 mi S on FDR 716. FACILITIES: Picnic Tables, Pets OK. ACTIVITIES: Fishing, Hiking. OPEN FOR USE: June through early Sept. CONTACT: Holy Cross Ranger District (970) 827-5715. NOTE: Camp is along the East Fork of the Eagle River, near the Colorado Trail. 7.5' TOPOGRAPHIC MAP: Pando. *Camp Hale East Fork Group ®.*

Map No.	Campground Name	Map Loc.	Fee	No. of Units	Max. Length	Elev.	Toilets	Water	Agency
15	**Cascade ®**	C-2	$	23	60'	9,000'	Yes	Yes	San Isabel National Forest

LOCATION: 1/2 mi S of Nathrop on Hwy 285, 8.5 mi W on Cty Rd 162. FACILITIES: Picnic Tables, Pets OK. ACTIVITIES: Fishing, Hiking. OPEN FOR USE: Late May through mid-Sept. CONTACT: Salida Ranger District (719) 539-3591 NOTE: Reservations Needed. Chalk Creek runs alongside campground. 7.5' TOPOGRAPHIC MAP: Mount Antero.

Map No.	Campground Name	Map Loc.	Fee	No. of Units	Max. Length	Elev.	Toilets	Water	Agency
16	**Chalk Lake ®**	C-2	$	21	35'	8,700'	Yes	Yes	San Isabel National Forest

LOCATION: 1/2 mi S of Nathrop on Hwy 285, 7.5 mi W on Cty Rd 162.. FACILITIES: Picnic Tables, Pets OK. ACTIVITIES: Fishing, Hiking. OPEN FOR USE: Late May through mid-Oct.. CONTACT: Salida Ranger District (719) 539-3591 NOTE: Reservations. Campground is one of three camps set along Chalk Creek. 7.5' TOPOGRAPHIC MAP: Mount Antero.

Map No.	Campground Name	Map Loc.	Fee	No. of Units	Max. Length	Elev.	Toilets	Water	Agency
17	**Chapman ®**	B-1	$	84	50'	8,300'	Yes	Yes	White River National Forest

LOCATION: 24 mi SE of Glenwood Springs on Hwy 82 to Basalt, E 24.5 mi on Cty Rd 105. FACILITIES: Picnic Tables, Pets OK. ACTIVITIES: Fishing, Hiking. OPEN FOR USE: Late May through late Sept. CONTACT: Sopris Ranger District (970) 963-2266. NOTE: Handicap Accessible, Reservations; Adjacent to *Chapman Group Campground ®.* Campground is near Frying Pan River. 7.5' TOPOGRAPHIC MAP: Meredith.

Map No.	Campground Name	Map Loc.	Fee	No. of Units	Max. Length	Elev.	Toilets	Water	Agency
18	**Clear Lake**	A-3	$	8	15'	10,000'	Yes	Yes	Arapaho/Roosevelt National Forest

LOCATION: 4 mi S of Georgetown on FDR 118. FACILITIES: Picnic Tables, Pets OK. ACTIVITIES: Fishing, Hiking. OPEN FOR USE: Late May through mid-Nov. CONTACT: Clear Creek Ranger District (303) 567-3000. NOTE: Campground is near South Clear Lake and Mount Evans Wilderness. 7.5' TOPOGRAPHIC MAP: Georgetown.

Map No.	Campground Name	Map Loc.	Fee	No. of Units	Max. Length	Elev.	Toilets	Water	Agency
19	**Coaldale**	D-3	$	11	20'	8,500'	Yes	No	San Isabel National Forest

LOCATION: 4.1 mi SW of Coaldale on Cty Rd 6. FACILITIES: Picnic Tables, Pets OK. ACTIVITIES: Fishing, Hiking. OPEN FOR USE: Late May through mid-Oct. CONTACT: Salida Ranger District (719) 539-3591. NOTE: Camp is along Hayden Creek with direct access to Rainbow Trail. 7.5' TOPOGRAPHIC MAP: Coaldale.

Map No.	Campground Name	Map Loc.	Fee	No. of Units	Max. Length	Elev.	Toilets	Water	Agency
20	**Cold Spring**	C-1	$	6	10'	9,000'	Yes	No	Gunnison National Forest

LOCATION: 11 mi N of Gunnison on Hwy 135 to Almont, 16.1 mi NE on FDR 742. FACILITIES: Picnic Tables. ACTIVITIES: Fishing, Hiking. OPEN FOR USE: Late May through late Sept. CONTACT: Gunnison Ranger District (970) 641-0471. NOTE: The Taylor River runs right past the campsite; near trailhead. 7.5' TOPOGRAPHIC MAP: Matchless Mountain.

Map No.	Campground Name	Map Loc.	Fee	No. of Units	Max. Length	Elev.	Toilets	Water	Agency
21	**Collegiate Peaks ®**	C-2	$	56	35'	9,800'	Yes	Yes	San Isabel National Forest

LOCATION: 10.6 mi W of Buena Vista on Hwy 306. FACILITIES: Picnic Tables, Pets OK. ACTIVITIES: Fishing, Hiking. OPEN FOR USE: Late May through late Oct. CONTACT: Salida Ranger District (719) 539-3591. NOTE: Reservations; Camp is on Cottonwood Creek. Near trailhead to Collegiate Peaks Wilderness. 7.5' TOPOGRAPHIC MAP: Mount Yale.

Map No.	Campground Name	Map Loc.	Fee	No. of Units	Max. Length	Elev.	Toilets	Water	Agency
22	**Comanche**	D-1	$	4	Short	8,900'	Yes	No	Gunnison National Forest

LOCATION: 2 mi N of Ohio on FDR 771. FACILITIES: Picnic Tables, Pets OK. ACTIVITIES: Fishing, Hiking. OPEN FOR USE: June through Sept. CONTACT: Gunnison Ranger District (970) 641-0471. NOTE: Near Gold Creek. 7.5' TOPOGRAPHIC MAP: Pitkin.

Map No.	Campground Name	Map Loc.	Fee	No. of Units	Max. Length	Elev.	Toilets	Water	Agency
23	**Cottonwood Lake**	C-2	$	28	40'	9,600'	Yes	Yes	San Isabel National Forest

LOCATION: 7 mi SW of Buena Vista on Hwy 306, 3.5 mi SW on Cty Rd 344. FACILITIES: Picnic Tables, Pets OK. ACTIVITIES: Fishing, Hiking. OPEN FOR USE: Late May through late Oct. CONTACT: Salida Ranger District (719) 539-3591. NOTE: Camp is set along Cottonwood Lake. 7.5' TOPOGRAPHIC MAP: Mount Yale.

Map No.	Campground Name	Map Loc.	Fee	No. of Units	Max. Length	Elev.	Toilets	Water	Agency
24	**Dillon Reservoir**	A-2	$			9,100'	Yes	Yes	White River National Forest
a.	Heaton Bay ®			72	90'				
b.	Peak One ®			79	50'				
c.	Pine Cove			55	50'				
d.	Prospector ®			108	32'				← ♿
e.	Windy Point Group ®			1	32'	*Construction 2001 - Call first.*			
f.	Lowry ®			29	50'				

LOCATION: S of I-70 at Dillon. FACILITIES: Fully developed campgrounds. ACTIVITIES: Fishing, Boating, Sailing - water contact sports are prohibited. OPEN FOR USE: Late May through mid-Nov. CONTACT: Dillon Ranger District (970) 468-5400. NOTE: Heaton Bay, Peak One, Windy Point - Reservations; Prospector - Handicap Accessible; Peak One, Pine Cove - Peninsula Recreation Area; The nearby towns of Dillon and Frisco offer a full range of services. Overnight boat camping at Dillon Marina. Windsurfing is allowed if wearing a wet suit. 7.5' TOPOGRAPHIC MAPS: Frisco, Dillon.

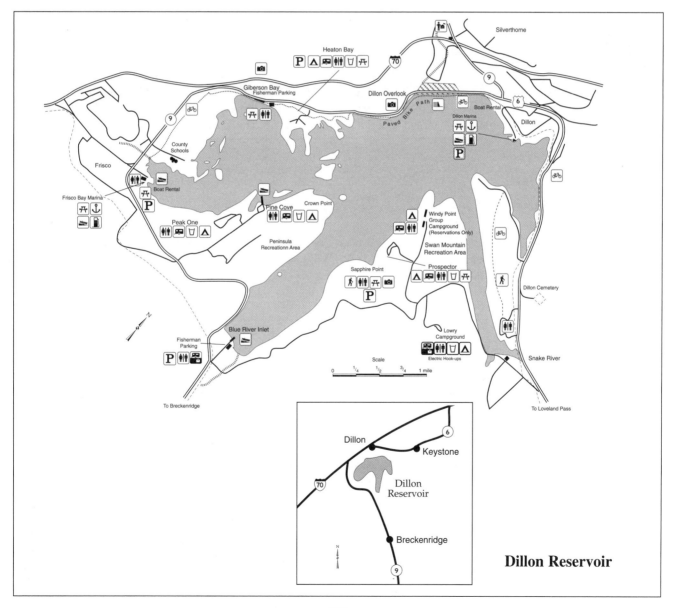

Dillon Reservoir

Map No.	Campground Name	Map Loc.	Fee	No. of Units	Max. Length	Elev.	Toilets	Water	Agency
25	**Dinner Station ®**	C-1	$	22	35'	9,600'	Yes	Yes	Gunnison National Forest

LOCATION: 11 mi N of Gunnison on Hwy 135 to Almont, 32.5 mi NE on FDR 742. FACILITIES: Picnic Tables. ACTIVI-TIES: Fishing, Hiking. OPEN FOR USE: Late May through late Oct. CONTACT: Gunnison Ranger District (970) 641-0471. NOTE: Reservations; Located on Taylor River 4 miles N of Taylor Reservoir. 7.5' TOPOGRAPHIC MAP: Pieplant.

Map No.	Campground Name	Map Loc.	Fee	No. of Units	Max. Length	Elev.	Toilets	Water	Agency
26	**Dorchester**	C-1	$	10	28'	9,800'	Yes	Yes	Gunnison National Forest

LOCATION: 11 mi N of Gunnison on Hwy 135 to Almont, 39.5 mi NE on FDR 742. FACILITIES: Picnic Tables. ACTIVI-TIES: Fishing, Hiking. OPEN FOR USE: Early June through late Sept. CONTACT: Gunnison Ranger District (970) 641-0471. NOTE: On Taylor River near Collegiate Peaks Wilderness. 7.5' TOPOGRAPHIC MAP: Italian Creek.

Map No.	Campground Name	Map Loc.	Fee	No. of Units	Max. Length	Elev.	Toilets	Water	Agency
27	**Echo Lake ®**	A-3	$	18	20'	10,600'	Yes	Yes	Arapaho/Roosevelt National Forest

LOCATION: 14 mi SW of Idaho Springs on Hwy 103. FACILITIES: Picnic Tables, Pets OK. ACTIVITIES: Fishing, Hiking. OPEN FOR USE: June through early Sept. CONTACT: Clear Creek Ranger District (303) 567-3000. NOTE: Handicap Accessible; Reservations; Campground is beside Little Echo Lake. Trailhead to Mount Evans. FDT 46. 7.5' TOPOGRAPHIC MAP: Idaho Springs.

Map No.	Campground Name	Map Loc.	Fee	No. of Units	Max. Length	Elev.	Toilets	Water	Agency
28	**Elbert Creek**	B-1	$	17	16'	10,000'	Yes	Yes	San Isabel National Forest

LOCATION: 3 mi. SW of Leadville on Hwy 24, 3/4 mi W on Cty Rd 300, 6 mi S on FDR 110. FACILITIES: Picnic Tables, Pets OK. ACTIVITIES: Fishing, Hiking. OPEN FOR USE: Late May through late Sept. CONTACT: Leadville Ranger District (719) 486-0749. NOTE: Campground is located at the confluence of Elbert Creek and Halfmoon Creek. It provides access to the Mount Massive Wilderness. FDT 1776 & 1486. 7.5' TOPOGRAPHIC MAP: Mount Massive.

Map No.	Campground Name	Map Loc.	Fee	No. of Units	Max. Length	Elev.	Toilets	Water	Agency
29	**Elk Wallow**	B1	0	7	30'	8,800'	Yes	No	White River National Forest

LOCATION: 24 mi SE of Glenwood Springs on Hwy 82 to Basalt, 23 mi E on Cty Rd 105, 3.3 mi E on FDR 501. FACILI-TIES: Picnic Tables, Pets OK. ACTIVITIES: Fishing, Hiking. OPEN FOR USE: Late May through early Nov. CONTACT: Sopris Ranger District (970) 963-2266. NOTE: Campground is along the North Fork of the Frying Pan River near Holy Cross Wilderness. 7.5' TOPOGRAPHIC MAP: Nast.

Map No.	Campground Name	Map Loc.	Fee	No. of Units	Max. Length	Elev.	Toilets	Water	Agency
30	**Fourmile**	B-2	$	14	22'	10,800'	Yes	Yes	Pike National Forest

LOCATION: 1.4 mi S of Fairplay on Hwy 285, 6.9 mi W on FDR 421. FACILITIES: Picnic Tables, Pets OK. ACTIVI-TIES: Fishing, Hiking. OPEN FOR USE: Mid-June through late Oct. CONTACT: South Park Ranger District (719) 836-2031. NOTE: Handicap Accessible; Camp is along Fourmile Creek. 7.5' TOPOGRAPHIC MAP: Fairplay West.

Map No.	Campground Name	Map Loc.	Fee	No. of Units	Max. Length	Elev.	Toilets	Water	Agency
31	**Fulford Cave**	A-1	$	7	20'	7,000'	Yes	Yes	White River National Forest

LOCATION: 12 mi S of Eagle on Cty Rd 307, 6 mi E on FDR 415. FACILITIES: Picnic Tables, Grills. ACTIVITIES: Fishing, Hiking. OPEN FOR USE: Mid-June through late Oct. CONTACT: Eagle Ranger District (970) 328-6388. NOTE: Handicap Accessible; Campground is at the end of the road at trailhead with access to lakes in the Holy Cross Wilderness. Fulford Cave TH, FDT 1875. 7.5' TOPOGRAPHIC MAP: Crooked Creek Pass.

Map No.	Campground Name	Map Loc.	Fee	No. of Units	Max. Length	Elev.	Toilets	Water	Agency
32	**Garfield**	D-2	$	11	35'	10,000'	Yes	Yes	San Isabel National Forest

LOCATION: 18 mi W of Salida on Hwy 50. FACILITIES: Picnic Tables, Pets OK. ACTIVITIES: Fishing, Hiking. OPEN FOR USE: June through early Oct. CONTACT: Salida Ranger District (719) 539-3591. NOTE:Campground near South Arkansas River. 4-Wheel Drive to High Lakes. 7.5' TOPOGRAPHIC MAP: Garfield.

Map No.	Campground Name	Map Loc.	Fee	No. of Units	Max. Length	Elev.	Toilets	Water	Agency
33	**Geneva Park**	A-3	$	26	20'	9,800'	Yes	Yes	Pike National Forest

LOCATION: 7 mi NW of Grant on County Rd 62, 1/4 mi NW on FDR 119. FACILITIES: Picnic Tables, Pets OK. ACTIVITIES: Fishing, Hiking. OPEN FOR USE: May through mid-Oct. CONTACT: South Platte Ranger District (303) 275-5610 NOTE: Campground is near Geneva Creek. 7.5' TOPOGRAPHIC MAP: Mount Evans.

Map No.	Campground Name	Map Loc.	Fee	No. of Units	Max. Length	Elev.	Toilets	Water	Agency
34	**Gold Creek**	D-1	$	6	Short	10,000'	Yes	No	Gunnison National Forest

LOCATION: 8 mi N of Ohio City on FDR 771. FACILITIES: Picnic Tables, Pets OK. ACTIVITIES: Fishing, Hiking. OPEN FOR USE: June through Sept. CONTACT: Gunnison Ranger District (970) 641-0471. NOTE: Campground is near Gold Creek and trails. Mill Creek TH, FDT 532, Gold Creek TH, FDT 427. 7.5' TOPOGRAPHIC MAP: Fairview Peak.

Map No.	Campground Name	Map Loc.	Fee	No. of Units	Max. Length	Elev.	Toilets	Water	Agency
35	**Gold Park**	A-1	$	14	40'	9,300'	Yes	Yes	White River National Forest

LOCATION: 3 mi S of Redcliffe on Hwy 24, 9 mi SW on FDR 703. FACILITIES: Picnic Tables, Pets OK. ACTIVITIES: Fishing, Hiking. OPEN FOR USE: June through early Sept. CONTACT: Holy Cross Ranger District (970) 827-5715. NOTE: On Homestake Creek, 3 mi N of Homestake Reservoir. Near Trailhead to Holy Cross Wilderness. 7.5' TOPOGRAPHIC MAP: Mount of the Holy Cross.

Map No.	Campground Name	Map Loc.	Fee	No. of Units	Max. Length	Elev.	Toilets	Water	Agency
36	**Gore Creek**	A-2	$	24	60'	8,700'	Yes	Yes	White River National Forest

LOCATION: 4 mi E of Vail on I-70, 2.5 mi S on the Frontage Rd. FACILITIES: Picnic Tables, Pets OK. ACTIVITIES: Fishing, Hiking. OPEN FOR USE: June through early Sept. CONTACT: Holy Cross Ranger District (970) 827-5715. NOTE: Campground is set along Gore Creek, with nearby trails up various creeks to small lakes in the Eagles Nest Wilderness. Deluge Crk TH, FDT 2014, Gore Crk TH, FDT 2015. 7.5' TOPOGRAPHIC MAP: Vail East.

Section 7

Map No.	Campground Name	Map Loc.	Fee	No. of Units	Max. Length	Elev.	Toilets	Water	Agency
37	Guanella Pass ®	A-3	$	18	35'	10,900'	Yes	Yes	Arapaho/Roosevelt National Forest

LOCATION: 8 mi S of Georgetown on FDR 118. FACILITIES: Picnic Tables, Pets OK. ACTIVITIES: Fishing, Hiking OPEN FOR USE: Late May through mid-Nov. CONTACT: Clear Creek Ranger District (303) 567-3000. NOTE: Handicap Accessible; Reservations; Near trailhead to Mount Evans Wilderness. Silver Dollar Lake TH, FDT 79. 7.5' TOPO-GRAPHIC MAP: Mount Evans.

Map No.	Campground Name	Map Loc.	Fee	No. of Units	Max. Length	Elev.	Toilets	Water	Agency
38	Halfmoon	B-1	$	22	16'	9,900'	Yes	Yes	San Isabel National Forest

LOCATION: 3.7 mi SW of Leadville on Hwy 24, 3/4 mi W on Hwy 300, 5.6 mi SW on FDR 110. FACILITIES: Picnic Tables, Pets OK. ACTIVITIES: Fishing, Hiking. OPEN FOR USE: Late May through late Sept. CONTACT: Leadville Ranger District (719) 486-0749. NOTE: Located 1 mi from Mt. Massive Wilderness. FDT 1486 & Colo.Tr. FDT 1776 nearby. 7.5' TOPOGRAPHIC MAP: Mount Massive.

Map No.	Campground Name	Map Loc.	Fee	No. of Units	Max. Length	Elev.	Toilets	Water	Agency
39	Hall Valley	A-3	$	9	20'	9,900'	Yes	Yes	Pike National Forest

LOCATION: 3.1 mi W of Grant on Hwy 285, 4.7 mi NW on FDR 120. FACILITIES: Picnic Tables, Pets OK. ACTIVI-TIES:Fishing, Hiking. OPEN FOR USE: May through mid-Oct. CONTACT: South Platte Ranger District (303) 275-5610. NOTE:Near North Fork of South Platte River 1 mi E of Colorado Trail. 7.5' TOPOGRAPHIC MAP: Jefferson.

Map No.	Campground Name	Map Loc.	Fee	No. of Units	Max. Length	Elev.	Toilets	Water	Agency
40	Handcart	A-3	$	10	Tent	9,800'	Yes	Yes	Pike National Forest

LOCATION: 3.1 mi W of Grant on Hwy 285, 4.9 mi NW on FDR 120. FACILITIES: Picnic Tables, Pets OK. ACTIVI-TIES: Fishing, Hiking. OPEN FOR USE: May through mid-Oct. CONTACT: South Platte Ranger District (303) 275-5610. NOTE:On the North Fork of the South Platte River. 7.5' TOPOGRAPHIC MAP: Jefferson.

Map No.	Campground Name	Map Loc.	Fee	No. of Units	Max. Length	Elev.	Toilets	Water	Agency
41	Hayden Creek	D-3	$	11	35'	8,000'	Yes	Yes	San Isabel National Forest

LOCATION: 5.1 mi SW of Coaldale on Cty Rd 6. FACILITIES: Picnic Tables, Pets OK. ACTIVITIES: Fishing, Hiking. OPEN FOR USE: Late May through mid-Oct. CONTACT: Salida Ranger District (719) 539-3591. NOTE: Campground is set near one of the trailheads for the Rainbow Trail, FDT 1336. 7.5' TOPOGRAPHIC MAP: Coaldale.

Map No.	Campground Name	Map Loc.	Fee	No. of Units	Max. Length	Elev.	Toilets	Water	Agency
42	Hornsilver	A-1	$	12	30'	8,800'	Yes	Yes	White River National Forest

LOCATION: 2.5 mi S of Redcliffe on Hwy 24. FACILITIES: Picnic Tables, Pets OK. ACTIVITIES: Fishing, Hiking. OPEN FOR USE: June through early Sept. CONTACT: Holy Cross Ranger District (970) 827-5715. NOTE: On Homestake Creek - Trailhead to Holy Cross Wilderness. 7.5' TOPOGRAPHIC MAP: Pando.

Map No.	Campground Name	Map Loc.	Fee	No. of Units	Max. Length	Elev.	Toilets	Water	Agency
43	**Horseshoe ®**	B-2	$	19	25'	10,600'	Yes	Yes	Pike National Forest

LOCATION: 1.4 mi S of Fairplay on Hwy 285, 6 mi W on FDR 421. FACILITIES: Picnic Tables, Pets OK. ACTIVITIES: Fishing, Hiking. OPEN FOR USE: May through mid-Oct. CONTACT: South Park Ranger District (719) 836-2031. NOTE: Set along Fourmile Creek. 7.5' TOPOGRAPHIC MAP: Fairplay West.

Map No.	Campground Name	Map Loc.	Fee	No. of Units	Max. Length	Elev.	Toilets	Water	Agency
44	**Iron City**	C-2	$	15	35'	9,900'	Yes	Yes	San Isabel National Forest

LOCATION: 1/2 mi S of Nathrop on Hwy 285, 15 mi W on Cty Rd 162, 1/2 mi N on FDR 292. FACILITIES: Picnic Tables, Pets OK. ACTIVITIES: Fishing, Hiking. OPEN FOR USE: Early June through late Sept. CONTACT: Salida Ranger District (719) 539-3591. NOTE: Camp is along Chalk Creek. 7.5' TOPOGRAPHIC MAP: St. Elmo.

Map No.	Campground Name	Map Loc.	Fee	No. of Units	Max. Length	Elev.	Toilets	Water	Agency
45	**Jefferson Creek ®**	A-3	$	17	25'	10,100'	Yes	Yes	Pike National Forest

LOCATION: 2 mi NW of Jefferson on Cty Rd 35, 1 mi N on Cty Rd 37, 2.9 mi NW on FDR 401. FACILITIES: Picnic Tables, Pets OK. ACTIVITIES: Fishing, Hiking. OPEN FOR USE: Late May through early Sept. CONTACT: South Park Ranger District (719) 836-2031. NOTE: Handicap Accessible. Reservations. Campground on Jefferson Creek 1 mi from Jefferson Lake, on Colorado Trail. 7.5' TOPOGRAPHIC MAP: Jefferson. ***Note: $3.00 parking fee.***

Map No.	Campground Name	Map Loc.	Fee	No. of Units	Max. Length	Elev.	Toilets	Water	Agency
46	**Kenosha Pass**	A-3	$	25	20'	10,000'	Yes	No	Pike National Forest

LOCATION: 4.2 mi NE of Jefferson on Hwy 285. FACILITIES: Picnic Tables, Pets OK. ACTIVITIES: Fishing, Hiking. OPEN FOR USE: May through mid-Oct. CONTACT: South Platte Ranger District (303) 275-5610. NOTE: Colorado Trail passes through campground, FDT 1776. 7.5' TOPOGRAPHIC MAP: Jefferson.

Map No.	Campground Name	Map Loc.	Fee	No. of Units	Max. Length	Elev.	Toilets	Water	Agency
47	**Kite Lake**	B-2	$	7	Tent	12,000'	Yes	No	Pike National Forest

LOCATION: 6 mi NW of Alma on FDR 416. FACILITIES: Picnic Tables, Pets OK. ACTIVITIES: Fishing, Hiking. OPEN FOR USE: Late May through early Sept. CONTACT: South Park Ranger District (719) 836-2031. NOTE: Last 1 mi designated as primitive road, check with forest service before trying this campground. 7.5' TOPOGRAPHIC MAPS: Climax, Alma. Note: $3.00 parking fee.

Map No.	Campground Name	Map Loc.	Fee	No. of Units	Max. Length	Elev.	Toilets	Water	Agency
48	**Lincoln Gulch**	B-1	$	7	30'	9,600'	Yes	Yes	White River National Forest

LOCATION: 10.4 mi SE of Aspen on Hwy 82, 0.2 mi W on FDR 106. FACILITIES: Picnic Tables, Pets OK. ACTIVITIES: Fishing, Hiking. OPEN FOR USE: July through mid-Sept. CONTACT: Aspen Ranger District (970) 925-3445. NOTE: Campground located between Hunter Frying Pan and Collegiate Peaks Wilderness, on Roaring Fork River. 7.5' TOPOGRAPHIC MAP: New York Peak.

Map No.	Campground Name	Map Loc.	Fee	No. of Units	Max. Length	Elev.	Toilets	Water	Agency
49	**Lodgepole ®**	C-1	$	16	35'	8,800'	Yes	Yes	Gunnison National Forest

LOCATION: 11 mi N of Gunnison on Hwy 135 to Almont, 14.7 mi NE on FDR 742. FACILITIES: Picnic Tables. ACTIVI-TIES: Fishing, Hiking. OPEN FOR USE: Late May through late Sept. CONTACT: Gunnison Ranger District (970) 641-0471. NOTE: Campground is near the Taylor River, near trailhead; Reservations. 7.5' TOPOGRAPHIC MAP: Matchless Mountain.

Map No.	Campground Name	Map Loc.	Fee	No. of Units	Max. Length	Elev.	Toilets	Water	Agency
50	**Lodgepole ®**	A-3	$	35	25'	9,900'	Yes	Yes	Pike National Forest

LOCATION: 2 mi NW of Jefferson on Cty Rd 35, 1 mi N on Cty Rd 37, 1.4 mi NW on FDR 401. FACILITIES: Picnic Tables, Pets OK. ACTIVITIES: Fishing, Hiking. OPEN FOR USE: Late May through early Sept. CONTACT: South Park Ranger District (719) 836-2031. NOTE: Reservations. Campground is near Jefferson Creek 2 miles South of Jefferson Lake on Colorado Trail. West Jefferson TH, FDT 643. Handicap Accessible. 7.5' TOPOGRAPHIC MAP: Jefferson. ♿
Note: $3.00 parking fee.

Map No.	Campground Name	Map Loc.	Fee	No. of Units	Max. Length	Elev.	Toilets	Water	Agency
51	**Lost Man**	B-1	$	10	30'	10,700'	Yes	Yes	White River National Forest

LOCATION: 14.2 mi SE of Aspen on Hwy 82. FACILITIES: Picnic Tables, Pets OK. ACTIVITIES: Fishing, Hiking. OPEN FOR USE: July through late Sept. CONTACT: Aspen Ranger District (970) 925-3445. NOTE: Campground is near Roaring Fork River, Trailhead for Hunter Fryingpan Wilderness. Lost Man TH, FDT 1996, Midway Creek TH, FDT 1993. 7.5' TOPOGRAPHIC MAP: New York Peak.

Map No.	Campground Name	Map Loc.	Fee	No. of Units	Max. Length	Elev.	Toilets	Water	Agency
52	**Lottis Creek**	C-1	$	27	35'	9,000'	Yes	Yes	Gunnison National Forest

LOCATION:11 mi N of Gunnison on Hwy 135 to Almont, 17.4 mi NE on FDR 742. FACILITIES: Picnic Tables. ACTIVI-TIES: Fishing, Hiking. OPEN FOR USE: Late May through late Sept. CONTACT: Gunnison Ranger District (970) 641-0471. NOTE: Handicap Accessible; Campground is near South Lottis Creek Trailhead, FDT 428. 7.5' TOPOGRAPHIC MAP: Matchless Mountain. ♿

Map No.	Campground Name	Map Loc.	Fee	No. of Units	Max. Length	Elev.	Toilets	Water	Agency
53	**Michigan Creek**	A-3	$	13	25'	10,000'	Yes	Yes	Pike National Forest

LOCATION: 3 mi NW of Jefferson on Cty Rd 35, 2.1 mi NW on Cty Rd 54, 1 mi NW on FDR 400. FACILITIES: Picnic Tables, Pets OK. ACTIVITIES: Fishing, Hiking. OPEN FOR USE: Mid-May through late Sept. CONTACT: South Park Ranger District (719) 836-2031. NOTE: Campground is a quiet spot on Michigan Creek. Handicap Accessible. 7.5' TOPOGRAPHIC MAP: Boreas Pass. ♿

Map No.	Campground Name	Map Loc.	Fee	No. of Units	Max. Length	Elev.	Toilets	Water	Agency
54	**Middle Quartz**	D-1	$	7	Short	10,200'	Yes	No	Gunnison National Forest

LOCATION: 56 mi W of Salida on Hwy 50 to Parlin, 18 mi NE on BLM Road 3101 to Pitkin, 1.5 mi NE on FDR 765, 5.5 mi E on FDR 767. FACILITIES: Picnic Tables, Pets OK. ACTIVITIES: Fishing, Hiking. OPEN FOR USE: Late June through late Sept. CONTACT: Gunnison Ranger District (970) 641-0471. NOTE: A primitive campground on Middle Quartz Creek. Near 4-Wheel Drive roads. 7.5' TOPOGRAPHIC MAP: Whitepine.

Map No.	Campground Name	Map Loc.	Fee	No. of Units	Max. Length	Elev.	Toilets	Water	Agency
55	**Mirror Lake**	C-1	$	10	16'	11,000'	Yes	No	Gunnison National Forest

LOCATION: 8 mi SE of Taylor Park Reservoir on FDR 765 to Tincup, 3 mi SE on FDR 267. FACILITIES: Picnic Tables. ACTIVITIES: Fishing, Hiking. OPEN FOR USE: Early June through August. CONTACT: Taylor River Ranger District (970) 641-0471. NOTE: 22 acre lake - Good Fishing. Timberline TH, FDT 414. 7.5' TOPOGRAPHIC MAP: Cumberland Pass.

Map No.	Campground Name	Map Loc.	Fee	No. of Units	Max. Length	Elev.	Toilets	Water	Agency
56	**Monarch Park ®**	D-2	$	38	40'	10,500'	Yes	Yes	San Isabel National Forest

LOCATION: 19.5 mi W of Salida on Hwy 50, 1 mi S on FDR 231. FACILITIES: Picnic Tables, Pets OK. ACTIVITIES: Fishing, Hiking. OPEN FOR USE: June through mid-Sept. CONTACT: Salida Ranger District (719) 539-3591. NOTE: Campground is near South Arkansas River and trails. 7.5' TOPOGRAPHIC MAP: Garfield.

Map No.	Campground Name	Map Loc.	Fee	No. of Units	Max. Length	Elev.	Toilets	Water	Agency
57	**Mosca**	C-1	$	16	35'	10,000'	Yes	Yes	Gunnison National Forest

LOCATION: 11 mi N of Gunnison on Hwy 135 to Almont, 7.2 mi NE on FDR 742, 12.1 mi N on FDR 744. FACILITIES: Picnic Tables, Boat Ramp nearby. ACTIVITIES: Fishing, Hiking. OPEN FOR USE: Early June through Sept. CONTACT: Gunnison Ranger District (970) 641-0471. NOTE: Campground is near Spring Creek Reservoir. 7.5' TOPOGRAPHIC MAP: Matchless Mountain.

Map No.	Campground Name	Map Loc.	Fee	No. of Units	Max. Length	Elev.	Toilets	Water	Agency
58	**Mount Princeton ®**	C-2	$	17	40'	8,000'	Yes	Yes	San Isabel National Forest

LOCATION: From Nathrop 1/2 mi S on Hwy 285, 7 mi W on Cty Rd 162. FACILITIES: Picnic Tables. ACTIVITIES: Fishing, Hiking. OPEN FOR USE: Late May through mid-Oct. CONTACT: Salida Ranger District (719) 539-3591. NOTE: Reservations. Campground is near Chalk Creek, along Spring Creek Reservoir. 7.5' TOPOGRAPHIC MAP: Mount Antero. *Construction 2001 - Call First*.

Map No.	Campground Name	Map Loc.	Fee	No. of Units	Max. Length	Elev.	Toilets	Water	Agency
59	**North Fork Reservoir**	D-2	$	8	25'	11,000'	Yes	Yes	San Isabel National Forest

LOCATION: 6 mi W of Poncha Springs on Hwy 50, 10.2 mi N on Cty Rd 240. FACILITIES: Picnic Tables, Boat Ramp, Pets OK. ACTIVITIES: Fishing, Hiking. OPEN FOR USE: Late June through late Sept. CONTACT: Salida Ranger District (719) 539-3591. NOTE: Campground is set along North Fork Lake. Last several miles to campground is primitive road. 7.5' TOPOGRAPHIC MAP: Garfield.

Map No.	Campground Name	Map Loc.	Fee	No. of Units	Max. Length	Elev.	Toilets	Water	Agency
60	**O'Haver Lake ®**	D-2	$	29	35'	9,200'	Yes	Yes	San Isabel National Forest

LOCATION: 4.5 mi S of Poncha Springs on Hwy 285, 4.6 mi SW on Cty Rd 200, 1/2 mi W on Cty Rd 202. FACILITIES: Picnic Tables, Pets OK. ACTIVITIES: Fishing, Hiking. OPEN FOR USE: Early May through mid-Oct. CONTACT: Salida Ranger District (719) 539-3591. NOTE: Reservations; Horse and hiking trails nearby. 7.5' TOPOGRAPHIC MAP: Mount Ouray.

Map No.	Campground Name	Map Loc.	Fee	No. of Units	Max. Length	Elev.	Toilets	Water	Agency
61	**Parry Peak**	B-1	$	26	32'	9,500'	Yes	Yes	San Isabel National Forest

LOCATION: 2.7 mi SW of Twin Lakes on Hwy 82. FACILITIES: Picnic Tables, Pets OK. ACTIVITIES: Fishing, Hiking. OPEN FOR USE: Late May through early Sept. CONTACT: Leadville Ranger District (719) 486-0749. NOTE: Campground is near Twin Lakes on Lake Creek. Colo.Tr. FDT 1776 nearby. 7.5' TOPOGRAPHIC MAP: Mount Elbert.

Map No.	Campground Name	Map Loc.	Fee	No. of Units	Max. Length	Elev.	Toilets	Water	Agency
62	**Pitkin**	D-1	$	22	35'	9,300'	Yes	Yes	Gunnison National Forest

LOCATION: 56 mi W of Salida on Hwy 50 to Parlin, 18 mi NE on BLM Rd 3101, 1 mi E on FDR 765. FACILITIES: Picnic Tables, Pets OK. ACTIVITIES: Fishing, Hiking. OPEN FOR USE: Late May through Sept. CONTACT: Gunnison Ranger District (970) 641-0471. NOTE: Handicap Accessible. Campground is along Quartz Creek. 7.5' TOPOGRAPHIC MAP: Whitepine.

Map No.	Campground Name	Map Loc.	Fee	No. of Units	Max. Length	Elev.	Toilets	Water	Agency
63	**Portal**	B-1	$	7	20'	10,500'	Yes	Yes	White River National Forest

LOCATION: 10.4 mi SE of Aspen on Hwy 82, 6.6 mi SE on Cty Rd 23. FACILITIES: Picnic Tables, Boat ramps, Pets OK. ACTIVITIES: Fishing, Hiking. OPEN FOR USE: Mid-July through late Sept. CONTACT: Aspen Ranger District (970) 925-3445. NOTE: Campground along Grizzly Reservoir, 4 wheel drive accessible. Grizzly Lake TH, FDT 1990. Flanked by Collegiate Peaks Wilderness. 7.5' TOPOGRAPHIC MAP: Independence Pass.

Map No.	Campground Name	Map Loc.	Fee	No. of Units	Max. Length	Elev.	Toilets	Water	Agency
64	**Quartz**	D-1	$	10	Short	9,800'	Yes	Yes	Gunnison National Forest

LOCATION: 56 mi W of Salida on Hwy 50 to Parlin, 18 mi NE on BLM Rd 3101, 4 mi NE on FDR 765. FACILITIES: Picnic Tables, Pets OK. ACTIVITIES: Fishing, Hiking. OPEN FOR USE: Late May through late Sept. CONTACT: Gunnison Ranger District (970) 641-0471. NOTE: North Quartz Creek runs next to camp. 7.5' TOPOGRAPHIC MAP: Cumberland Pass.

Map No.	Campground Name	Map Loc.	Fee	No. of Units	Max. Length	Elev.	Toilets	Water	Agency
65	**Selkirk**	A-3	$	15	25'	10,500'	Yes	No	Pike National Forest

LOCATION: 3.5 mi NW of Como on Cty Rd 33, 1 mi NW on Cty Rd 50, 1.8 mi NW on FDR 406. FACILITIES: Picnic Tables, Pets OK. ACTIVITIES: Fishing, Hiking. OPEN FOR USE: Mid-May through late Sept. CONTACT: South Park Ranger District (719) 836-2031. NOTE: Campground is near North Tarryall Creek. Near Gold Dust TH, FDT 653. 7.5' TOPOGRAPHIC MAP: Como.

Map No.	Campground Name	Map Loc.	Fee	No. of Units	Max. Length	Elev.	Toilets	Water	Agency
66	**Snowblind**	D-1	$	23	Short	9,300'	Yes	Yes	Gunnison National Forest

LOCATION: 1.1 mi NE of Sargents on Hwy 50, 6.9 mi N on FDR 888. FACILITIES: Picnic Tables, Pets OK. ACTIVITIES: Fishing, Hiking. OPEN FOR USE: June through late Sept. CONTACT: Gunnison Ranger District (970) 641-0471. NOTE: Campground is located on Canyon Creek. 4-Wheel drive road nearby. 7.5' TOPOGRAPHIC MAP: Whitepine.

Map No.	Campground Name	Map Loc.	Fee	No. of Units	Max. Length	Elev.	Toilets	Water	Agency
67	**Taylor Park Reservoir**	C-1	$		35'	9,330'	Yes	Yes	Gunnison National Forest
a.	Lakeview/Bighorn ®			46					
b.	Rivers End			15					

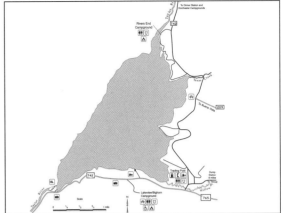

LOCATION: N 11 mi from Gunnison to Almont, NE on FDR 742, 23 mi to Reservoir.
FACILITIES: Boat Ramp, Picnic Tables, Pets OK.
ACTIVITIES: Fishing, Hiking.
OPEN FOR USE: May through Sept.
CONTACT: Gunnison Ranger District (970) 641-0471.
NOTE: Lakeview - Reservations.
7.5' TOPOGRAPHIC MAP: Taylor Park Reservoir.

Map No.	Campground Name	Map Loc.	Fee	No. of Units	Max. Length	Elev.	Toilets	Water	Agency
68	**Tigiwon**	A-1	$	9	25	9,900'	Yes	Yes	White River National Forest

LOCATION: Exit I-70 at Dowd's Junction, S 5 mi on Hwy 24, S on FDR 100 approx. 4 mi. FACILITIES: Picnic Tables, Pets OK. ACTIVITIES: Fishing, Hiking. OPEN FOR USE: Mid-June through late Oct. CONTACT: Holy Cross Ranger District (970) 827-5715. NOTE: On Brush Creek near trailhead to Holy Cross Wilderness. 7.5' TOPOGRAPHIC MAP: Minturn. *Tigiwon Community House Group ®.*

Map No.	Campground Name	Map Loc.	Fee	No. of Units	Max. Length	Elev.	Toilets	Water	Agency
69	**Turquoise Lake**	B-2	$			9,900'	Yes	Yes	San Isabel National Forest
a.	Baby Doe ®			50	32'				
b.	Belle of Colorado			19	Tent				
c.	Father Dyer ®			25	32'				
d.	May Queen ®			27	32'				
e.	Molly Brown ®			49	32'				
f.	Printer Boy Group ®			---	---				
g.	Silver Dollar ®			43	22'				
h.	Tabor			44	37'				

LOCATION: 4 mi W of Leadville on FDR 105.
FACILITIES: Full service campgrounds, Boat ramps, Picnic Tables, some Barrier Free Access, Pets OK.
ACTIVITIES: Fishing, Hiking.
OPEN FOR USE: Late May through early Sept.
CONTACT: Leadville Ranger District (719) 486-0749.
NOTE: Handicap Accessible; Baby Doe, Father Dyer, Printer Boy, Silver Dollar, Tabor - Reservations. On Colorado Trail.
7.5' TOPOGRAPHIC MAPS: Leadville North, Leadville South.

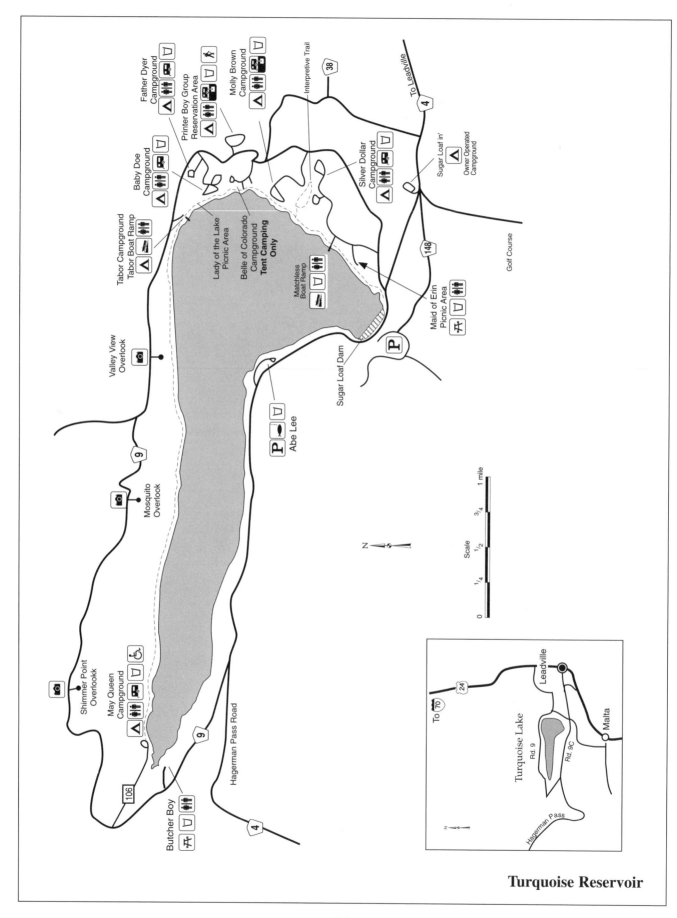

Turquoise Reservoir

Map No.	Campground Name	Map Loc.	Fee	No. of Units	Max. Length	Elev.	Toilets	Water	Agency
70	**Twin Lakes Reservoir**	B-2	$			9,500'	Yes	Yes	San Isabel National Forest
a.	Lakeview ®			59	32'				
b.	White Star ®			68	32'				
c.	Dexter			24	37'				
d.	Lakeview Group ®			---	---				

LOCATION: S of Leadville on Hwy 24, exit at Balltown, 5 mi W on Hwy 82. FACILITIES: Boat ramps, Picnic Tables. ACTIVITIES: Fishing, Hiking. OPEN FOR USE: Late May through early Sept. CONTACT: Leadville Ranger District (719) 486-0749. NOTE: Handicap Accessible. Lakeview - Reservations. Colo.Tr. FDT 1776 nearby. 7.5' TOPOGRAPHIC MAPS: Granite, South Peak.

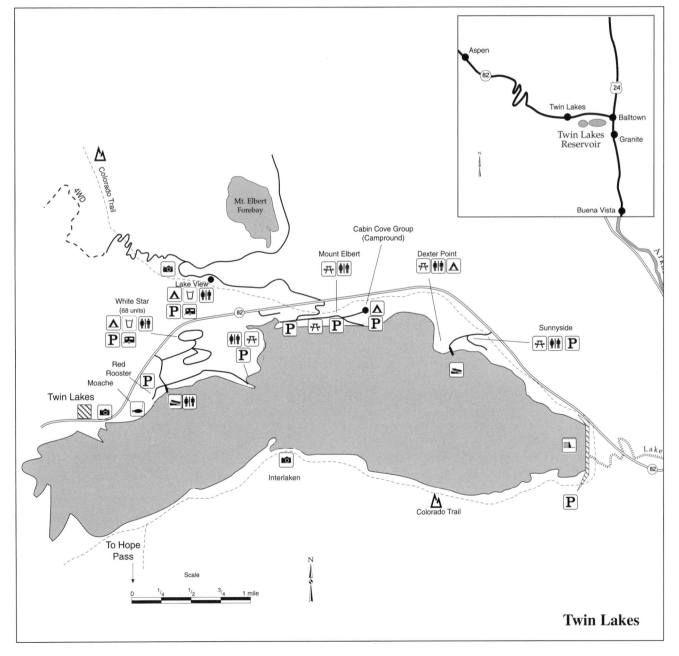

Twin Lakes

Map No.	Campground Name	Map Loc.	Fee	No. of Units	Max. Length	Elev.	Toilets	Water	Agency
71	**Twin Peaks**	B-1	$	39	32'	9,600'	Yes	Yes	San Isabel National Forest

LOCATION: 3 mi W of Twin Lakes on Hwy 82. FACILITIES: Picnic Tables, Boat ramps nearby, Pets OK. ACTIVITIES: Fishing, Hiking. OPEN FOR USE: Late May through early Sept. CONTACT: Leadville Ranger District (719) 486-0749. NOTE: Campground is along Lake Creek near Collegiate Peaks Wilderness and Twin Lakes. 7.5' TOPOGRAPHIC MAP: Mount Elbert.

Map No.	Campground Name	Map Loc.	Fee	No. of Units	Max. Length	Elev.	Toilets	Water	Agency
72	**Weller**	B-1	$	11	40'	9,400'	Yes	Yes	White River National Forest

LOCATION: 11.4 mi SE of Aspen on Hwy 82, 100 yards S on FDR 104. FACILITIES: Picnic Tables, Pets OK. ACTIVITIES: Fishing, Hiking. OPEN FOR USE: Mid-June through Late Sept. CONTACT: Aspen Ranger District (970) 925-3445. NOTE: Campground is on the Roaring Fork River, between Hunter Fryingpan and Collegiate Peaks Wilderness. Weller Lake TH, FDT 1989. 7.5' TOPOGRAPHIC MAP: New York Peak.

Map No.	Campground Name	Map Loc.	Fee	No. of Units	Max. Length	Elev.	Toilets	Water	Agency
73	**West Chicago Creek ®**	A-3	$	16	30'	9,600'	Yes	Yes	Arapaho/Roosevelt National Forest

LOCATION: 6 mi SW of Idaho Springs on Hwy 103, 4 mi SW on FDR 188. FACILITIES: Picnic Tables, Pets OK. ACTIVITIES: Fishing, Hiking. OPEN FOR USE: Late May through mid-Nov. CONTACT: Clear Creek Ranger District (303) 567-3000. NOTE: Handicap Accessible; Reservations; Trailhead to Mount Evans Wilderness. West Chicago Creek TH, FDT 53. 7.5' TOPOGRAPHIC MAP: Georgetown.

Map No.	Campground Name	Map Loc.	Fee	No. of Units	Max. Length	Elev.	Toilets	Water	Agency
74	**Weston Pass**	B-2	$	14	25'	10,200'	Yes	Yes	Pike National Forest

LOCATION: 5 mi S of Fairplay on Hwy 285, 11 mi SW on FDR 425. FACILITIES: Picnic Tables, Pets OK. ACTIVITIES: Fishing, Hiking. OPEN FOR USE: Late May through early Sept. CONTACT: South Park Ranger District (719) 836-2031. NOTE: Campground is on the South Fork of the South Platte River. Rich Creek TH, FDT 616. 7.5' TOPOGRAPHIC MAP: South Peak.

Map No.	Campground Name	Map Loc.	Fee	No. of Units	Max. Length	Elev.	Toilets	Water	Agency
75	**Whiteside**	A-3	$	5	Tent	8,900'	Yes	Yes	Pike National Forest

LOCATION: 2.2 mi NW of Grant on Cty Rd 62. FACILITIES: Picnic Tables, Pets OK. ACTIVITIES: Fishing, Hiking. OPEN FOR USE: May through mid-Oct. CONTACT: South Platte Ranger District (303) 275-5610. NOTE: Near the confluence of Bear Creek and Scott Gomer Creek and trailhead to Mount Evans Wilderness. 7.5' TOPOGRAPHIC MAP: Mount Logan.

Map No.	Campground Name	Map Loc.	Fee	No. of Units	Max. Length	Elev.	Toilets	Water	Agency
76	**Yeoman Park**	A-1	$	24	36'	9,000'	Yes	Yes	White River National Forest

LOCATION: 12 mi S of Eagle on Cty Rd 307, 5 mi E on FDR 415. FACILITIES: Picnic Tables, Pets OK. ACTIVITIES: Fishing, Hiking, Hunting, Wildlife Viewing. OPEN FOR USE: Mid-June through late Oct. CONTACT: Eagle Ranger District (970) 328-6388. NOTE: Near Brush Creek, near trailhead to Holy Cross Wilderness. 7.5' TOPOGRAPHIC MAP: Fulford.

<table>
<tr><td></td><td>AGENCY</td><td>PHONE NO.</td></tr>
</table>

BUREAU OF LAND MANAGEMENT		

Colorado Outdoor Recreation Information Phone Numbers
- U.S. Forest Service • Bureau of Land Management
- Colorado State Parks • Colorado Div. of Wildlife
- National Parks Service • Other Agencies

NATIONAL FOREST	PHONE NO.

APAPAHO/ROOSEVELT NATIONAL FOREST
BOULDER RANGER DISTRICT . . . . (303) 444-6600
CANYON LAKES RANGER DISTRICT . . . . (970) 498-2770
CLEAR CREEK RANGER DISTRICT . . . . (303) 567-3000
PAWNEE RANGER DISTRICT . . . . (970) 353-5004
SULPHUR RANGER DISTRICT . . . . (970) 887-4100

GRAND MESA NATIONAL FOREST
COLLBRAN RANGER DISTRICT . . . . (970) 487-3534
GRAND JUNCTION RANGER DISTRICT . . . . (970) 242-8211

GUNNISON NATIONAL FOREST
GUNNISON RANGER DISTRICT . . . . (970) 641-0471
PAONIA RANGER DISTRICT . . . . (970) 527-4131

PIKE NATIONAL FOREST
PIKES PEAK RANGER DISTRICT . . . . (719) 636-1602
SOUTH PARK RANGER DISTRICT . . . . (719) 836-2031
SOUTH PLATTE RANGER DISTRICT . . . . (303) 275-5610

RIO GRANDE/SAN JUAN NATIONAL FOREST
CONEJOS PEAK RANGER DISTRICT . . . . (719) 274-8971
DIVIDE RANGER DISTRICT (Creede) . . . . (719) 658-2556
DIVIDE RANGER DIST. (Del Norte) . . . . (719) 657-3321
SAGUACHE RANGER DISTRICT . . . . (719) 655-2547

ROUTT NATIONAL FOREST
HAHNS PEAK/BEAR EARS RANGER DIST. . . . . (970) 879-1870
THE PARKS RANGER DISTRICT . . . . (970) 723-8204
YAMPA RANGER DISTRICT . . . . (970) 638-4516

SAN ISABEL NATIONAL FOREST
LEADVILLE RANGER DISTRICT . . . . (719) 486-0749
SALIDA RANGER DISTRICT . . . . (719) 539-3591
SAN CARLOS RANGER DISTRICT . . . . (719) 269-8500

SAN JUAN/RIO GRANDE NATIONAL FOREST
COLUMBINE RANGER DIST.(BAYFIELD) . . . . . (970) 884-2512
COLUMBINE RANGER DIST. (DURANGO) . . . . . (970) 247-4874
MANCOS/DOLORES RANGER DIST. . . . . (970) 882-7296
PAGOSA RANGER DISTRICT . . . . (970) 264-2268

UNCOMPAHGRE NATIONAL FOREST
GRAND JUNCTION RANGER DISTRICT . . . . (970) 242-8211
NORWOOD RANGER DISTRICT . . . . (970) 327-4261
OURAY RANGER DISTRICT . . . . (970) 240-5300

WHITE RIVER NATIONAL FOREST
ASPEN RANGER DISTRICT . . . . (970) 925-3445
BLANCO RANGER DISTRICT . . . . (970) 878-4039
DILLON RANGER DISTRICT . . . . (970) 468-5400
EAGLE RANGER DISTRICT . . . . (970) 328-6388
HOLY CROSS RANGER DISTRICT . . . . (970) 827-5715
RIFLE RANGER DISTRICT . . . . (970) 625-2371
SOPRIS RANGER DISTRICT . . . . (970) 963-2266

REGIONAL FOREST SERVICE OFFICE
LAKEWOOD COLORADO . . . . (303) 275-5350

BUREAU OF LAND MANAGEMENT
GRAND JUNCTION RESOURCE AREA . . . . (970) 244-3000
GUNNISON RESOURCE AREA . . . . (970) 641-0471
GLENWOOD SPRINGS RESOURCE AREA . . . . . . (970) 947-2800
LA JARA RESOURCE AREA . . . . (719) 274-8971
LITTLE SNAKE RESOURCE AREA . . . . (970) 824-5000
SAGUACHE RESOURCE AREA . . . . (719) 655-2547
SAN JUAN RESOURCE AREA . . . . (970) 247-4874
UNCOMPAHGRE BASIN RESOURCE AREA . . . . (970) 240-5300

BOULDER MTN. PARKS . . . . (303) 441-3440

CORP OF ENGINEERS
JOHN MARTIN RESERVOIR . . . . (719) 336-3476

CITY OF LAKEWOOD
BEAR CREEK LAKE PARK . . . . (303) 697-6159

CITY OF RIFLE
RIFLE MOUNTAIN PARK . . . . (970) 625-2121

CITY OF TRINIDAD
MONUMENT LAKE RESORT . . . . (719) 868-2226

COLORADO DIVISION OF WILDLIFE
CENTRAL REGION, DENVER . . . . (303) 297-1192
NORTHEAST REGION, FORT COLLINS . . . . (970) 472-4300
NORTHWEST REGION, GRAND JUNCTION . . . . (970) 255-6100
SOUTHEAST REGION, COLORADO SPRINGS . . . (719) 227-5200
SOUTHWEST REGION, MONTROSE . . . . (970) 252-6000

COLORADO STATE PARKS
DIRECTORS OFFICE, DENVER . . . . (303) 866-3437
METRO DENVER, LITTLETON . . . . (303) 791-1957
NORTH REGION, FORT COLLINS . . . . (970) 226-6641
SOUTH REGION, COLORADO SPRINGS . . . . . . (719) 471-0900
WEST REGION, CLIFTON . . . . (970) 434-6862

U.S. FISH AND WILDLIFE SERVICE
BROWNS PARK NATIONAL WILDLIFE REFUGE . . . . . . (970) 365-3613

HINSDALE COUNTY
COUNTY OFFICE, LAKE CITY . . . . (970) 944-2225

LARIMER COUNTY PARKS & OPEN LAND
PARKS OFFICE, FORT COLLINS . . . . (970) 679-4570

LONGMONT CITY PARKS DEPARTMENT
UNION RESERVOIR PARK OFFICE . . . . (303) 772-1265

NATIONAL PARKS SERVICE
BLACK CANYON OF THE GUNNISON . . . . (970) 641-2337
COLORADO NATIONAL MONUMENT . . . . (970) 858-3617
CURECANTI NATIONAL RECREATION AREA . . . . . . (970) 641-2337
DINOSAUR NATIONAL MONUMENT . . . . (970) 374-3000
GREAT SAND DUNES NATIONAL MON. . . . . . . (719) 378-2312
MESA VERDE NATIONAL PARK . . . . (970) 529-4465
ROCKY MOUNTAIN NATIONAL PARK . . . . (970) 586-1200

US GEOL. SURVEY MAP SALES (800) HELP MAP . . . . (303) 202-4657
. . . .
CAMPING RESERVATIONS:
NATIONAL FOREST SERVICE . . . . (877) 444-6777

STATE PARKS (From outside Metro Denver Area) . . . . (800) 678-2267
(From inside Metro Denver Area) . . (303) 470-1144
Note: Reservation period for State Parks, April through September.

NATIONAL PARKS SERVICE . . . . (800) 365-2267
(Rocky Mountain National Park)

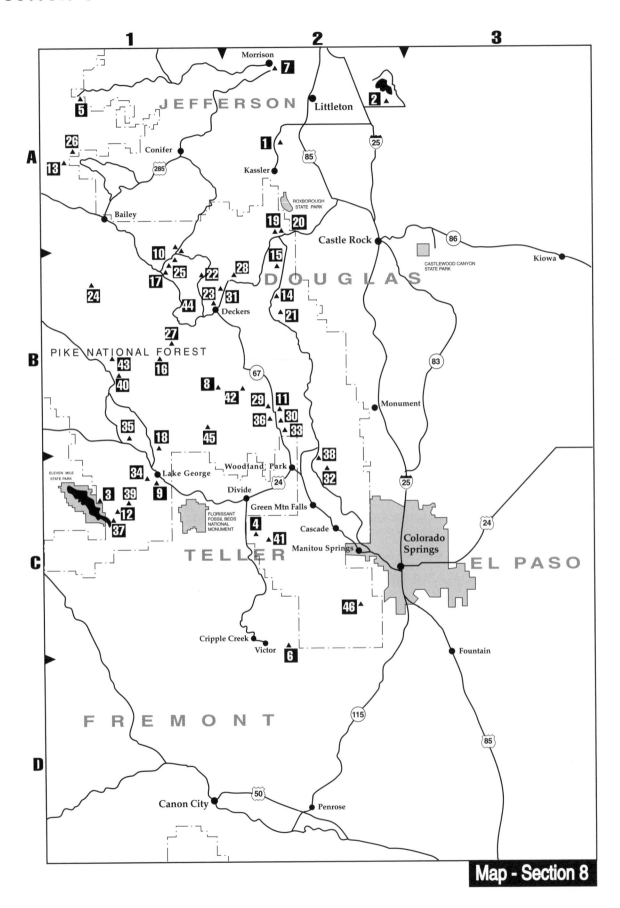

Rampart Reservoir

Section 8

Map No.	Name	Map Loc.	Fee	No. of Units	Max. Length	Elev.	Toilets	Water	Agency
1	**Chatfield State Park ®**	A-2	$	153	Open	5,430'	Yes	Yes	Colorado State Parks

Chatfield State Park located in Littleton, south of Interstate 470, is fully accessible to persons with disabilities. Twenty-five miles of paved trails are wide enough and level enough to accommodate wheelchairs. A handicapped fishing pier is located near the marina on the east side of the lake, and an access trail is located at the South Platte River.

Camping

Water faucet's are conveniently located throughout the campground and each of the 153 individual sites has a fire ring and grill. A camping permit is required in addition to the parks pass for persons using the campgrounds. Campers may stay a maximum of 14 days in any 45 day period, and immediate occupancy of sites is required. Quiet hours are observed from 10 pm to 6 am and generators may not be operated during these hours. A sewage dump station is located near the campground. Please use this facility. It is illegal to dump waste or sewage, including dishwater, anywhere else. Individual sites can be reserved, and group sites are by reservation only. Further information can be obtained by calling the park office.

Wildlife

Chatfield's thousands of acres of prairie grasses, water and ground cover support a multitude of wildlife species. Over 180 species of birds have been sighted at Chatfield, most notably Great Blue herons. A 27 acre heron rookery is the breeding area for over 50 pair of the large birds.

Fishing

In addition to a healthy population of trout and bass Chatfield has channel catfish, yellow perch, crappie, bluegill, sunfish and carp. The lake is periodically stocked with rainbow trout and other fish by the Division of Wildlife, and with a 15 inch minimum size limit is in effect for largemouth bass to allow the little ones to grow big!

Water Sports

Boating, waterskiing, sailing and swimming. Areas are set aside for different activities to ensure maximum safety for everyone. There are designed water beaches and a swim beach.

Trails

A series of trails winds through the Chatfield area and provides the park visitor with an abundance of opportunities.

Other Activities

Horseback Riding, Model planes, Balloons, and Ice Fishing.

Daily Fee/Annual Pass
For more information contact:
Chatfield State Park
11500 N. Roxborough Park Road
Littleton, CO 80125 -- (303)791-7275

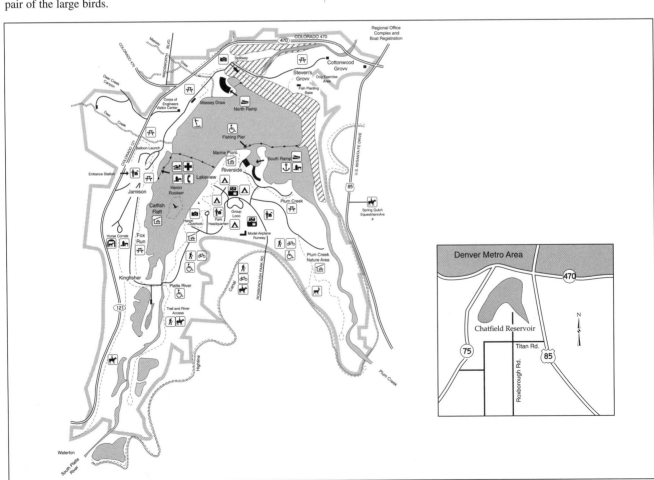

Map No.	Name	Map Loc.	Fee	No. of Units	Max. Length	Elev.	Toilets	Water	Agency
2	**Cherry Creek State Park** ®	A-2	$	102	Open	5,550'	Yes	Yes	Colorado State Parks

Over 1.5 million visitors can't be wrong! Cherry Creek State Park, located in SE Denver one and half miles south of 1-225 on Parker Road, is an oasis for boaters, fishermen and swimmers alike. The recreation opportunities are unlimited at this 4800 acre park. There's excitement on the 880 acre reservoir with water skiers, windsurfers and boaters. Yet solitude can be found fishing in a cove or walking the nature trails.

During the summer colorful masts from sailboats and windsurfers dot the lake in summer against a backdrop of the Rockies. It's a unique place. It offers a fast gateway for city dwellers to unwind. It provides a place to learn about nature, a place to have a family picnic and even a special area to train your dog. Then there's the unexpected - a herd of over 20 deer - plus coyotes, pheasant, cottontail and jack rabbits.

Facilities for the Disabled
Special facilities to accommodate handicapped persons are located at the fishing access areas, the Dixon Grove picnic area, the campground, the group picnic sites and the swim beach. Parking for handicapped visitors is signed throughout the park.

Camping
Cherry Creek offers metro Denver area residents the convenience of close-in camping at its 102 sites located on the east side of the reservoir. Showers, laundry facilities and electrical hook-ups are available. Campsites can be reserved in advance. A holding tank dump station is located across from the campground entrance.

Fishing
Fisherman head out to Cherry Creek to catch trout, walleye, bass, crappie, pike, carp and catfish. The Tower Loop area near the dam is a popular spot as well as the quiet of the south end of the reservoir.

Other Activities
Nature Study, Horseback Riding, and Bicycle Trails.

Daily Fee/Annual Pass
For more information contact:
Cherry Creek State Park
4201 S. Parker Rd.
Aurora CO, 80014 -- (303) 699-3860

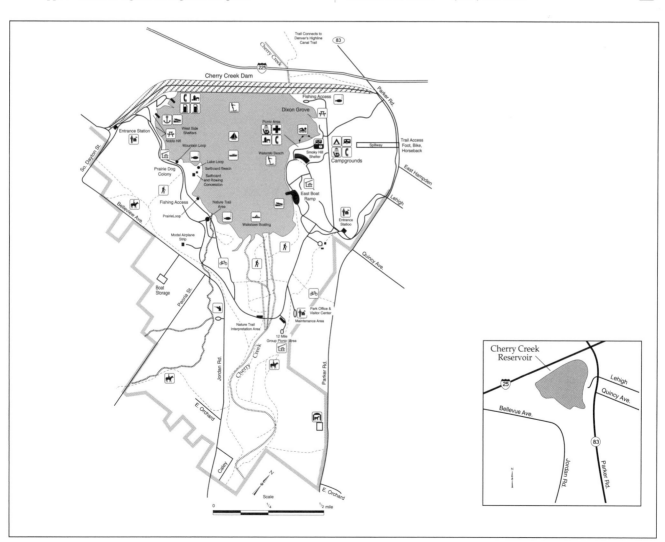

Map No.	Name	Map Loc.	Fee	No. of Units	Max. Length	Elev.	Toilets	Water	Agency
3	**Eleven Mile State Park ®**	C-1	$	300	Open	8,600'	Yes	Yes	Colorado State Parks

Located 39 mi W of Colorado Springs on U.S. 24 to Lake George south on County Road 247. Eleven Mile exemplifies the beauty and drama of this part of Colorado. The Pike National Forest borders the park on two sides. In the distance, Pike's Peak and the Tarryall Range to the east and the snowy Continental Divide to the west form an imposing setting for the reservoir, short grass and rocky outcroppings of the park.

Eleven Mile's 8,600 foot altitude means that the temperatures can vary widely in any season. Sunburn can occur rapidly in the thin air.

Accessibility
Some areas and campgrounds have been adapted for use by persons with disabilities. Ask at the Park Office or northeast entrance station for more information.

Camping
Eleven Mile's 300 campsites can accommodate tent, pickups, campers, trailers and motor homes. A camping permit is required for all vehicles parked overnight. Holding tank dump stations are located at the entrance to North Shore and Witches Cove.

Fishing
Brown and rainbow trout, mackinaw, kokanee, northern pike and carp are found in the reservoir. Fishing is prohibited in the restricted area near the dam, but is permitted everywhere else on the reservoir. Bow fishing for carp is permitted year round.

Wildlife
Many species of waterfowl are abundant at the reservoir and the surrounding area. Antelope, elk, deer, bear, coyote, mountain lion, bobcat and several varieties of small mammals frequent the park.

Activities
Boating, Ice fishing, cross-country skiing, and ice boating. All water contact sports including swimming, waterskiing, wading, scuba diving, and windsurfing are prohibited.

Daily Fee/Annual Pass
For more information contact:
Eleven Mile State Park
4229 County Rd. 92
Star Rt, 2 Box 4229
Lake George, CO 80827 -- (719) 748-3401

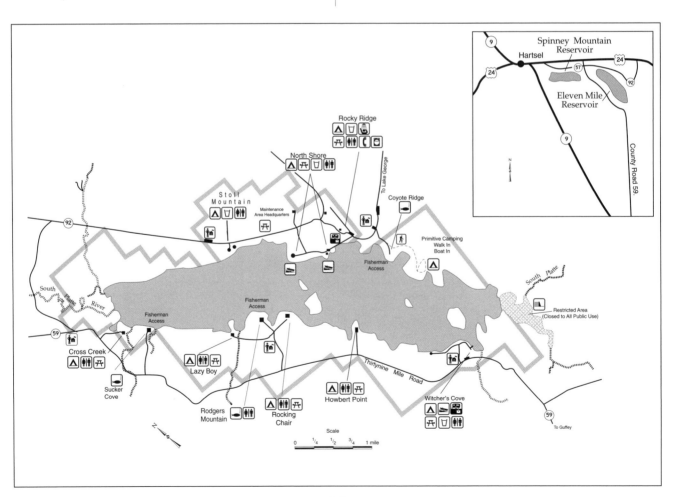

Map No.	Campground Name	Map Loc.	Fee	No. of Units	Max. Length	Elev.	Toilets	Water	Agency
4	**Mueller State Park & Wildlife Area ®**	C-2	$	90	Open	9,500'	Yes	Yes	Colorado State Parks

Mueller State Park and Wildlife area is located on Colorado Highway 67, S of Divide 4.5 miles. You are surrounded by 12,l03 acres of spring fed meadows, forested ridges and massive Pikes Peak granite.

The park's topography varies from rolling timber and grasslands interrupted by dramatic rock outcroppings in the north, to the south portion of the park where Fourmile Creek spills through the rugged terrain dominated by Sheep Nose and the impressive Dome Rock.

Camping
The campground is located in a picturesque forested setting of spruce, fir, and aspen with panoramic views of the Rocky Mountains. The park has 90 sites including 12 walk-in tent sites and a group campground. The campground can accommodate motor home's, trailers and tents. A camper services facility with modern restrooms, hot showers and laundry facilities is centrally located in the campground. All sites, except the walk-in tent sites, have electrical hookups, and drinking water is available. There are no sewer hookups, but a dump station is available.

Trails
Approximately 90 miles of trails invite exploration of wildlife habitat shared by elk, big horn sheep, mule deer, eagles hawks and a variety of small mammals and song birds. In remote areas, bears, bobcats and mountain lions are able to live in freedom. Trails vary from short, leisurely walks to challenging, full day hikes. Most trails are open to hikers and cyclists with a few ecologically fragile areas restricted to hikers only.

Other Activities
Fishing, Hunting and Picnicking.

Dally Fee/Annual Pass
For more information contact:
Mueller State Park and Wildlife Area
P.O. Box 49
Divide, CO 80814 -- (719) 687-2366

Map No.	Campground Name	Map Loc.	Fee	No. of Units	Max. Length	Elev.	Toilets	Water	Agency
5	**Mount Evans State Wildlife Area**	A-1	0	---	---	9,500'	Yes	Yes	Colorado Division of Wildlife

LOCATION:From Denver W on I-70 to El Rancho exit, 6 miles S on Hwy 74 to Evergreen Lake. (3,438 ACRES.) Turn right on Upper Bear Creek Rd for 6.5 mi. to Cty Rd 480. Turn Right, 3 mi. to property. FACILITIES: None, Pets OK. ACTIVITIES: Fishing, Hiking, Hunting in Fall. OPEN FOR USE: Mid-June thru Dec. CONTACT: Colorado Division of Wildlife (303) 297-1192. NOTE: Campground is in the Mount Evans Wildlife Area, near Mount Evans Wilderness. Camping limited to 5 days in any 45 day period except in big game season. Camp in designated areas.

Map No.	Campground Name	Map Loc.	Fee	No. of Units	Max. Length	Elev.	Toilets	Water	Agency
6	**Skagway Reservoir State Wildlife Area**	C-2	0	Dispersed	Open	9,000'	Yes	No	Colorado Division of Wildlife

LOCATION: 1/2 mi E of Victor on Cty Rd 67, 6 1/2 mi E on Cty Rd 441. FACILITIES: Boat ramp. ACTIVITIES: Fishing, Hiking. OPEN FOR USE: Year Round. CONTACT: Colorado Division of Wildlife SE Region (719) 227-5200. 7.5' TOPO-GRAPHIC MAP: Big Bull Mountain.

Map No.	Campground Name	Map Loc.	Fee	No. of Units	Max. Length	Elev.	Toilets	Water	Agency
7	**Bear Creek Lake Park**	A-2	$	52	Open	5,775'	Yes	Yes	City of Lakewood

LOCATION: Bear Creek Lake Park entrance 1/8 mi E of C-470 on Morrison Rd (State Hwy 8). After hours entrance (Use after 9:45 pm) located 1/8 mi N of State Hwy 285 on Westbound C-470. FACILITIES: (Indian Paintbrush Campground) Picnic Tables, Firepits. Reduced fees for seniors and special group area and rates available to Boy/Girl Scout troops and other special interest groups by reservation. ACTIVITIES: Fishing, Hiking, Sailing/Canoeing, Outdoor Archery Range, Camping, Mountain Biking, Roller Blading, Horseback Riding, Picnicking (both group areas and individual sites), Evening Campfire Programs, and a Summer Nature Camp for 10, 11, and 12 year old's. OPEN FOR USE: Year Round. CON-TACT: Park Office (303) 697-6159.

Map No.	Campground Name	Map Loc.	Fee	No. of Units	Max. Length	Elev.	Toilets	Water	Agency
8	**Big Turkey**	B-1	$	10	16'	8,000'	Yes	Yes	Pike National Forest

LOCATION: 13.5 mi NW of Woodland Park on Hwy 67 to Westcreek, 3/4 mi SW on FDR 200, 3.9 mi SW on FDR 360. FACILITIES: Picnic Tables, Pets OK. ACTIVITIES: Fishing, Hiking, Mountain Biking. OPEN FOR USE: May through mid-Oct. CONTACT: South Platte Ranger District (303) 275-5610. NOTE: Campground is near Turkey Creek. 7.5' TOPOGRAPHIC MAPS: Signal Butte, Westcreek.

Map No.	Campground Name	Map Loc.	Fee	No. of Units	Max. Length	Elev.	Toilets	Water	Agency
9	**Blue Mountain ®**	C-1	$	21	35'	8,200'	Yes	Yes	Pike National Forest

LOCATION: 1.3 mi SW of Lake George on FDR 245, 1/2 mi S on FDR 240. FACILITIES: Picnic Tables, Pets OK. ACTIVITIES: Fishing, Hiking. OPEN FOR USE: Mid-May through late Sept. CONTACT: South Park Ranger District (719) 836-2031. NOTE: Handicap Accessible. Campground is along South Platte River in Eleven Mile Canyon and near Florissant Fossil Beds National Monument. 7.5' TOPOGRAPHIC MAP: Lake George. ♿

Map No.	Campground Name	Map Loc.	Fee	No. of Units	Max. Length	Elev.	Toilets	Water	Agency
10	**Buffalo ®**	B-1	$	41	20'	7,400'	Yes	Yes	Pike National Forest

LOCATION: 1/2 mi SE of the town of Buffalo Creek on Cty Rd 126, 5.7 mi SW on FDR 543, 1/4 mi E on FDR 550. FACILITIES: Picnic Tables, Pets OK. ACTIVITIES: Fishing, Hiking, Mountain Biking. OPEN FOR USE: April through mid-Nov. CONTACT: South Platte Ranger District (303) 275-5610. NOTE: Handicap Accessible. Reservations. Campground is near Buffalo Creek and on the Colorado Trail, FDT 1776. 7.5' TOPOGRAPHIC MAP: Green Mountain. ♿

Map No.	Campground Name	Map Loc.	Fee	No. of Units	Max. Length	Elev.	Toilets	Water	Agency
11	**Colorado ®**	B-2	$	81	30'	7,800'	Yes	Yes	Pike National Forest

LOCATION: 6.9 mi N of Woodland Park on Hwy 67. FACILITIES: Picnic Tables, Dump Station, Pets OK. ACTIVITIES: Fishing, Hiking. OPEN FOR USE: Late May through early Sept. CONTACT: Pikes Peak Ranger District (719) 636-1602. NOTE: Handicap Accessible. Fishing @ 34 ac. Manitou Lake and Trout Creek. Paved bike trail, hiking trail at Manitou Park Recreation Area. 7.5' TOPOGRAPHIC MAP: Mount Deception. ♿

Map No.	Campground Name	Map Loc.	Fee	No. of Units	Max. Length	Elev.	Toilets	Water	Agency
12	**Cove ®**	C-1	$	4	16'	8,400'	Yes	Yes	Pike National Forest

LOCATION: 8 mi SW of Lake George on Cty Rd 96. FACILITIES: Picnic Tables, Fire Rings, Pets OK. ACTIVITIES: Fishing, Hiking. OPEN FOR USE: Mid-May through late Sept. CONTACT: South Park Ranger District (719) 836-2031. NOTE: 1 mi from Eleven Mile Reservoir State Park. Parking Fee. 7.5' TOPOGRAPHIC MAP: Eleven Mile Canyon. Note: *$3.00 parking fee.*

Map No.	Campground Name	Map Loc.	Fee	No. of Units	Max. Length	Elev.	Toilets	Water	Agency
13	**Deer Creek**	A-1	$	13	20'	9,000'	Yes	Yes	Pike National Forest

LOCATION: 2.4 mi N of Bailey on Hwy 285, 8 mi NW on FDR 100. FACILITIES: Picnic Tables, Pets OK. ACTIVITIES: Fishing, Hiking. OPEN FOR USE: April through mid-Nov. CONTACT: South Platte Ranger District (303) 275-5610. NOTE: Camp is near Deer Creek and trailhead to Mount Evans Wilderness. Tanglewood TH, FDT 636. 7.5' TOPOGRAPHIC MAP: Harris Park.

Map No.	Campground Name	Map Loc.	Fee	No. of Units	Max. Length	Elev.	Toilets	Water	Agency
14	**Devils Head**	B-2	$	21	20'	8,800'	Yes	Yes	Pike National Forest

LOCATION: 10 mi SW of Sedalia on Hwy 67, 9.1 mi S on FDR 300, 4/10 mi SE on Devils Head Rd. FACILITIES: Picnic Tables, Pets OK. ACTIVITIES: Fishing, Hiking. OPEN FOR USE: May through mid-Oct. CONTACT: South Platte Ranger District (303) 275-5610. NOTE: Devils Head Fire Lookout is 1 mi S of campground. Devils Head TH, FDT 611. 7.5' TOPOGRAPHIC MAP: Devils Head.

Map No.	Campground Name	Map Loc.	Fee	No. of Units	Max. Length	Elev.	Toilets	Water	Agency
15	**Flat Rocks**	B-2	$	19	20'	8,200'	Yes	Yes	Pike National Forest

LOCATION: 10 mi SW of Sedalia on Hwy 67, 4.8 mi S on FDR 300. FACILITIES: Picnic Tables, Pets OK. ACTIVITIES: Fishing, Hiking, Mountain Biking. OPEN FOR USE: May through mid-Oct. CONTACT: South Platte Ranger District (303) 275-5610. NOTE: Secluded camping spot. TH, FDT 673. 7.5' TOPOGRAPHIC MAP: Devils Head.

Map No.	Campground Name	Map Loc.	Fee	No. of Units	Max. Length	Elev.	Toilets	Water	Agency
16	**Goose Creek**	B-1	$	10	20'	8,100'	Yes	Yes	Pike National Forest

LOCATION: 2.5 mi SW of Deckers on Cty Rd 126, 10 mi SW on FDR 211. FACILITIES: Picnic Tables, Pets OK. ACTIVITIES: Fishing, Hiking, Mountain Biking. OPEN FOR USE: May through mid-Oct. CONTACT: South Platte Ranger District (303) 275-5610. NOTE: Near trailhead to Lost Creek Wilderness. 7.5' TOPOGRAPHIC MAP: Cheesman Lake.

Map No.	Campground Name	Map Loc.	Fee	No. of Units	Max. Length	Elev.	Toilets	Water	Agency
17	**Green Mountain**	B-1	$	6	Tent	7,600'	Yes	No	Pike National Forest

LOCATION: 1/2 mi SE of the town of Buffalo Creek on Cty Rd 126, 7.7 mi SW on FDR 543. FACILITIES: Picnic Tables, Pets OK. ACTIVITIES: Fishing, Hiking, Mountain Biking. OPEN FOR USE: May through mid-Oct. CONTACT: South Platte Ranger District (303) 275-5610. NOTE: Campground is near Wellington Lake, Buffalo Creek and trailhead to Lost Creek Wilderness. 7.5' TOPOGRAPHIC MAP: Green Mountain.

Map No.	Campground Name	Map Loc.	Fee	No. of Units	Max. Length	Elev.	Toilets	Water	Agency
18	**Happy Meadows**	B-1	$	7	22'	7,900'	Yes	Yes	Pike National Forest

LOCATION: 1.2 mi NW of Lake George on Hwy 24, 1.2 mi N on Cty Rd 77, 3/4 mi NE on FDR 207. FACILITIES: Picnic Tables, Pets OK. ACTIVITIES: Fishing, Hiking. OPEN FOR USE: Mid-May through late Sept. CONTACT: South Park Ranger District (719) 836-2031. NOTE: Campground is near South Platte River. Near Platte River TH, FDT 654. 7'5 TOPOGRAPHIC MAP: Hackett Mountain.

Map No.	Campground Name	Map Loc.	Fee	No. of Units	Max. Length	Elev.	Toilets	Water	Agency
19	**Indian Creek**	A-2	$	11	20'	7,500'	Yes	Yes	Pike National Forest

LOCATION: 10 mi W of Sedalia on Hwy 67, 1/4 mi W on Cty Rd 67. FACILITIES: Picnic Tables, Pets OK. ACTIVITIES: Fishing, Hiking, Mountain Biking. OPEN FOR USE: April through mid-Nov. CONTACT: South Platte Ranger District (303) 275-5610. NOTE: First campground S of Denver in Pike National Forest. 7.5' TOPOGRAPHIC MAP: Kassler.

Map No.	Campground Name	Map Loc.	Fee	No. of Units	Max. Length	Elev.	Toilets	Water	Agency
20	**Indian Creek Equestrian ®**	A-2	$	8	Four Horse Trailer	7,500'	Yes	Yes	Pike National Forest

LOCATION: 10 mi W of Sedalia on Hwy 67, 1/4 mi W on Cty Rd 67. FACILITIES: Picnic Tables, Pets OK. ACTIVITIES: Horse Trail FDT 800. OPEN FOR USE: April through mid-Nov. CONTACT: South Platte Ranger District (303) 275-5610. NOTE: First campground S of Denver in Pike National Forest. 7.5' TOPOGRAPHIC MAP: Kassler. ♿
Note: FDT 800 will open late June 2001. Trail will be 13 miles long at completion. Hitching posts are available.

Map No.	Campground Name	Map Loc.	Fee	No. of Units	Max. Length	Elev.	Toilets	Water	Agency
21	**Jackson Creek**	B-2	$	9	20'	8,100'	Yes	Yes	Pike National Forest

LOCATION: 10 mi W of Sedalia on Hwy 67, 13.9 mi S on FDR 300, 1.5 mi NE on FDR 502. FACILITIES: Picnic Tables, Pets OK. ACTIVITIES: Fishing, Hiking. OPEN FOR USE: May through mid-Oct. CONTACT: South Platte Ranger District (303) 275-5610. NOTE: Campground is near Jackson Creek. 7.5' TOPOGRAPHIC MAP: Devils Head, Dakan Mountain.

Map No.	Campground Name	Map Loc.	Fee	No. of Units	Max. Length	Elev.	Toilets	Water	Agency
22	**Kelsey ®**	B-1	$	17	20'	8,000'	Yes	Yes	Pike National Forest

LOCATION: 7.9 mi S of the town of Buffalo Creek on Cty Rd 126. FACILITIES: Picnic Tables, Pets OK. ACTIVITIES: Fishing, Hiking, Mountain Biking. OPEN FOR USE: May through mid-Oct. CONTACT: South Platte Ranger District (303) 275-5610. NOTE: Reservations; Campground is near Sixmile Creek N of Cheesman Lake. 7.5' TOPOGRAPHIC MAP: Green Mountain.

Map No.	Campground Name	Map Loc.	Fee	No. of Units	Max. Length	Elev.	Toilets	Water	Agency
23	**Lone Rock ®**	B-1	$	19	20'	6,400'	Yes	Yes	Pike National Forest

LOCATION: 17 mi SE of the town of Buffalo Creek on Cty Rd 126. FACILITIES: Picnic Tables, Pets OK. ACTIVITIES: Fishing, Hiking, Mountain Biking. OPEN FOR USE: April through Oct. CONTACT: South Platte Ranger District (303) 275-5610. NOTE: Campground is near South Platte River, just W of Deckers. Reservations; Handicap Accessible. 7.5' TOPOGRAPHIC MAP: Deckers. ♿

Map No.	Campground Name	Map Loc.	Fee	No. of Units	Max. Length	Elev.	Toilets	Water	Agency
24	**Lost Park**	B-1	$	12	22'	10,000'	Yes	Yes	Pike National Forest

LOCATION: 1.2 mi NE of Jefferson on Hwy 285, 19.7 mi E on FDR 127. FACILITIES: Picnic Tables, Pets OK. ACTIVITIES: Fishing, Hiking. OPEN FOR USE: Mid-May through late Sept. CONTACT: South Park Ranger District (719) 836-2031. NOTE: Handicap Accessible; Campground near Lost Creek and trailhead to Lost Creek Wilderness and Colorado Trail. 7.5' TOPOGRAPHIC MAP: Topas Mountain. ♿

Map No.	Campground Name	Map Loc.	Fee	No. of Units	Max. Length	Elev.	Toilets	Water	Agency
25	**Meadows Group ®**	B-1	$	---	Open	7,000'	Yes	Yes	Pike National Forest

LOCATION: 1/2 mi SE of the town Buffalo Creek on Cty Rd 126, 5.7 mi SW on FDR 543. FACILITIES: Picnic Tables, Pets OK. ACTIVITIES: Fishing, Hiking. OPEN FOR USE: April through mid-Nov. CONTACT: South Platte Ranger District (303) 275-5610. NOTE: Reservations. Campground near Redskin Creek and Colorado Trail, FDT 1776, to Lost Creek Wilderness (5 mi). 7.5' TOPOGRAPHIC MAP: Green Mountain.

Map No.	Campground Name	Map Loc.	Fee	No. of Units	Max. Length	Elev.	Toilets	Water	Agency
26	**Meridian**	A-1	$	18	20'	9,000'	Yes	Yes	Pike National Forest

LOCATION: 2.4 mi N of Bailey on Hwy 285, 6.6 mi NW on Cty Rd 43 to FDR 100, 1 mi N on FDR 102. FACILITIES: Picnic Tables, Pets OK. ACTIVITIES: Fishing, Hiking. OPEN FOR USE: May through Sept. CONTACT: South Platte Ranger District (303) 275-5610. NOTE: Along Elk Creek, near Mt. Evans Wilderness. 7.5' TOPOGRAPHIC MAP: Harris Park.

Map No.	Campground Name	Map Loc.	Fee	No. of Units	Max. Length	Elev.	Toilets	Water	Agency
27	**Molly Gulch**	B-1	$	15	20'	7,500'	Yes	Yes	Pike National Forest

LOCATION: 9 mi SW of Deckers on FDR 211. FACILITIES: Picnic Tables, Pets OK. ACTIVITIES: Fishing, Hiking. OPEN FOR USE: May through mid-Oct. CONTACT: South Platte Ranger District (303) 275-5610. NOTE: Camp is along Goose Creek and near Lost Creek Wilderness. 7.5' TOPOGRAPHIC MAP: Cheesman Lake.

Map No.	Campground Name	Map Loc.	Fee	No. of Units	Max. Length	Elev.	Toilets	Water	Agency
28	**1. Ouzel** **2. Osprey**	B-2	$	13 10	Tent	8,100'	Yes	Yes	Pike National Forest

LOCATION: **Ouzel** 5 mi N of Deckers on County Road 67. **Osprey** 7 mi N of Deckers on Cty Rd 67. FACILITIES: Picnic Tables, Fire Rings, Pets OK. ACTIVITIES: Fishing, Hiking. OPEN FOR USE: Mid-May through late Sept. CONTACT: South Platte Ranger District (303) 275-5610. NOTE: Located on South Platte River, FDT 695. 7.5' TOPOGRAPHIC MAP: Deckers.

Map No.	Campground Name	Map Loc.	Fee	No. of Units	Max. Length	Elev.	Toilets	Water	Agency
29	**Painted Rocks ®**	B-2	$	18	21'	7,900'	Yes	Yes	Pike National Forest

LOCATION: 8 mi N of Woodland Park on Hwy 67, 1/2 mi W on FDR 342. FACILITIES: Picnic Tables, Pets OK. ACTIVITIES: Fishing, Hiking. OPEN FOR USE: Late May through early Sept. CONTACT: Pikes Peak Ranger District (719) 636-1602. NOTE: Fishing @ 34 ac. Manitou Lake and Trout Creek. Paved bike trail, hiking trail at Manitou Park Recreation Area. 7.5' TOPOGRAPHIC MAP: Mount Deception.

Map No.	Campground Name	Map Loc.	Fee	No. of Units	Max. Length	Elev.	Toilets	Water	Agency
30	**Pike Community Group ®**	B-2	$	---	Open	7,700'	Yes	Yes	Pike National Forest

LOCATION: 5.3 mi N of Woodland Park on County Road 67. FACILITIES: Picnic Tables, Grills. ACTIVITIES: Hiking. OPEN FOR USE: May through Oct. CONTACT: Pikes Peak Ranger District (719) 636-1602. NOTE: Reservations; Fishing @ 34 ac. Manitou Lake and Trout Creek. Paved bike trail, hiking trail at Manitou Recreation Area. 7.5' TOPOGRAPHIC MAP: Mount Deception. ♿

Map No.	Campground Name	Map Loc.	Fee	No. of Units	Max. Length	Elev.	Toilets	Water	Agency
31	**Platte River**	B-2	$	10	Tent	6,300'	Yes	Yes	Pike National Forest

LOCATION: 3.5 mi N of Deckers on County Road 67. FACILITIES: Picnic Tables, Fire Rings, Pets OK. ACTIVITIES: Fishing, Hiking. OPEN FOR USE: Mid-May through late Sept. CONTACT: South Platte Ranger District (303) 275-5610. NOTE: Located on South Platte River, FDT 695. 7.5' TOPOGRAPHIC MAP: Deckers.

Map No.	Campground Name	Map Loc.	Fee	No. of Units	Max. Length	Elev.	Toilets	Water	Agency
32	**Rampart Reservoir**	C-2	$		21'	9,200'	Yes	Yes	Pike National Forest
a.	Meadow Ridge ®			19					
b.	Thunder Ridge ®			21					

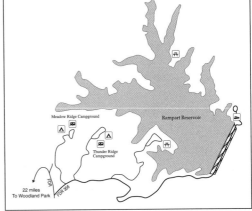

LOCATION: 3 mi NE from Woodland Park on FDR 393, 1.5 mi E on FDR 300, 2.5 mi E on FDR 306. FACILITIES: Picnic Tables, Grills, Fireplaces, Boat Ramps. ACTIVITIES: Fishing for rainbow trout on 500 acre lake. Hiking Trails FDT 700, 709, 712, 721 in the area. Mountain Biking. OPEN FOR USE: May through Oct. CONTACT: Pikes Peak Ranger District (719) 636-1602. NOTE: Handicap Accessible; Reservations. 7.5' TOPOGRAPHIC MAP: Cascade.

Map No.	Campground Name	Map Loc.	Fee	No. of Units	Max. Length	Elev.	Toilets	Water	Agency
33	**Red Rocks Group ®**	B-2	$	1	Open	8,200'	Yes	Yes	Pike National Forest

LOCATION: 4 mi N of Woodland Park on Hwy 67. FACILITIES: Picnic Tables, Grills. ACTIVITIES: Hiking, Biking. CONTACT: Pikes Peak Ranger District (719) 636-1602. NOTE: Reservations; Fishing @ 34 ac. Manitou Lake and Trout Creek. Paved bike trail, hiking trail at Manitou Park Recreation Area. 7.5' TOPOGRAPHIC MAP: Mount Deception.

Map No.	Campground Name	Map Loc.	Fee	No. of Units	Max. Length	Elev.	Toilets	Water	Agency
34	**Riverside ®**	C-1	$	19	25'	8,000'	Yes	Yes	Pike National Forest

LOCATION: 2.5 mi SW of Lake George on FDR 245. FACILITIES: Picnic Tables, Pets OK. ACTIVITIES: Fishing, Hiking. OPEN FOR USE: Mid-May through late Sept. CONTACT: South Park Ranger District (719) 836-2031. NOTE: Campground is near Eleven Mile Reservoir State Park and the Florissant Fossil Beds National Monument; Parking Fee. 7.5' TOPOGRAPHIC MAP: Lake George. *Note: $3.00 parking fee.*

Map No.	Campground Name	Map Loc.	Fee	No. of Units	Max. Length	Elev.	Toilets	Water	Agency
35	**Round Mountain ®**	B-1	$	17	30'	8,500'	Yes	Yes	Pike National Forest

LOCATION: 5.4 mi NW of Lake George on Hwy 24. FACILITIES: Picnic Tables, Pets OK. ACTIVITIES: Fishing, Hiking. OPEN FOR USE: Mid-May through late Sept. CONTACT: South Park Ranger District (719) 836-2031. NOTE: Handicap Accessible. 7.5' TOPOGRAPHIC MAP: Tarryall.

Map No.	Campground Name	Map Loc.	Fee	No. of Units	Max. Length	Elev.	Toilets	Water	Agency
36	**South Meadows ®**	B-2	$	64	30'	8,000'	Yes	Yes	Pike National Forest

LOCATION: 5.8 mi N of Woodland Park on Hwy 67. FACILITIES: Picnic Tables, Pets OK. ACTIVITIES: Biking, Fishing, Hiking. OPEN FOR USE: May through mid-Oct. CONTACT: Pikes Peak Ranger District (719) 636-1602. NOTE: Fishing @ 34 ac Manitou Lake and Trout Creek. Paved bike trail, hiking trail, FDT 669. 7.5' TOPOGRAPHIC MAP: Mount Deception.

Map No.	Campground Name	Map Loc.	Fee	No. of Units	Max. Length	Elev.	Toilets	Water	Agency
37	**Spillway ®**	C-1	$	24	25'	8,500'	Yes	Yes	Pike National Forest

LOCATION: 8 mi SW of Lake George on Cty Rd 96. FACILITIES: Picnic Tables, Fire Rings, Pets OK. ACTIVITIES: Fishing, Hiking. OPEN FOR USE: Mid-May through late Sept. CONTACT: South Park Ranger District (719) 836-2031. NOTE: 1/2 mi from Eleven Mile Reservoir. Overlook TH, FDT 641. 7.5' TOPOGRAPHIC MAP: Eleven Mile Canyon.

Map No.	Campground Name	Map Loc.	Fee	No. of Units	Max. Length	Elev.	Toilets	Water	Agency
38	**Springdale**	C-2	$	14	16'	9,100'	Yes	Yes	Pike National Forest

LOCATION: 3 mi N of Woodland Park on FDR 393, 2.5 mi S on FDR 300. FACILITIES: Picnic Tables, Pets OK. ACTIVITIES: Fishing, Hiking. OPEN FOR USE: May through mid-Oct. CONTACT: Pikes Peak Ranger District (719) 636-1602. NOTE: Campground is 3.5 mi from Rampart Reservoir. 7.5' TOPOGRAPHIC MAP: Woodland Park.

Map No.	Campground Name	Map Loc.	Fee	No. of Units	Max. Length	Elev.	Toilets	Water	Agency
39	**Springer Gulch ®**	C-1	$	15	25'	8,300'	Yes	Yes	Pike National Forest

LOCATION: 6.6 mi SW of Lake George on FDR 245. FACILITIES: Picnic Tables, Pets OK. ACTIVITIES: Fishing, Hiking. OPEN FOR USE: Mid-May through late Sept. CONTACT: South Park Ranger District (719) 836-2031. NOTE: Handicap Accessible. 3 mi from Eleven Mile Reservoir. 7.5' TOPOGRAPHIC MAP: Eleven Mile Canyon. Note: $3.00 parking fee.

Map No.	Campground Name	Map Loc.	Fee	No. of Units	Max. Length	Elev.	Toilets	Water	Agency
40	**Spruce Grove**	B-1	$	26	35'	8,600'	Yes	Yes	Pike National Forest

LOCATION: 1.2 mi NW of Lake George on Hwy 24, 12.2 mi NW on Cty Rd 77. FACILITIES: Picnic Tables, Piped Water, Flush Toilets, Pets OK. ACTIVITIES: Fishing, Hiking. OPEN FOR USE: Mid-May through late Sept. CONTACT: South Park Ranger District (719) 836-2031. NOTE: Campground is near Tarryall Creek and Twin Eagles Trailhead to Lost Creek Wilderness. Lizard Rock TH, FDT 658. 7.5' TOPOGRAPHIC MAP: McCurdy Mountain.

Map No.	Campground Name	Map Loc.	Fee	No. of Units	Max. Length	Elev.	Toilets	Water	Agency
41	**The Crags**	C-2	$	17	No Trailers	10,100'	Yes	Yes	Pike National Forest

LOCATION: 4.25 mi S of Divide on Hwy 67, 3 mi E on FDR 383. FACILITIES: Picnic Tables, Pets OK. ACTIVITIES: Fishing, Hiking. OPEN FOR USE: Mid-May through Sept. CONTACT: Pikes Peak Ranger District (719) 636-1602. NOTE: 2.5 mi to Mueller State Park, 15 mi S is the historic Cripple Creek-Victor mining District, limited stakes gambling. Crags TH, FDT 664. 7.5' TOPOGRAPHIC MAPS: Woodland Park, Pikes Peak.

Map No.	Campground Name	Map Loc.	Fee	No. of Units	Max. Length	Elev.	Toilets	Water	Agency
42	**Trail Creek**	B-2	$	7	---	7,800'	Yes	No	Pike National Forest

LOCATION: 13 mi SW of Deckers to Westcreek, 3 mi S on Cty Rd 3. FACILITIES: Picnic Tables, Pets OK. ACTIVITIES: Fishing, Hiking. OPEN FOR USE: Late May through Oct. CONTACT: Pikes Peak Ranger District (719) 636-1602. NOTE: East of Cheesman Lake, South Platte River and a number mtn. biking trails. 7.5' TOPOGRAPHIC MAP: Signal.

Map No.	Campground Name	Map Loc.	Fee	No. of Units	Max. Length	Elev.	Toilets	Water	Agency
43	**Twin Eagles Trailhead**	B-1	$	9	22'	8,550'	Yes	No	Pike National Forest

LOCATION: 1.2 mi NW of Lake George on Hwy 24, 13 mi NW on Cty Rd 77. FACILITIES: Picnic Tables, Pets OK. ACTIVITIES: Fishing, Hiking. OPEN FOR USE: Mid-May through late Sept. CONTACT: South Park Ranger District (719) 836-2031. NOTE: Campground near Tarryall Creek and Twin Eagles Trailhead to Lost Creek Wilderness. 7.5' TOPOGRAPHIC MAP: McCurdy Mountain.

Map No.	Campground Name	Map Loc.	Fee	No. of Units	Max. Length	Elev.	Toilets	Water	Agency
44	**Wigwam**	B-1	$	10	20'	6,600'	Yes	Yes	Pike National Forest

LOCATION: 3 mi S of Deckers on Hwy 126. FACILITIES: Picnic Tables, Pets OK. ACTIVITIES: Fishing, Hiking. OPEN FOR USE: Late May through late Sept. CONTACT: South Platte Ranger District (303) 275-5610. NOTE: Handicap Accessible. Campground 2 mi N of Chessman Lake. Gill TH, FDT 610. 7.5' TOPOGRAPHIC MAP: Chessman Lake.

Map No.	Campground Name	Map Loc.	Fee	No. of Units	Max. Length	Elev.	Toilets	Water	Agency
45	**Wildhorn**	B-1	$	9	16'	9,100'	Yes	Yes	Pike National Forest

LOCATION: 13 mi SW of Deckers on Hwy 67, 9 mi SW on Cty Rd 3. FACILITIES: Picnic Tables, Fire rings, Pets OK. ACTIVITIES: Hiking. OPEN FOR USE: Late May through Sept. CONTACT: Pikes Peak Ranger District (719) 636-1602. NOTE: North of Florissant Fossil Beds National Monument, approximately 10 miles. 7.5' TOPOGRAPHIC MAP: Hackett Mountain.

Map No.	Campground Name	Map Loc.	Fee	No. of Units	Max. Length	Elev.	Toilets	Water	Agency
46	**Wye**	C-2	$	21	---	10,300'	Yes	Yes	Pike National Forest

LOCATION: From Colo. Springs take the Old Stage Coach Rd S to the Gold Camp Road 7 mi. Turn right, 5 mi to FDR 381, right for 1/2 mi. FACILITIES: Tables, Fireplaces. No firewood or shelters. ACTIVITIES: Fishing at Rosemont Reservoir 1 1/2 mi W of campground, Hiking. OPEN FOR USE: Mid- May through mid-Sept. CONTACT: Pikes Peak Ranger District (719) 636-1602. 7.5' TOPOGRAPHIC MAP: Mount Big Chief.

YOUR RESPONSIBILITY

The National Forests are public lands in joint ownership by all citizens, their management requires different laws and regulations based on local conditions. Please be familiar with restrictions by checking with local offices and reading signs and bulletin boards.

It is your responsibility to be aware of the potential risks and take safety precautions at all times when you visit National Forest areas. Changing terrain, forest, and weather conditions present a wide variety of hazards. Hazards include, but are not limited to: snow and ice fields, landslides, falling trees or limbs, high or rushing water, contaminated water, wild animals, severe weather, becoming lost or over-exerted, hypothermia, and exposure to unreasonable acts of other people.

NO-TRACE CAMPING

Trail travel tends to concentrate camping use. You can help preserve the natural setting and quality of an area by practicing no-trace camping. By practicing no-trace camping techniques, hikers and horsemen leave the landscape appearing untouched when they move on their way. Check with Forest Service offices for more no-trace camping ideas.

SANITATION-Keep soaps and detergents out of lakes and streams. Wash dishes and clothes in a pot and dispose of the waste water on rocky soil at least 100 feet from the nearest water supply. Bathe in the same manner. Do not bathe in lakes or streams. Protect your drinking and cooking water.

TOILETS-Locate toilets at least 100 feet away from the nearest water supply. Dig a small, 6 inch-deep hole and cover after use.

TRASH-Do not bury trash. Burn it or pack it out.

PACK STOCK AND HORSES-Pack and saddle stock can seriously damage soil and vegetation if not properly cared for. Pack in a good supply of pelletized feed-forage is scarce in many areas and hay is discouraged because it is a source of undesirable weed seeds. Use a "hitchline" or hobbles in lieu of tying stock to trees-they can kill the tree by pawing up roots and stripping bark.

CAMPSITES-Never camp in meadows or soft grassy areas that compact easily. Pick a place where you won't have to clear vegetation or level a tent site. Before leaving camp, naturalize the area. Try to make the site look as if no one had been there.

TRAVELING-Don't pick flowers, dig up plants, cut live branches from trees, or take short cuts off the trails.

ENJOY AND HELP PRESERVE YOUR AMERICAN HERITAGE

Archaeological and historical sites hold clues to America's past. If disturbed, a part of our heritage may be lost forever. The Antiquities Act of 1906 and the Archaeological Resource Protection Act of 1979 protect cultural resources on public lands for the benefit of all Americans. If you discover such remains, please leave them undisturbed.

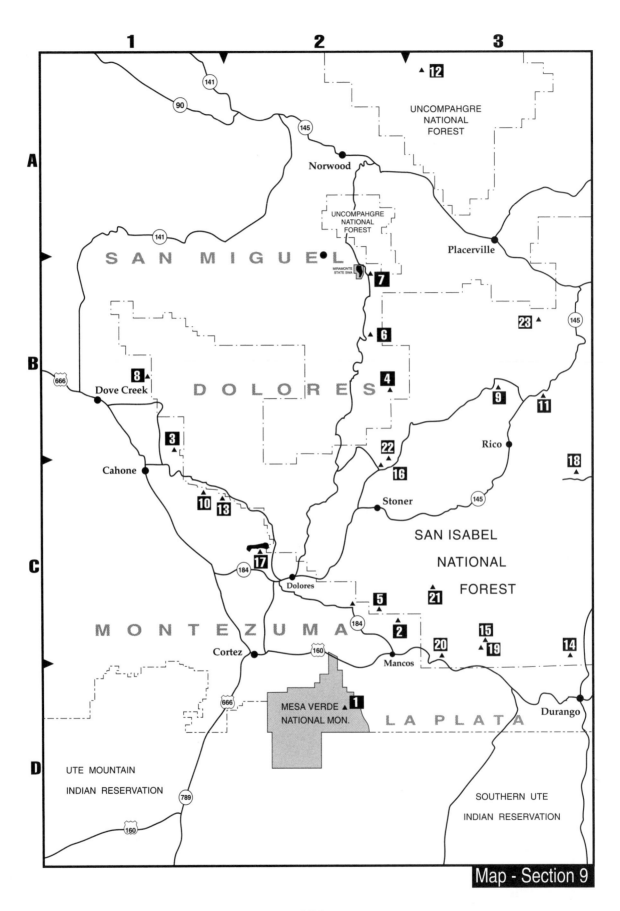

Section 9

Map No.	Name	Map Loc.	Fee	No. of Units	Max. Length	Elev.	Toilets	Water	Agency
1	Mesa Verde National Park	D-2	$	477	70'	7,000'	Yes	Yes	National Parks Service

About Your Visit

Mesa Verde National Park, located in the high plateau country of Southwestern Colorado contains Anasazi (Ancient Ones) Cliff Dwellings dating back to 1200 A.D. The park entrance is midway between Cortez and Mancos, off U.S. 160. It is 21 miles from the entrance to park headquarters and the Chapin Mesa ruins. Morefield Campground is four miles from the entrance; Far View Visitors Center is 15 miles. Allow at least 45 minutes for the drive to Chapin Mesa. Park roads are scenic drives with sharp curves, steep grades, and reduced speed limits. For your safety, do not park on any roadway.

To See The Park

To get the most out of your visit, go first to either the Far View Visitors Center (open only in the summer) or the Chapin Mesa Museum (open from 8 a.m. to 6:30 p.m. in summer and 8 a.m. to 5 p.m. the rest of the year). Rangers there will help you plan your visit.

Services

Food, gasoline, and lodging are available only from mid-May to mid-October. No services are available the rest of the year. Full interpretive services begin in mid-June and continue through Labor Day.

Camping

Morefield Campground ®, open early May through mid-October, has single and group campsites. Six campsites (with restrooms) are accessible to physically impaired persons. Each campsite has table, benches and a grill. The gathering of firewood or injuring of trees or shrubs is prohibited. Camps should not be left unattended for more than 24 hours. There are 15 utility hook-ups and a disposal station for dumping trailer tanks. Commercial campgrounds are located near the park entrance. Services at the campground include groceries, carry-out food, gasoline, firewood, showers, and a laundromat. Evening programs are given daily from early June to Labor day. During the summer non-denominational religious services are held. Three hiking trails originate in the Morefield area. Morfield Group ® has 17 Campsites. Park Point offers superb views of the entire Four Corners region. The fire lookout station here is staffed during the fire season. A brochure describes the natural features of the area.

Far View is a major center of visitor service. The visitor center displays contemporary Indian arts and crafts. Commercial tours of Mesa leave from the Far View Motor Lodge. The Motor Lodge is open mid-May to mid-October.

Chapin Mesa - Three major cliff dwellings are located on Chapin Mesa (Spruce Tree House, Cliff Palace, and Balcony House) and are open seasonally for visits and many others are visible from Ruins Road. An archaeological museum with dioramas and exhibits interpret the life of the ancient Anasazi. In summer, rangers conduct tours through cliff dwellings. Current schedules are available at the museum or Far View Visitor Center.

Two hiking trails lead into Spruce Canyon. The Petroglyph Point Trail, 2.8 miles, and Spruce Canyon trail, 2.1 miles, begin at points on the Spruce Tree Trail. Hikers must register at the rangers office before attempting these trails.

Other cliff dwellings can be seen from canyon-rim vantage points by taking the self-guiding loop drives on Ruins Road. Wayside exhibits interpret the development of Anasazi culture from the Basket makers through the Classic period. These roads are open from 8:00 a.m. until sunset, but are often closed during the winter months. Visitors may snowshoe or cross-country ski as snow conditions permit.

At Spruce Tree Terrace, open from early spring through fall, light snacks, gifts, souvenirs, and bicycle rentals are available. In winter, guided tours are offered to Spruce tree House, weather and trail conditions permitting.

Administration
For more information please write:
Mesa Verde National Park
Box 8 Mesa Verde
National Park Colorado 81330
(970) 529-4465

Map No.	Name	Map Loc.	Fee	No. of Units	Max. Length	Elev.	Toilets	Water	Agency
2	**Mancos State Park ®**	C-2	$	34	40'	7,800'	Yes	Yes	Colorado State Parks

Scenic Mancos Lake State Park is located only ten miles from historic Mesa Verde National Monument in southwest Colorado, north of Mancos on Forest Road 561. Situated at an elevation of 7,800 feet on the San Juan Skyway scenic byway, Mancos State Park is surrounded by the majestic Sun Juan Mountain Range. The area has more than 300 land acres and the reservoir, which was once called Jackson Gulch, provides 216 surface acres of water for recreation.

Jackson Gulch Dam at Mancos Lake was constructed in 1948 by the Bureau of Reclamation in conjunction with the Young Adult Conversation Corps. It supplies the drinking water for Mesa Verde and the surrounding rural area.

There is a beautiful campground here, nestled within a mature ponderosa pine forest. Wakeless boating and excellent year round fishing, await the recreationist looking for a relaxing day. Picnickers and hikers will find sites and trails sure to please.

Camping
Mancos State Park has 24 campsites, most located on the south side of the reservoir in a mature ponderosa pine forest. There are vault toilets and drinking water, but no electrical hookups. Along the northwest side of the reservoir, there are nine campsites, primarily for tent campers, with a restroom, but no drinking water nearby. Check-out time is noon. A dump station is located at the campground exit.

Wildlife
Deer, elk, small game animals, migrating bald eagles and waterfowl, hawks, raptors and hummingbirds are among the wildlife seen at Mancos.

Hiking & Nature Trails
A four-mile trail weaves through Mancos, meeting Chicken Creek trail which connects with a network of trails on US Forest land. The trail system is for hikers, horseback riding and mountain bikes.

Other Activities
Cross-Country Skiing, Ice Fishing, and Snowmobiling.

Daily Fee/Annual Pass
For information contact:
Mancos Lake State Park
Box 1697
Arboles, CO 81121
(970) 883-2208

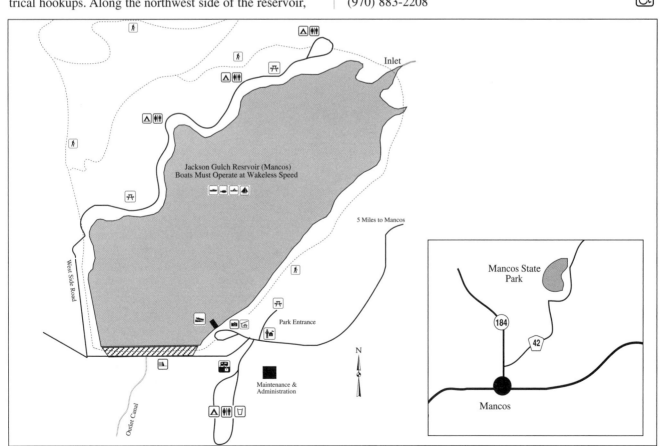

Section 9

Map No.	Campground Name	Map Loc.	Fee	No. of Units	Max. Length	Elev.	Toilets	Water	Agency
3	**Bradfield Bridge**	B-1	$	22	45'	6,400'	Yes	Yes	BLM/San Juan National Forest

LOCATION: 25 mi NW of Cortez on Hwy 666 to Cahone, at N end of town, turn E on FDR for 5 mi to the Dolores River. Follow signs to recreation site. FACILITIES: Picnic Tables, Fire Grills. ACTIVITIES: Fishing, Hiking, Rafting, Hunting. OPEN FOR USE: May thru Oct. CONTACT: Mancos/Dolores Ranger District (970) 882-7296. NOTE: Along Dolores River adjacent to National Forest. 7.5' TOPOGRAPHIC MAP: Doe Canyon.

Map No.	Campground Name	Map Loc.	Fee	No. of Units	Max. Length	Elev.	Toilets	Water	Agency
4	**Groundhog Reservoir State Wildlife Area**	B-2	0	13	Open	8,740'	Yes	No	Colorado Division of Wildlife

LOCATION: 25 mi N of Dolores on FDR 526 to FDR 533, then 5 mi NE. FACILITIES: Boat ramp (boating is prohibited in a manner that creates a whitewater wake). ACTIVITIES: Fishing, Hiking. OPEN FOR USE: Year Round. CONTACT: Colorado Division of Wildlife SW Region (970) 252-6000. NOTE: 670 acre lake, good Fishing for cutthroat, brown and rainbow trout. 7.5' TOPOGRAPHIC MAP: Groundhog Reservoir.

Map No.	Campground Name	Map Loc.	Fee	No. of Units	Max. Length	Elev.	Toilets	Water	Agency
5	**Joe Moore Reservoir State Wildlife Area**	C-2	0	Dispersed	Open	7,520'	Yes	No	Colorado Division of Wildlife

LOCATION: 2.5 mi NW of Mancos on Hwy 184, 2.5 mi N on Cty. Rd. 40. (170 acres.) FACILITIES: Boat ramp. ACTIVITIES: Fishing, Hiking, Hunting. OPEN FOR USE: Year Round. CONTACT: Colorado Division of Wildlife SW Region (970) 252-6000. NOTE: 35 acre lake - Good Fishing for cutthroat, browns and rainbow trout. 7.5' TOPOGRAPHIC MAP: Millwood. Wakeless boating.

Map No.	Campground Name	Map Loc.	Fee	No. of Units	Max. Length	Elev.	Toilets	Water	Agency
6	**Lone Cone State Wildlife Area**	B-2	0	---	---	7,963'	Yes	Yes	Colorado Division of Wildlife

LOCATION: 1.5 mi E of Norwood on Hwy 145, 24 mi S on FDR 610. FACILITIES: Boat ramp. ACTIVITIES: Fishing, Hiking, Hunting. OPEN FOR USE: Year Round. CONTACT: Colorado Division of Wildlife SW Region (970) 252-6000. NOTE: Designated camping. Two horse corrals. Morrison Creek runs through property. North of Groundhog Reservoir. 7.5' TOPOGRAPHIC MAP: Groundhog Reservoir.

Map No.	Campground Name	Map Loc.	Fee	No. of Units	Max. Length	Elev.	Toilets	Water	Agency
7	**Miramounte Reservoir State Wildlife Area**	B-2	0	---	---	7,755'	Yes	Yes	Colorado Division of Wildlife

LOCATION: 1.5 mi E of Norwood on Hwy 145, 17 mi S on FDR 610. (831 acres.) FACILITIES: Boat ramp, Shelters, Dump Station. ACTIVITIES: Fishing, Hiking, Boating, Waterskiing. OPEN FOR USE: All Year. CONTACT: Colorado Division of Wildlife SW Region (970) 252-6000. NOTE: Designated camping. 420 acre reservoir considered best fishing in area. 7.5' TOPOGRAPHIC MAP: Lone Cone.

Map No.	Campground Name	Map Loc.	Fee	No. of Units	Max. Length	Elev.	Toilets	Water	Agency
8	**Mountain Sheep Point**	B-1	$	3	30'	6,100'	Yes	Yes	Bureau of Land Management

LOCATION: E from Dove Creek, follow Dolores River access road 5 miles to river. Follow signs to recreation site. FACILITIES: Picnic Tables, Fire Grills. ACTIVITIES: Fishing, Hiking, Rafting, Hunting, Mountain Biking. OPEN FOR USE: May thru Oct. CONTACT: San Juan Resource Area (970) 247-4874. NOTE: Along Dolores River adjacent to National Forest. 7.5' TOPOGRAPHIC MAP: Secret Canyon.

Map No.	Campground Name	Map Loc.	Fee	No. of Units	Max. Length	Elev.	Toilets	Water	Agency
9	**Burro Bridge**	B-3	$	15	35'	9,000'	Yes	Yes	San Juan National Forest

LOCATION: 12.5 mi NE of Dolores on Hwy 145, 23 mi NE on Cty Rd 535. FACILITIES: Picnic Tables, Grills, Pets OK. ACTIVITIES: Fishing, Hiking. OPEN FOR USE: Mid-May thru mid-Nov. CONTACT: Mancos/Dolores Ranger District (970) 882-7296. NOTE: Camp is on West Dolores River, near Navajo Lake Trailhead to Lizard Head Wilderness. 7.5' TOPOGRAPHIC MAP: Dolores Peak.

Map No.	Campground Name	Map Loc.	Fee	No. of Units	Max. Length	Elev.	Toilets	Water	Agency
10	**Cabin Canyon**	C-1	$	11	45'	6,500'	Yes	Yes	San Juan National Forest

LOCATION: 25 miles NW of Cortez on Hwy 666 to Cahone, at N end of town turn E on FDR for 5 mi to the Dolores River, S on FDR 504 3.5 miles. FACILITIES: Picnic Tables, Fire Grills. ACTIVITIES: Fishing, Hiking, Rafting, Hunting. OPEN FOR USE: May thru Oct. CONTACT: Mancos/Dolores Ranger District (970) 882-7296. NOTE: Along Dolores River. 7.5' TOPOGRAPHIC MAP: Yellow Jacket.

Map No.	Campground Name	Map Loc.	Fee	No. of Units	Max. Length	Elev.	Toilets	Water	Agency
11	**Cayton**	B-3	$	27	35'	9,400'	Yes	Yes	San Juan National Forest

LOCATION: 6 mi NE of Rico on Hwy 145, 0.5 mi E on Cty Rd 578. FACILITIES: Picnic Tables, Grills, Pets OK. ACTIVITIES: Fishing, Hiking. OPEN FOR USE: Mid-May thru mid-Nov. CONTACT: Mancos/Dolores Ranger District (970) 882-7296. NOTE: Several miles to Lizard Head Wilderness. 7.5' TOPOGRAPHIC MAP: Mount Wilson.

Map No.	Campground Name	Map Loc.	Fee	No. of Units	Max. Length	Elev.	Toilets	Water	Agency
12	**Iron Springs**	A-3	$	7	20'	9,500'	Yes	No	Uncompahgre National Forest

LOCATION: Approx. 27 miles southwest of Montrose. Take old Hwy 90 south to forest boundary, FDR 540 four miles to Campground. FACILITIES: Picnic Tables, Fire Grills. ACTIVITIES: Fishing, Hiking. OPEN FOR USE: May thru Labor Day. CONTACT: Ouray District (970) 240-5300. 7.5' TOPOGRAPHIC MAP: Antone Spring.

Map No.	Campground Name	Map Loc.	Fee	No. of Units	Max. Length	Elev.	Toilets	Water	Agency
13	**Ferris Canyon**	C-1	$	6	45'	6,500'	Yes	Yes	San Juan National Forest

LOCATION: 25 mi NW of Cortez on Hwy 666 to Cahone, at North end of town turn E on FDR for 5 mi to the Dolores River, S on FDR 504 5.5 mi. FACILITIES: Picnic Tables, Fire Grills. ACTIVITIES: Fishing, Hiking, Rafting, Hunting. OPEN FOR USE: May thru Oct. CONTACT: Mancos/Dolores Ranger District (970) 882-7296. NOTE: Along Dolores River. 7.5' TOPOGRAPHIC MAP: Yellow Jacket.

Map No.	Campground Name	Map Loc.	Fee	No. of Units	Max. Length	Elev.	Toilets	Water	Agency
14	**Junction Creek**	C-3	$	34	50'	7,500'	Yes	Yes	San Juan National Forest

LOCATION: 1 mi NW from Durango on Hwy 550, 3.5 mi NW on Cty Rd 204, 1 mi NW on FDR 171. FACILITIES: Picnic Tables, Grills, Pets OK. ACTIVITIES: Fishing, Hiking. OPEN FOR USE: May thru mid-Nov. CONTACT: Columbine Ranger District (Durango) (970) 247-4874. NOTE: Handicap Accessible Camp is along Junction Creek. Trailhead for Colorado Trail, FDT 1776. 7.5' TOPOGRAPHIC MAP: Durango West. ♿

Map No.	Campground Name	Map Loc.	Fee	No. of Units	Max. Length	Elev.	Toilets	Water	Agency
15	**Kroeger**	C-3	$	11	35'	9,000'	Yes	Yes	San Juan National Forest

LOCATION: 11 mi W of Durango on Hwy 160 to Hesperus, 200 yards NW on Hwy 160, 7 mi N on FDR 571. FACILITIES: Picnic Tables, Grills, Firewood, Pets OK. ACTIVITIES: Fishing, Hiking. OPEN FOR. USE: Mid-June thru mid-Oct. CONTACT: Columbine Ranger District (970) 247-4874. NOTE: Camp is in the La Plata River Canyon. 7.5' TOPOGRAPHIC MAP: LaPlata.

Map No.	Campground Name	Map Loc.	Fee	No. of Units	Max. Length	Elev.	Toilets	Water	Agency
16	**Mavresso**	C-2	$	14	35'	7,600'	Yes	Yes	San Juan National Forest

LOCATION: 13 mi NE of Dolores on Hwy 145, 6 mi NE on FDR 535. FACILITIES: Picnic Tables, Grills, Pets OK. ACTIVITIES: Fishing, Hiking. OPEN FOR USE: Mid-May thru mid-Nov. CONTACT: Mancos/Dolores Ranger District (970) 882-7296. NOTE: Campground is near West Dolores River. 7.5' TOPOGRAPHIC MAP: Nipple Mountain.

Map No.	Campground Name	Map Loc.	Fee	No. of Units	Max. Length	Elev.	Toilets	Water	Agency
17	**McPhee Reservoir**	C-2	$		50'	7,100'	Yes	Yes	San Juan National Forest
a.	House Creek ®			72	(Also House Creek Group ®)				
b.	McPhee ®			73					

LOCATION: House Creek - 6 mi N of Dolores on FDR 526, 6 mi SW on FDR 526, 6 mi SW on FDR 528; McPhee - 2.5 mi W of Dolores on Hwy 145, 4.5 mi NW on Hwy 184, 2.5 mi NE on FDR 271. FACILITIES: Picnic Tables, Grills, Boat ramps, Dump Station 5 sites with electric hook-ups, sites can be reserved, group sites at both camps, hook-ups at McPhee, Pets OK. ACTIVITIES: Fishing, Hiking. OPEN FOR USE: Mid-May thru mid-Nov. CONTACT: Mancos/Dolores Ranger District (970) 882-7296. NOTE: Handicap Accessible. Reservations. Good fishing with a great view. 7.5' TOPOGRAPHIC MAPS: Dolores East, Boggy Draw. ♿

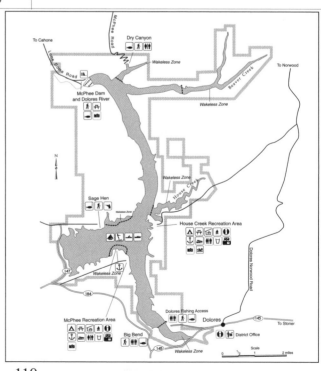

Map No.	Campground Name	Map Loc.	Fee	No. of Units	Max. Length	Elev.	Toilets	Water	Agency
18	**Sig Creek**	C-3	$	9	30'	9,000'	Yes	Yes	San Juan National Forest

LOCATION: 21 mi SW of Silverton on Hwy 550, 6 mi W on FDR 578. FACILITIES: Picnic Tables, Grills, Pets OK. ACTIVITIES: Fishing, Hiking. OPEN FOR USE: Mid-May thru Nov. CONTACT: Columbine Ranger District (Durango) (970) 247-4874. NOTE: Camp is along East Fork of Hermosa Creek - 2 mi E of Upper Hermosa trailhead. 7.5' TOPOGRAPHIC MAP: Hermosa Peak.

Map No.	Campground Name	Map Loc.	Fee	No. of Units	Max. Length	Elev.	Toilets	Water	Agency
19	**Snowslide**	C-3	$	13	30'	9,000'	Yes	No	San Juan National Forest

LOCATION: 11 mi W of Durango 160 to Hesperus, 200 yards NW on Hwy 160, 6.5 mi N on FDR 571. FACILITIES: Picnic Tables, Grills, Pets OK. ACTIVITIES: Fishing, Hiking. OPEN FOR USE: Mid-June thru Oct. CONTACT: Columbine Ranger District (970) 247-4874. NOTE: Campground is in LaPlata River Canyon. Formerly Potato Patch Campground. 1/2 mi S of Kroeger CG. 7.5' TOPOGRAPHIC MAP: Hesprus.

Map No.	Campground Name	Map Loc.	Fee	No. of Units	Max. Length	Elev.	Toilets	Water	Agency
20	**Target Tree**	C-3	$	25	45'	7,800'	Yes	Yes	San Juan National Forest

LOCATION: 7 mi E of Mancos on Hwy 160. FACILITIES: Picnic Tables, Grills, Pets OK. ACTIVITIES: Fishing, Hiking. OPEN FOR USE: Mid-May thru early Nov. CONTACT: Mancos/ Dolores Ranger District (970) 882-7296. NOTE: Interpretative Site of Ute Indian history and use of Ponderosa pine trees for food and targets. 7.5' TOPOGRAPHIC MAP: Thompson Park.

Map No.	Campground Name	Map Loc.	Fee	No. of Units	Max. Length	Elev.	Toilets	Water	Agency
21	**Transfer**	C-3	$	12	45'	8,500'	Yes	Yes	San Juan National Forest

LOCATION:13 mi NE of Dolores on Hwy 145, 7.5 mi NE on FDR 535. FACILITIES: Picnic Tables, Grills, Pets OK. ACTIVITIES: Fishing, Hiking. OPEN FOR USE: Mid-May thru mid-Nov. CONTACT: Mancos/Dolores Ranger District (970) 882-7296. NOTE: Campground near West Dolores River. West Mancos TH, FDT 565. 7.5' TOPOGRAPHIC MAP: Nipple Mountain.

Map No.	Campground Name	Map Loc.	Fee	No. of Units	Max. Length	Elev.	Toilets	Water	Agency
22	**West Dolores**	C-2	$	13	35'	7,800'	Yes	Yes	San Juan National Forest

LOCATION:13 mi NE of Dolores on Hwy 145, 7.5 mi NE on FDR 535. FACILITIES: Picnic Tables, Grills, Pets OK. ACTIVITIES: Fishing, Hiking. OPEN FOR USE: Mid-May thru mid-Nov. CONTACT: Mancos/Dolores Ranger District (970) 882-7296. NOTE: Campground near West Dolores River. 7.5' TOPOGRAPHIC MAP: Nipple Mountain.

Map No.	Campground Name	Map Loc.	Fee	No. of Units	Max. Length	Elev.	Toilets	Water	Agency
23	**Woods Lake**	B-3	$	41	---	9,400'	Yes	Yes	Uncompahgre National Forest

LOCATION: Southwest of Ridgway on Hwy 62 24 mi to Hwy 145. Southeast 4 miles to FDR 618, south approx. 10 mi to campground. FACILITIES: Picnic Tables, Fire Grates, RV hook-ups, Pets OK. ACTIVITIES: Fishing, Hiking. OPEN FOR USE: Mid-May to after Labor Day. CONTACT: Norwood Ranger District (970) 327-4261. NOTE: Near Woods Lake and trailhead to Lizard Head Wilderness. TOPOGRAPHIC MAP: Little Cone.

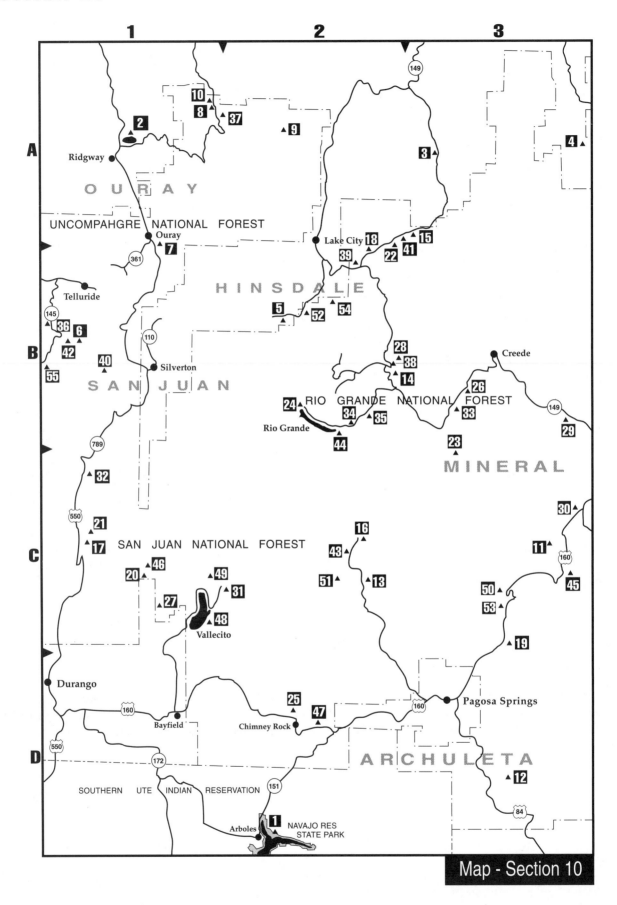

Map - Section 10

Navajo Res. Boat ramp

Map No.	Name	Map Loc.	Fee	No. of Units	Max. Length	Elev.	Toilets	Water	Agency
1	**Navajo State Park** ®	D-2	$	70	30'	6,100'	Yes	Yes	Colorado State Parks

At Navajo State Park visitors have an unparalleled opportunity to capture history and beauty of southwestern Colorado. Situated near Arboles, 35 miles southwest of Pagosa Springs, 45 miles southeast of Durango, the area is unpolluted and sparsely populated. The park's main attraction is the 35 mile long Navajo reservoir which extends well in to New Mexico. The 15,000 acres, including 3,000 acres on the Colorado side offer a challenge to the angler and unlimited pleasure to the boater and waterskier. Navajo boasts Colorado's largest boat ramp 80' wide, a quarter mile long and a good recreational airstrip, used frequently by flying clubs and fly-in campers.

Camping
Navajo's modern campground offers 70 sites, showers and flush toilets. Many sites are pull through, all can accommodate tents, trailers or pick-up campers. A dump station is located in the campground.

Wildlife
Waterfowl, shorebirds, birds of prey including the bald eagle are found at Navajo along with game birds like doves, grouse and turkeys. Visitors may also see beaver, mink, foxes, deer, elk, rabbits and in remote areas, its possible to glimpse coyote, bobcat or lion.

Fishing
Bluegill, catfish, crappie and largemouth bass lie in the shallows and near the lake surface. Kokanee salmon and many varieties of trout are found in the depths.

Other Activities: Hunting, Boating and Winter Recreation.

Daily Fee/Annual Pass
For more information contact:
Navajo State Park
Box 1697, Arboles, CO 81121
(970) 883-2208

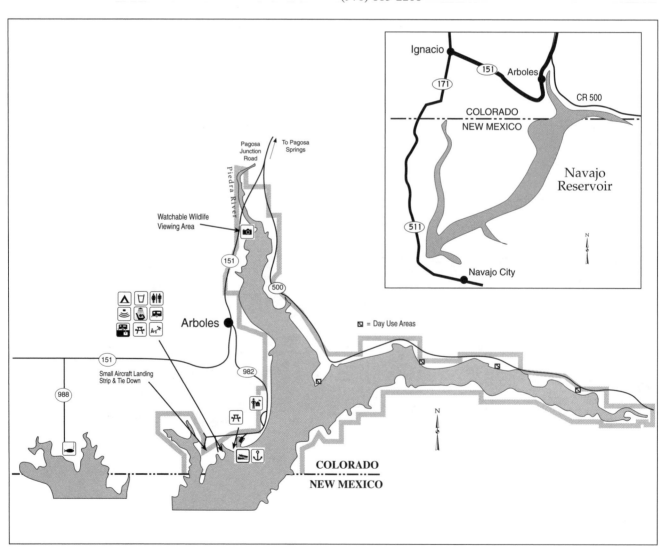

Map No.	Name	Map Loc.	Fee	No. of Units	Max. Length	Elev.	Toilets	Water	Agency
2	**Ridgway Reservoir State Park ®**	A-1	$	283	35'	6,880'	Yes	Yes	Colorado State Parks

Ridgway State Park, located 2 miles north of Ridgway on US Highway 550, more than 90 percent of the facilities are accessible to disabled people. A wheelchair walkway leading to the swim beach is available as well as table and grills constructed on cement high-use pads. Call for specific information on the disabled accessibility.

Camping
Ridgway has two picturesque campgrounds, Dakota Terrace and Elk Ridge. Dakota Terrace is within walking distance to the lake and swim beach. Elk Ridge is located in a pinion-juniper forest with panoramic views of the San Juan Mountains. There are 283 campsites, including 25 walk-in tent areas. The campgrounds can also accommodate trailers, campers and motor home's. A camper's service building with modem restrooms, hot showers and laundry facilities is also on the premises. All sites, except the tent sites, have electrical hookups and drinking water is available. There are no sewer hookups, but there is a dump station available. Ridgway campgrounds are open all year round.

Fishing
Rainbow trout are stocked annually by the Division of Wildlife. Rainbow and brown trout, which inhabited the Uncompahgre River prior to construction of the dam are also in the reservoir.

Hiking Nature Trails
Four miles of developed trails wind through the recreation area connecting the various facilities. These trails range from a moderate walk to a challenging hike.

Other Activities
Hunting, Boating and Winter Recreation.

Daily Fee/Annual Pass
For more information contact:
Ridgway State Park
28555 Highway 550
Ridgway, CO 81432
(970) 626-5822

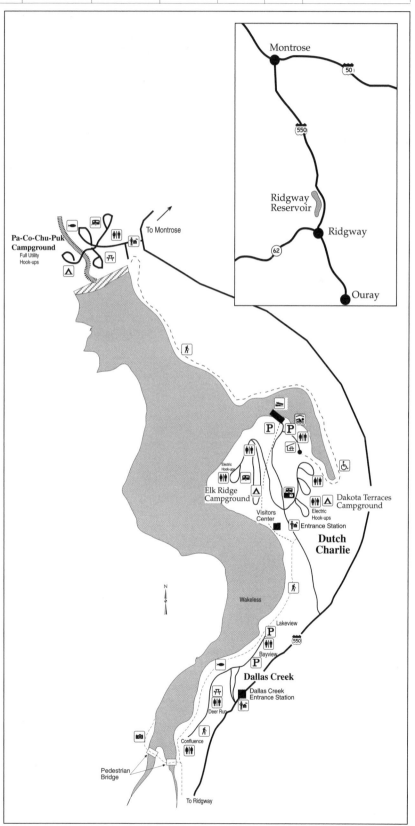

115

Map No.	Campground Name	Map Loc.	Fee	No. of Units	Max. Length	Elev.	Toilets	Water	Agency
3	**Cebolla Creek**	A-3	0	3	30'	9,500'	Yes	Yes	Bureau of Land Management

LOCATION: 9 mi W from Gunnison on Hwy 50, 17 mi S on Hwy 149 toward Lake City, 8 mi S on Cty Rd 27 along Cebolla Creek, turn right to campground. FACILITIES: None. ACTIVITIES: Fishing, Hiking, Hunting. OPEN FOR USE: June thru mid-Oct. CONTACT: Gunnison Resource Area (970) 641-0471. NOTE: 10 mi from Powderhorn Wilderness Trailhead. 7.5' TOPOGRAPHIC MAP: Rudolph Hill.

Map No.	Campground Name	Map Loc.	Fee	No. of Units	Max. Length	Elev.	Toilets	Water	Agency
4	**Dome Lakes State Wildlife Area**	A-3	0	Dispersed	Open	9,129'	Yes	Yes	Colorado Division of Wildlife

LOCATION: 8 mi SE from Gunnison on Hwy 50, 22 mi S on Hwy 114. FACILITIES: Picnic Tables. ACTIVITIES: Fishing, Hiking, Hunting. OPEN FOR USE: June through Oct. CONTACT: DOW SW Region (970) 252-6000. NOTE: Cochetopa Creek and Dome Reservoir - fishing, open camping on east & west of Upper Dome Lake and in Cochetopa Canyon. 7.5' TOPOGRAPHIC MAP: Cochetopa Park. Camping prohibited Oct.1, thru end waterfowl season.

Map No.	Campground Name	Map Loc.	Fee	No. of Units	Max. Length	Elev.	Toilets	Water	Agency
5	**Mill Creek**	B-2	$	22	21'	9,500'	Yes	Yes	Bureau of Land Management

LOCATION: 3 mi S from Lake City on Hwy 149, 11 W on BLM Rd 3306, following the Lake Fork of the Gunnison. FACILITIES: Picnic Tables, Fire Grills. ACTIVITIES: Fishing, Hiking, Historical Ruins, Off-Road Vehicles. OPEN FOR USE: June through Oct.. CONTACT: Gunnison Resource Area (970) 614-0471. NOTE: Riverine - On Alpine Loop National Backcountry Byway. 7.5' TOPOGRAPHIC MAP: Redcloud Peak (CALL FIRST).

Map No.	Campground Name	Map Loc.	Fee	No. of Units	Max. Length	Elev.	Toilets	Water	Agency
6	**Alta Lakes**	B-1	$	Dispersed	Open	11,216'	Yes	No	Uncompahgre National Forest

LOCATION: 3 mi W from Telluride on Hwy 145, 5 mi S on Hwy 145 to FDR 632, E approx. 4 mi to Alta Lakes. FACILITIES: Grills, Pets OK. ACTIVITIES: Fishing, Hiking. OPEN FOR USE: Late May through early Sept. CONTACT: Norwood Ranger District (970) 327-4261. NOTE: Dispersed camping near Alta Lakes. 7.5' TOPOGRAPHIC MAP: Telluride.

Map No.	Campground Name	Map Loc.	Fee	No. of Units	Max. Length	Elev.	Toilets	Water	Agency
7	**Amphitheater ®**	A-1	$	30	20'	8,400'	Yes	Yes	Uncompahgre National Forest

LOCATION: 1/2 mi S of Ouray on Hwy 550, 1/2 mi E on FDR 885. FACILITIES: Picnic Tables, Grills, Pets OK. ACTIVITIES: Fishing, Hiking. OPEN FOR USE: Late May through early Sept. CONTACT: Ouray Ranger District (970) 240-5300. NOTE: Campground is near Uncompahgre Primitive Area. Cascade Falls TH, FDT 213, Portland TH, FDT 238. Reservations Needed. 7.5' TOPOGRAPHIC MAP: Ouray. *Construction 2001- Call first.*

Map No.	Campground Name	Map Loc.	Fee	No. of Units	Max. Length	Elev.	Toilets	Water	Agency
8	**Beaver Lake**	A-1	$	11	20'	8,800	Yes	Yes	Uncompahgre National Forest

LOCATION: 20 mi E of Montrose on Hwy 50, 20 mi S on Cty Rd 69. FACILITIES: Picnic Tables, Grills, Store, Ice, Boat ramp, Pets OK. ACTIVITIES: Fishing, Hiking. OPEN FOR USE: Early June through late Sept. CONTACT: Ouray Ranger District (970) 240-5300. NOTE: Near Beaver Lake. Non-motorized boats are permitted. 7.5' TOPOGRAPHIC MAP: Washboard Rock.

Map No.	Campground Name	Map Loc.	Fee	No. of Units	Max. Length	Elev.	Toilets	Water	Agency
9	**Big Blue**	A-2	$	11	Short	9,600'	Yes	No	Gunnison National Forest

LOCATION:10 mi W of Gunnison on Hwy 50, 36 mi S on Hwy 149, 9 mi NW on FDR 868 FACILITIES: Picnic Tables, Grills, Pets OK. ACTIVITIES: Fishing, Hiking. OPEN FOR USE: Mid-June through late Sept. CONTACT: Gunnison Ranger District (970) 641-0471. NOTE: Campground is at the trailhead of Big Blue TH, FDT 232 and near Uncompahgre Wilderness. 7.5' TOPOGRAPHIC MAP: Sheep Mountain.

Map No.	Campground Name	Map Loc.	Fee	No. of Units	Max. Length	Elev.	Toilets	Water	Agency
10	**Big Cimarron**	A-1	$	10	20'	8,600'	Yes	No	Uncompahgre National Forest

LOCATION: 20 mi E of Montrose on Hwy 50, 20 mi S on Cty Rd 69. FACILITIES: Picnic Tables, Grills, Pets OK. ACTIVITIES: Fishing, Hiking. OPEN FOR USE: Early June through late Sept. CONTACT: Ouray Ranger District (970) 240-5300. NOTE: Campground is along Cimarron River and near several small lakes. 7.5' TOPOGRAPHIC MAP: Washboard Rock.

Map No.	Campground Name	Map Loc.	Fee	No. of Units	Max. Length	Elev.	Toilets	Water	Agency
11	**Big Meadows ®**	C-3	$	52	35'	9,500'	Yes	Yes	Rio Grande National Forest

LOCATION: 12.5 mi SW of South Fork on Hwy 160, 1.8 mi SW on FDR 410. FACILITIES: Picnic Tables, Boat Ramp & Dock, Pets OK. ACTIVITIES: Fishing, Hiking, Boating. OPEN FOR USE: Mid-June through late Sept. CONTACT: Divide/ Del Norte Ranger District (719) 657-3321. NOTE: Reservations; Campground is beside Big Meadows Reservoir and near Weminuche Wilderness Trailhead. 7.5' TOPOGRAPHIC MAP: Mount Hope.

Map No.	Campground Name	Map Loc.	Fee	No. of Units	Max. Length	Elev.	Toilets	Water	Agency
12	**Blanco River**	D-3	$	6	35'	7,200'	Yes	Yes	San Juan National Forest

LOCATION: 13.1 mi SE of Pagosa Springs on Hwy 84, 1.8 mi E on FDR 656. FACILITIES: Picnic Tables, Pets OK. ACTIVITIES: Fishing, Hiking. OPEN FOR USE: Mid-May through mid-Nov. CONTACT: Pagosa Ranger District (970) 264-2268. NOTE: Campground is along the Rio Blanco River. Inquire about water, it may not be available. 7.5' TOPOGRAPHIC MAP: Serviceberry Mountain.

Map No.	Campground Name	Map Loc.	Fee	No. of Units	Max. Length	Elev.	Toilets	Water	Agency
13	**Bridge**	C-2	$	19	50'	7,800'	Yes	Yes	San Juan National Forest

LOCATION: 3 mi W of Pagosa Springs on Hwy 160, 17 mi NW on FDR 631. FACILITIES: Picnic Tables, Fire Rings, Pets OK. ACTIVITIES: Fishing, Hiking. OPEN FOR USE: June through mid-Sept. CONTACT: Pagosa Ranger District (970) 264-2268. NOTE: 3.5 mi SE of Williams Creek Reservoir. 7.5' TOPOGRAPHIC MAP: Oakbrush Ridge.

Map No.	Campground Name	Map Loc.	Fee	No. of Units	Max. Length	Elev.	Toilets	Water	Agency
14	**Bristol Head**	B-2	$	16	30'	9,500'	Yes	Yes	Rio Grande National Forest

LOCATION: 27.5 mi W of Creede on Hwy 149, N approx 1/4 mi on FDR 510. FACILITIES: Picnic Tables, Pets OK. ACTIVITIES: Fishing, Hiking. OPEN FOR USE: May through Sept. CONTACT: Divide/Creede Ranger District (719) 658-2556. 7.5' TOPOGRAPHIC MAP: Bristol Head.

Map No.	Campground Name	Map Loc.	Fee	No. of Units	Max. Length	Elev.	Toilets	Water	Agency
15	**Cebolla**	A-3	$	5	Short	9,200'	Yes	Yes	Gunnison National Forest

LOCATION: 9 mi SE of Lake City on Hwy 149, 8.8 mi NE on FDR 788. FACILITIES: Picnic Tables, Pets OK. ACTIVITIES: Fishing, Hiking. OPEN FOR USE: Mid-June through late Sept. CONTACT: Gunnison Ranger District (970) 641-0471. NOTE: Camp near trailhead to La Garita Wilderness on Cebolla Creek. 7.5' TOPOGRAPHIC MAP: Mineral Mountain.

Map No.	Campground Name	Map Loc.	Fee	No. of Units	Max. Length	Elev.	Toilets	Water	Agency
16	**Cimarrona**	C-2	$	21	35'	8,400'	Yes	Yes	San Juan National Forest

LOCATION: 3 mi W of Pagosa Springs on Hwy 160, 22 mi NW on FDR 631, 4 mi N on FDR 640. FACILITIES: Picnic Tables, Fire Ring, Pets OK. ACTIVITIES: Fishing, Hiking. OPEN FOR USE: June through mid Sept. CONTACT: Pagosa Ranger District (970) 264-2268. NOTE: On Williams Creek-Trailhead for Weminuche Wilderness, FDT 586. 7.5' TOPOGRAPHIC MAP: Cimarrona Peak.

Map No.	Campground Name	Map Loc.	Fee	No. of Units	Max. Length	Elev.	Toilets	Water	Agency
17	**Chris Park Group ®**	C-1	$	----	----	8,000'	Yes	Yes	San Juan National Forest

LOCATION: 16.5 mi N of Durango on Hwy 550, 1 mi SE from Haviland Lake turn off. FACILITIES: Picnic Tables, Grills, Pets OK. ACTIVITIES: Fishing, Hiking. OPEN FOR USE: Mid-May through Oct. CONTACT: Columbine Ranger District/ Durango (970) 247-4874. NOTE: Reservations Required; Group Only. 7.5' TOPOGRAPHIC MAP: Electra Lake.

Map No.	Campground Name	Map Loc.	Fee	No. of Units	Max. Length	Elev.	Toilets	Water	Agency
18	**Deer Lakes**	A-2	$	12	30'	10,400'	Yes	Yes	Gunnison National Forest

LOCATION: 9 mi SE of Lake City on Hwy 149, 4 mi NE on FDR 788. FACILITIES: Picnic Tables, Pets OK. ACTIVITIES: Fishing, Hiking. OPEN FOR USE: June through Sept. CONTACT: Gunnison Ranger District (970) 641-0471. NOTE: On Mill Creek near La Garita Wilderness. FDT 458. 7.5' TOPOGRAPHIC MAP: Cannibal Plateau. Note: Handicapped accessible fishing platform.

Map No.	Campground Name	Map Loc.	Fee	No. of Units	Max. Length	Elev.	Toilets	Water	Agency
19	**East Fork**	C-3	$	26	35'	7,600'	Yes	Yes	San Juan National Forest

LOCATION: 9.7 mi NE of Pagosa Springs on Hwy 160, 0.8 mi E on FDR 667. FACILITIES: Picnic Tables, Pets OK. ACTIVITIES: Fishing, Hiking. OPEN FOR USE: Mid-May through mid-Nov. CONTACT: Pagosa Ranger District (970) 264-2268. NOTE: Campground is on East Fork of the San Juan River at the base of Turner Peak. 7.5' TOPOGRAPHIC MAPS: Jackson Mountain/ Saddle Mountain.

Map No.	Campground Name	Map Loc.	Fee	No. of Units	Max. Length	Elev.	Toilets	Water	Agency
20	**Florida**	C-1	$	20	35'	8,500'	Yes	Yes	San Juan National Forest

LOCATION: 14 mi NE of Durango on Cty Rd 240, 9 mi N on Cty Rd 243. FACILITIES: Picnic Tables, Grills, Pets OK. ACTIVITIES: Fishing, Hiking. OPEN FOR USE: May through Oct. CONTACT: Columbine Ranger District (970) 884-2512. NOTE: Campground is N of Lemon Reservoir, near trailhead to Weminuche Wilderness. 7.5' TOPOGRAPHIC MAP: Lemon Reservoir.
FLORIDA GROUP ®: Reservations. Restrooms and Water. Capacity 100 persons.

Map No.	Campground Name	Map Loc.	Fee	No. of Units	Max. Length	Elev.	Toilets	Water	Agency
21	**Haviland Lake**	C-1	$	45	45'	8,000'	Yes	Yes	San Juan National Forest

LOCATION: 16.5 mi N of Durango on Hwy 550, 1 mi E on FDR 671. FACILITIES: Picnic Tables, Grills, Boat Dock. ACTIVITIES: Fishing, Hiking. OPEN FOR USE: Mid-May through Oct. CONTACT: Columbine Ranger District (Durango) (970) 247-4874. NOTE: Reservations; Campground is along Haviland Lake, South of Electra Lake. 7.5' TOPOGRAPHIC MAP: Electra Lake.

Map No.	Campground Name	Map Loc.	Fee	No. of Units	Max. Length	Elev.	Toilets	Water	Agency
22	**Hidden Valley**	A-2	$	3	Tent	9,700'	Yes	Yes	Gunnison National Forest

LOCATION: 9 mi SE of Lake City on Hwy 149, 6.8 mi NE on FDR 788. FACILITIES: Picnic Tables, Pets OK. ACTIVITIES: Fishing, Hiking. OPEN FOR USE: Mid-June through late Sept. CONTACT: Gunnison Ranger District (970) 641-0471. NOTE: Campground is near Mineral Creek trailhead to La Garita Wilderness on Cebolla Creek. 7.5' TOPOGRAPHIC MAP: Cannibal Plateau.

Map No.	Campground Name	Map Loc.	Fee	No. of Units	Max. Length	Elev.	Toilets	Water	Agency
23	**Ivy Creek**	C-3	0	4	25	9,500'	Yes	No	Rio Grande National Forest

LOCATION: 7 mi SW of Creed SW on Hwy 149, 4.5 mi S on FDR 523, 3 mi SE on FDR 528, 3 mi SW on FDR 526. FACILITIES: Picnic Tables, Pets OK. ACTIVITIES: Fishing, Hiking. OPEN FOR USE: June through Sept. CONTACT: Divide/Creede Ranger District (719) 658-2556. NOTE: Trailhead for Weminuche Wilderness, Ivy Creek TH, FDT 805. 7.5' TOPOGRAPHIC MAPS: Workman Creek, Star City.

Map No.	Campground Name	Map Loc.	Fee	No. of Units	Max. Length	Elev.	Toilets	Water	Agency
24	**Lost Trail**	B-2	0	7	25'	9,500'	Yes	Yes	Rio Grande National Forest

LOCATION: 20 mi SW of Creede on Hwy 149, 18 mi SW on FDR 520. FACILITIES: Picnic Tables, Grills, Pets OK. ACTIVITIES: Fishing, Hiking. OPEN FOR USE: May through Oct. CONTACT: Divide/ Creede Ranger District (719) 658-2556. NOTE: Campground is on NW end of Rio Grande Reservoir and near Lost Creek Trailhead, FDT 821. Lots of trails near camp. 7.5' TOPOGRAPHIC MAP: Finger Mesa.

Map No.	Campground Name	Map Loc.	Fee	No. of Units	Max. Length	Elev.	Toilets	Water	Agency
25	**Lower Piedra**	D-2	$	17	35'	7,200'	Yes	No	San Juan National Forest

LOCATION: 25 mi W of Creede on Hwy 149, W on FDR 520 approx. 19 mi . FACILITIES: Picnic Tables, Grills, Boat Ramp, Pets OK. ACTIVITIES: Fishing, Hiking. OPEN FOR USE: May through Oct. CONTACT: Pagosa Ranger District (970) 264-2268. NOTE: Campground is along the Piedra River. 7.5' TOPOGRAPHIC MAP: Chimney Rock.

Map No.	Campground Name	Map Loc.	Fee	No. of Units	Max. Length	Elev.	Toilets	Water	Agency
26	**Marshall Park**	B-3	$	15	30'	8,800'	Yes	Yes	Rio Grande National Forest

LOCATION: 7 mi SW of Creede on Hwy 149. FACILITIES: Picnic Tables, Grills, Fire Rings, Pets OK. ACTIVITIES: Fishing, Hiking. OPEN FOR USE: June through mid-Sept. CONTACT: Divide/Creede Ranger District (719) 658-2556. NOTE: Campground near Rio Grande River. 7.5' TOPOGRAPHIC MAP: Creede.

Map No.	Campground Name	Map Loc.	Fee	No. of Units	Max. Length	Elev.	Toilets	Water	Agency
27	**Miller Creek**	C-1	$	12	35'	8,150'	Yes	Yes	San Juan National Forest

LOCATION: 15 mi E of Durango on Cty Rd 240, 4 mi N on Cty Rd 243. FACILITIES: Picnic Tables, Grills, Boat Ramp, Pets OK. ACTIVITIES: Fishing, Hiking. OPEN FOR USE: May through Oct. CONTACT: Columbine Ranger District (Bayfield) (970) 884-2512. NOTE: Camp is on Lemon Reservoir near the trailhead to Weminuche Wilderness. 7.5' TOPO-GRAPHIC MAP: Lemon Reservoir. *Construction beginning July 2001 - Call first.*

Map No.	Campground Name	Map Loc.	Fee	No. of Units	Max. Length	Elev.	Toilets	Water	Agency
28	**North Clear Creek**	B-2	$	25	30'	9,900'	Yes	Yes	Rio Grande National Forest

LOCATION: 33 mi W of Creede on Hwy 149, 3 mi SE on FDR 509. FACILITIES: Picnic Tables, Pets OK. ACTIVITIES: Fishing, Hiking. OPEN FOR USE: June through Sept. CONTACT: Divide/Creede Ranger District (719) 658-2556. NOTE: On North Clear Creek. 7.5' TOPOGRAPHIC MAP: Hermit Lakes.

Map No.	Campground Name	Map Loc.	Fee	No. of Units	Max. Length	Elev.	Toilets	Water	Agency
29	**Palisade**	B-3	$	12	30'	8,300'	Yes	Yes	Rio Grande National Forest

LOCATION: 8 mi NW of South Fork on Hwy 149. FACILITIES: Picnic Tables, Fire Rings, Pets OK. ACTIVITIES: Fishing, Hiking. OPEN FOR USE: June through mid-Oct. CONTACT: Divide/ Creede Ranger District (719) 658-2556. NOTE: 2 mi SW of Wagon Wheel Gap. 7.5' TOPOGRAPHIC MAP: Wagon Wheel Gap.

Map No.	Campground Name	Map Loc.	Fee	No. of Units	Max. Length	Elev.	Toilets	Water	Agency
30	**Park Creek**	C-3	$	16	35'	8,500'	Yes	Yes	Rio Grande National Forest

LOCATION: 8.9 mi SW of South Fork on Hwy 160. FACILITIES: Picnic Tables, Boat Ramps, Boat Docks, Pets OK. ACTIVITIES: Fishing, Hiking. OPEN FOR USE: Mid-June through mid-Sept. CONTACT: Divide/Del Norte Ranger District (719) 657-3321. NOTE: Campground located where Park Creek enters South Fork of the Rio Grande. 7.5' TOPO-GRAPHIC MAP: Beaver Creek Reservoir.

Map No.	Campground Name	Map Loc.	Fee	No. of Units	Max. Length	Elev.	Toilets	Water	Agency
31	**Pine River**	C-2	$	6	20'	8,100'	Yes	No	San Juan National Forest

LOCATION: 25 mi NE of Bayfield on Cty Rd 501. FACILITIES: Picnic Tables, Grills, Pets OK. ACTIVITIES: Fishing, Hiking. OPEN FOR USE: May through Oct. CONTACT: Columbine Ranger District (Bayfield) (970) 884-2512. NOTE: Campground is near trailhead to Weminuche Wilderness, FDT 523, on Los Pinos River. **BEST SUITED FOR TENTS.** 7.5' TOPOGRAPHIC MAP: Vallecito Reservoir.

Map No.	Campground Name	Map Loc.	Fee	No. of Units	Max. Length	Elev.	Toilets	Water	Agency
32	**Purgatory**	C-1	$	14	30'	8,800'	Yes	Yes	San Juan National Forest

LOCATION: 22 mi SW of Silverton on Hwy 550. FACILITIES: Picnic Tables, Grills, Pets OK. ACTIVITIES: Fishing, Hiking. OPEN FOR USE: Mid-May through mid-Nov. CONTACT: Columbine Ranger District (Durango) (970) 247-4874. NOTE: Trailhead to Weminuche Wilderness, FDT 511. 7.5' TOPOGRAPHIC MAP: Engineer Mountain.

Map No.	Campground Name	Map Loc.	Fee	No. of Units	Max. Length	Elev.	Toilets	Water	Agency
33	**Rio Grande**	B-3	0	4	25'	9,300'	Yes	Yes	Rio Grande National Forest

LOCATION: 9 mi SW of Creede on Hwy 149, 1 mi E on access road to river. FACILITIES: Picnic Tables, Pets OK. ACTIVITIES: Fishing, Hiking. OPEN FOR USE: Mid-May through Sept. CONTACT: Divide/ Creede Ranger District (719) 658-2556. NOTE: On Rio Grande River, 2 mi of open fishing. 7.5' TOPOGRAPHIC MAP: Bristol Head.

Map No.	Campground Name	Map Loc.	Fee	No. of Units	Max. Length	Elev.	Toilets	Water	Agency
34	**River Hill**	B-2	$	20	30'	9,200'	Yes	Yes	Rio Grande National Forest

LOCATION: 20 mi W from Creede on Hwy 149, 10 mi SW on FDR 520. FACILITIES: Picnic Tables, Pets OK. ACTIVITIES: Fishing, Hiking. OPEN FOR USE: June through Sept. CONTACT: Divide/ Creede Ranger District (719) 658-2556. NOTE: On Rio Grande River. 7.5' TOPOGRAPHIC MAP: Little Squaw Creek.

Map No.	Campground Name	Map Loc.	Fee	No. of Units	Max. Length	Elev.	Toilets	Water	Agency
35	**Road Canyon**	B-2	0	6	---	9,500'	Yes	No	Rio Grande National Forest

LOCATION: 25 mi W from Creede on Hwy 149, 7 mi SW FDR 520. FACILITIES: Picnic Tables, Pets OK. ACTIVITIES: Fishing, Hiking. OPEN FOR USE: Mid-May through Sept. CONTACT: Divide/ Creede Ranger District (719) 658-2556. NOTE: South of 100 acre Road Canyon Reservoir - good fishing. 7.5' TOPOGRAPHIC MAP: Hermit Lakes.

Map No.	Campground Name	Map Loc.	Fee	No. of Units	Max. Length	Elev.	Toilets	Water	Agency
36	**Sheep Corral**	B-1	$	8	17'	8,400'	Yes	Yes	Uncompahgre National Forest

LOCATION: 6 mi W from Telluride on Hwy 145 to FDR 623, S 5 mi to CG. FACILITIES: Grills, Pets OK. ACTIVITIES: Fishing, Hiking. OPEN FOR USE: Late May through early Sept. CONTACT: Norwood Ranger District (970) 327-4261. NOTE: On South Fork San Miguel River. 7.5' TOPOGRAPHIC MAP: Gray Head.

Map No.	Campground Name	Map Loc.	Fee	No. of Units	Max. Length	Elev.	Toilets	Water	Agency
37	**Silver Jack**	A-1	$	60	30'	8,900'	Yes	Yes	Uncompahgre National Forest

LOCATION: 20 mi E of Montrose on Hwy 50, 22 mi S on Cty Rd 69. FACILITIES: Picnic Tables, Grills, Store, Ice, Pets OK. ACTIVITIES: Fishing, Hiking. OPEN FOR USE: Early June through mid-Sept. CONTACT: Ouray Ranger District (970) 240-5300. NOTE: Handicap Accessible; Campground is near Silver Jack Reservoir. No motorized boats allowed. Best fishing in spring. 7.5' TOPOGRAPHIC MAPS: Courthouse Mountain, Sheep. Mountain.

Map No.	Campground Name	Map Loc.	Fee	No. of Units	Max. Length	Elev.	Toilets	Water	Agency
38	**Silver Thread**	B-2	$	11	30'	9,500'	Yes	Yes	Rio Grande National Forest

LOCATION: 29 mi W of Creede on Hwy 149, at Junction of FDR 515. FACILITIES: Picnic Tables, Pets OK. ACTIVITIES: Fishing, Hiking. OPEN FOR USE: May through Sept. CONTACT: Divide/Creede Ranger District (719) 658-2556. NOTE: 7.5' TOPOGRAPHIC MAP: Hermit Lake.

Map No.	Campground Name	Map Loc.	Fee	No. of Units	Max. Length	Elev.	Toilets	Water	Agency
39	**Slumgullion**	B-2	$	21	Short	11,200'	Yes	Yes	Gunnison National Forest

LOCATION: 9 mi SE of Lake City on Hwy 149, 200 yards NE on FDR 788. FACILITIES: Picnic Tables, Pets OK. ACTIVITIES: Fishing, Hiking. OPEN FOR USE: Mid-June through late Sept. CONTACT: Gunnison Ranger District (970) 641-0471. NOTE: Campground near Slumgullion Pass and Mill Creek. Trailhead to La Garita Wilderness. 7.5' TOPOGRAPHIC MAP: Slumgullion Pass.

Map No.	Campground Name	Map Loc.	Fee	No. of Units	Max. Length	Elev.	Toilets	Water	Agency
40	**South Mineral**	B-1	$	26	45'	10,000'	Yes	Yes	San Juan National Forest

LOCATION: 4 mi NW of SIlverton on Hwy 550, 5 mi SW on FDR 585. FACILITIES: Picnic Tables, Grills, Pets OK. ACTIVITIES: Fishing, Hiking. OPEN FOR USE: Late May through mid-Oct. CONTACT: Columbine Ranger District (Durango) (970) 247-4874. NOTE: Campground is along South Fork of Mineral Creek near trailhead to small lakes along Continental Divide, Ice Lake TH, FDT 505. 7.5' TOPOGRAPHIC MAP: Ophir.

Map No.	Campground Name	Map Loc.	Fee	No. of Units	Max. Length	Elev.	Toilets	Water	Agency
41	**Spruce**	A-2	$	9	Short	9,300'	Yes	Yes	Gunnison National Forest

LOCATION: 9 mi SE of Lake City on Hwy 149, 8 mi NE on FDR 788. FACILITIES: Picnic Tables, Pets OK. ACTIVITIES: Fishing, Hiking. OPEN FOR USE: Mid-June through late Sept. CONTACT: Gunnison Ranger District (970) 641-0471. NOTE: Campground is along Cebolla Creek and near La Garita Wilderness. 7.5' TOPOGRAPHIC MAP: Mineral Mountain.

Map No.	Campground Name	Map Loc.	Fee	No. of Units	Max. Length	Elev.	Toilets	Water	Agency
42	**Sunshine**	B-1	0	14	---	9,500'	Yes	Yes	Uncompahgre National Forest

LOCATION: 8 mi SW of Telluride on Hwy 145. FACILITIES: Picnic Tables, Grills, Boat Ramp, Pets OK. ACTIVITIES: Fishing, Hiking. OPEN FOR USE: Late May through late Sept. CONTACT: Norwood Ranger District (970) 327-4261. NOTE: Campground is near Cushman Lake and the South San Miguel River, Lizard Head Wilderness. 7.5' TOPOGRAPHIC MAP: Gray Head.

Map No.	Campground Name	Map Loc.	Fee	No. of Units	Max. Length	Elev.	Toilets	Water	Agency
43	**Teal**	C-2	$	16	35'	8,300'	Yes	Yes	San Juan National Forest

LOCATION: 3 mi W of Pagosa Springs on Hwy 160, 22 mi N on Cty Rd 600 (FDR 631), 2 mi N to Williams Creek Res. FACILITIES: Picnic Tables, Grills, Fire Rings, Boat Ramp, Pets OK. ACTIVITIES: Fishing, Hiking. OPEN FOR USE: June through mid-Sept. CONTACT: Pagosa Ranger District (970) 264-2268. NOTE: Campground near Williams Creek Reservoir. 7.5' TOPOGRAPHIC MAP: Cimarrona Peak.

Map No.	Campground Name	Map Loc.	Fee	No. of Units	Max. Length	Elev.	Toilets	Water	Agency
44	**Thirty Mile ®**	B-2	$	35	30'	9,300'	Yes	Yes	Rio Grande National Forest

LOCATION: 25 mi W of Creede on Hwy 149, 12 mi W on FDR 520 to Rio Grande Reservoir. FACILITIES: Picnic Tables, Pets OK. ACTIVITIES: Fishing, Hiking. OPEN FOR USE: May through Sept. CONTACT: Divide/ Creede Ranger District (719) 658-2556. NOTE: On E end of Rio Grande Reservoir - Trailhead for Weminuche Wilderness, Weminuche TH, FDT 818, Squaw Creek TH, FDT 814. 7.5' TOPOGRAPHIC MAP: Weminuche Pass.

Map No.	Campground Name	Map Loc.	Fee	No. of Units	Max. Length	Elev.	Toilets	Water	Agency
45	**Tucker Ponds**	C-3	$	16	35'	9,600'	Yes	No	Rio Grande National Forest

LOCATION: 14.4 mi SW of South Fork on Hwy 160, 2.6 mi S on FDR 390. FACILITIES: Picnic Tables, Pets OK. ACTIVITIES: Fishing, Hiking. OPEN FOR USE: Late June through mid-Sept. CONTACT: Divide/ Del Norte Ranger District (719) 657-3321. NOTE: On Pass Creek with several ponds to fish. 7.5' TOPOGRAPHIC MAP: Wolf Creek Pass.

Map No.	Campground Name	Map Loc.	Fee	No. of Units	Max. Length	Elev.	Toilets	Water	Agency
46	**Transfer Park ®**	C-1	$	25	35'	8,600'	Yes	Yes	San Juan National Forest

LOCATION: 14 mi NE of Durango on Cty Rd 240, 8 mi N on Cty Rd 243. FACILITIES: Picnic Tables, Grills, Pets OK. ACTIVITIES: Fishing, Hiking. OPEN FOR USE: May through Oct. CONTACT: Columbine Ranger District (Bayfield) (970) 884-2512. NOTE: Reservations. Trailhead Weminuche Wilderness, FDT 667. 7.5' TOPOGRAPHIC MAP: Lemon Reservoir.

Map No.	Campground Name	Map Loc.	Fee	No. of Units	Max. Length	Elev.	Toilets	Water	Agency
47	**Ute**	D-2	$	24	35'	7,150'	Yes	Yes	San Juan National Forest

LOCATION: 18 mi W of Pagosa Springs on Hwy 160. FACILITIES: Picnic Tables, Grills, Pets OK. ACTIVITIES: Fishing, Hiking. OPEN FOR USE: May through Oct. CONTACT: Pagosa Ranger District (970) 264-2268. NOTE: Reservations Near Chimney Rock Archeological Area. 7.5' TOPOGRAPHIC MAP: Chimney Rock.

Map No.	Campground Name	Map Loc.	Fee	No. of Units	Max. Length	Elev.	Toilets	Water	Agency
48	**Vallecito Reservoir**	C-1	$		35'	7,900'	Yes	Yes	San Juan National Forest
a.	Graham Creek			25					
b.	Middle Mountain			24					
c.	North Canyon			21					
d.	Pine Point			30					
e.	Old Timer			10					

LOCATION: 14 mi N of Bayfield on Cty Rd 501. FACILITIES: Picnic Tables, Grills, Pets OK. ACTIVITIES: Fishing, Hiking. OPEN FOR USE: May through Oct. CONTACT: Columbine Ranger District (Bayfield) (970) 884-2512. NOTE: Campgrounds are near 2,700 acre reservoir - Full range of services available - Coldwater fishing. 7.5' TOPOGRAPHIC MAP: Vallecito Reservoir. *See map page 125.*

Map No.	Campground Name	Map Loc.	Fee	No. of Units	Max. Length	Elev.	Toilets	Water	Agency
49	**Vallecito**	C-1	$	80	35'	8,000'	Yes	Yes	San Juan National Forest

LOCATION: 18 mi N of Bayfield on Cty Rd 501, 2.5 mi N on Cty Rd 500. FACILITIES: Picnic Tables, Grills, Pets OK. ACTIVITIES: Fishing, Hiking. OPEN FOR USE: May through Oct. CONTACT: Columbine Ranger District (Bayfield) (970) 884-2512. NOTE: 3 mi N of Vallecito Reservoir - Trailhead to Weminuche Wilderness. 7.5' TOPOGRAPHIC MAP: Vallecito Reservoir.

Map No.	Campground Name	Map Loc.	Fee	No. of Units	Max. Length	Elev.	Toilets	Water	Agency
50	**West Fork**	C-3	$	28	35'	8,000'	Yes	Yes	San Juan National Forest

LOCATION: 13.7 mi NE of Pagosa Springs on Hwy 160, 1.6 mi N on FDR 684. FACILITIES: Picnic Tables, Pets OK. ACTIVITIES: Fishing, Hiking. OPEN FOR USE: Mid-May through mid-Nov. CONTACT: Pagosa Ranger District (970) 264-2268. NOTE: Near Hatcher Lakes - Trailhead Weminuche Wilderness. 7.5' TOPOGRAPHIC MAP: Saddle Mountain.

Map No.	Campground Name	Map Loc.	Fee	No. of Units	Max. Length	Elev.	Toilets	Water	Agency
51	**Williams Creek**	C-2	$	67	45'	8,300'	Yes	Yes	San Juan National Forest

LOCATION: 3 mi W of Pagosa Springs on Hwy 160, 22 mi NW on FDR 631. FACILITIES: Picnic Tables, Pets OK. ACTIVITIES: Fishing, Hiking, 4-Wheel Drive Roads. OPEN FOR USE: June through Sept. CONTACT: Pagosa Ranger District (970) 264-2268. NOTE: 1 mi S of Williams Creek Reservoir; Reservations. 7.5' TOPOGRAPHIC MAP: Lake San Cristobol.

Map No.	Campground Name	Map Loc.	Fee	No. of Units	Max. Length	Elev.	Toilets	Water	Agency
52	**Williams Creek**	B-2	$	23	20'	9,200'	Yes	Yes	Gunnison National Forest

LOCATION: 3 mi S of Lake City on Hwy 149, 7 mi SW on BLM Rd 3306. FACILITIES: Picnic Tables, Pets OK. ACTIVITIES: Fishing, Hiking. OPEN FOR USE: Mid-May through Sept. CONTACT: Gunnison Ranger District (970) 641-0471. NOTE: On Lake Fork Gunnison River near 350 acre Lake San Cristobal. 7.5' TOPOGRAPHIC MAP: Oakbrush Ridge.

Map No.	Campground Name	Map Loc.	Fee	No. of Units	Max. Length	Elev.	Toilets	Water	Agency
53	**Wolf Creek**	C-3	$	26	35'	8,000'	Yes	Yes	San Juan National Forest

LOCATION: 13.7 mi NE of Pagosa Springs on Hwy 160, 1/2 mi N on FDR 684. FACILITIES: Picnic Tables, Pets OK. ACTIVITIES: Fishing, Hiking. OPEN FOR USE: Mid-May through mid-Nov. CONTACT: Pagosa Ranger District (970) 264-2268. NOTE: On Wolf Creek near Hatcher Lakes - near several trails. 7.5' TOPOGRAPHIC MAP: Wolf Creek Pass.

Map No.	Campground Name	Map Loc.	Fee	No. of Units	Max. Length	Elev.	Toilets	Water	Agency
54	**Wupperman**	B-2	$	40	24'	8,000'	Yes	Yes	Hinsdale County

LOCATION: 2.5 mi S of Lake City on Hwy 149, 1 mi S on BLM 3306, 1 mi SE on east side of lake. FACILITIES: Picnic Tables, Fire rings, Dump Station, Boat Ramp, Pets OK. ACTIVITIES: Fishing, Hiking. OPEN FOR USE: Mid-May through mid-Nov. CONTACT: Hinsdale County (970) 944-2225. NOTE: Camp on bluff overlooking Lake San Cristobal - Beautiful view. 7.5' TOPOGRAPHIC MAP: Lake San Cristobol.

Map No.	Campground Name	Map Loc.	Fee	No. of Units	Max. Length	Elev.	Toilets	Water	Agency
55	**Matterhorn**	B-1	$	28	35'	9,500'	Yes	Yes	Uncompahgre National Forest

LOCATION: 15 mi SW of Telluride on Hwy 145. FACILITIES: Picnic Tables, Grills, RV hook-ups Pets OK. ACTIVITIES: Fishing, Hiking. OPEN FOR USE: Late May through late Sept. CONTACT: Grand Junction Ranger District (970) 242-8211. NOTE: Campground is near Trout Lake, Lizard Head Wilderness. 7.5' TOPOGRAPHIC MAP: Gray Head.

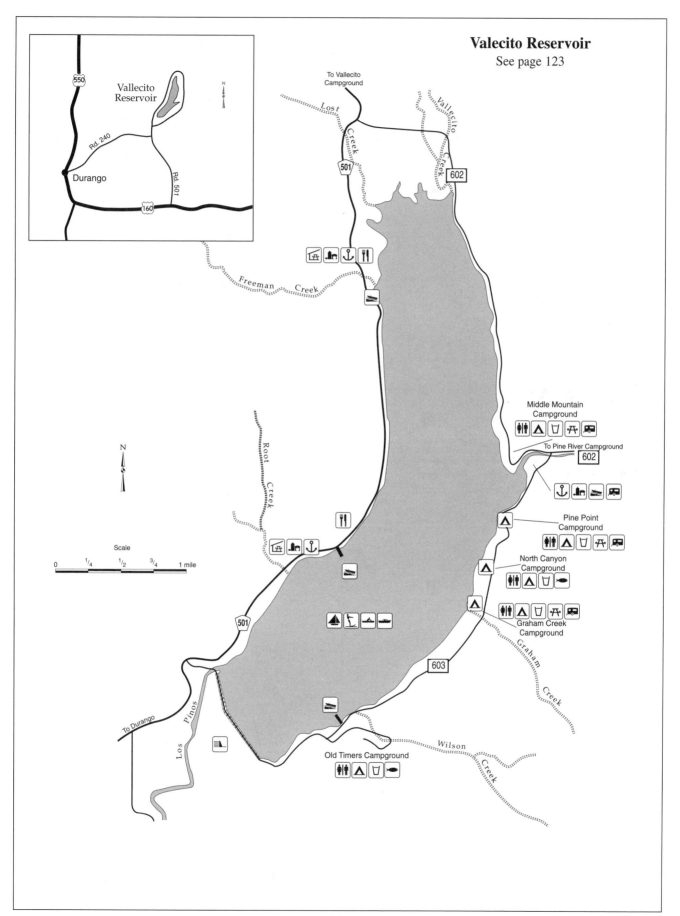

Valecito Reservoir
See page 123

Vallecito Reservoir

550

Rd. 240

Durango

Rd. 501

160

N

To Vallecito
Campground

Lost

Creek

Vallecito

Creek

501

602

Freeman   Creek

Root

Creek

Middle Mountain
Campground

To Pine River Campground

602

N

Scale

0   1/4   1/2   3/4   1 mile

Pine Point
Campground

North Canyon
Campground

501

Graham Creek
Campground

Graham

Creek

603

Pinos

To Durango

Los

Old Timers Campground

Wilson

Creek

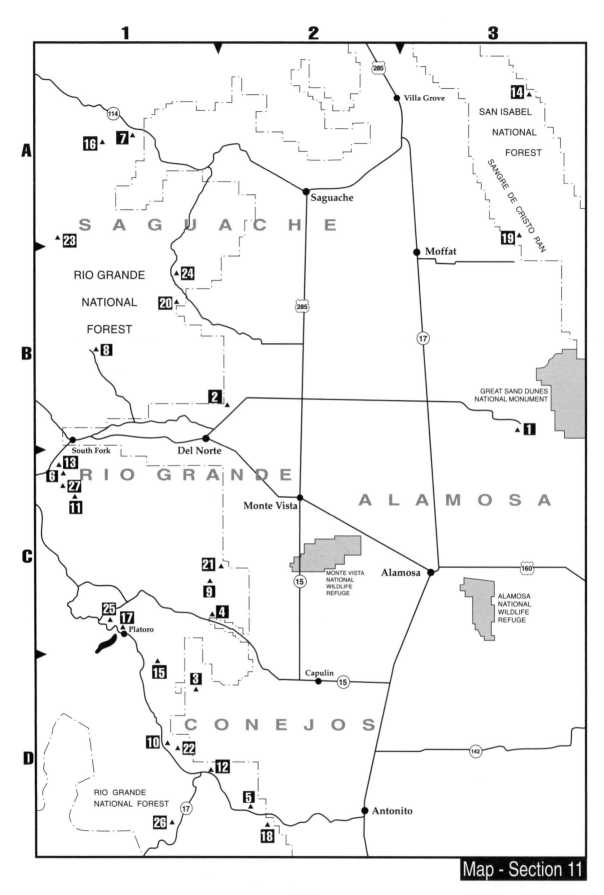

Map - Section 11

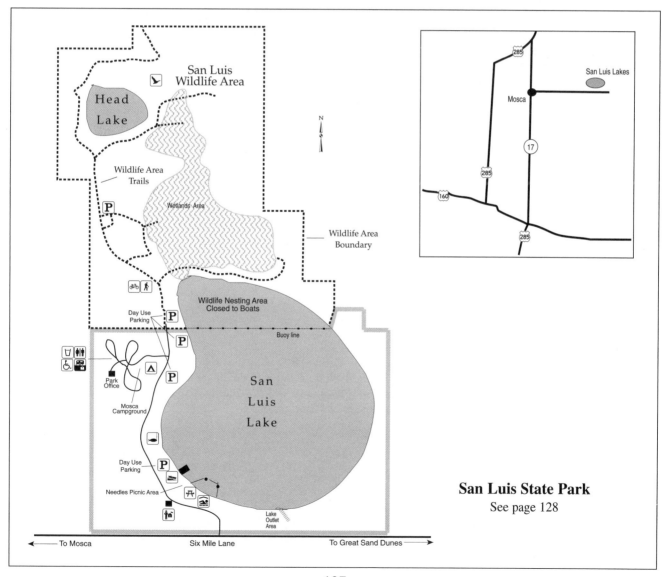

San Luis State Park

See page 128

Map No.	Campground Name	Map Loc.	Fee	No. of Units	Max. Length	Elev.	Toilets	Water	Agency
1	**San Luis Lakes State Park ®**	B-3	$	51	45'	7,525'	Yes	Yes	Colorado State Parks

Known as "The Valley" by Coloradan's, the San Luis Valley has outstanding natural features combined with unique cultural heritage, that provides the perfect backdrop for visitors with an interest in frontier history and an eye for spectacular scenery. Take Hwy l60 west from Walsenburg for 60 miles. North on Hwy 150 13.5 miles. Left on Sixmile Lane 8 miles, north 1/8 mile to park entrance. Visitors can search for lost gold mines of the Conquistadors, follow the trail of past trains, visit ghost towns and historic districts or relive the life of a soldier at a frontier fort, all within an hours drive from San Luis Lakes State Park.

Camping

The Mosca Campground is located in the low sand dunes just west of San Luis Lake. Campsites have electrical hookups, sheltered tables and fire grates, and drinking water is available. A bathhouse with modern restrooms, hot showers and laundry facilities is located in the campground. There are no individual sewer hookups, but a dump station is available. The campground can accommodate motor homes, trailers and tents. For information about group camping contact the park office. See map page 127.

Wildlife

Wildlife watching is year around activity at San Luis State Park. The San Luis Valley is extremely popular for bird watching and provides one of the best viewing opportunities in the state for migratory birds like sandhill cranes, whopping cranes, bald eagles and waterfowl. Many types of raptors and songbirds spend part of the year either nesting or wintering in the San Luis Valley. Small mammals, amphibians, reptiles and predators are also common to this unique riparian area. Mule deer, pronghorn and elk live nearby.

Hiking

The wide, level trails in the wildlife area provide a pleasant experience at the edge of the dunes and wetlands.

Other Activities:

Fishing, sailing windsurfing.

Daily Fee/Annual Pass
For more information contact:
San Luis Lakes State Park
PO Box l75, Mosca, CO 81146
(719) 378-2020

Map No.	Campground Name	Map Loc.	Fee	No. of Units	Max. Length	Elev.	Toilets	Water	Agency
2	**Penitente Canyon**	B-2	0	10	NA	7,800'	Yes	Yes	Bureau of Land Management

LOCATION: 2.5 mi NE of Del Norte on Hwy 112, N on Cty Rd 33/38 approx. 8 mi to area. FACILITIES: Fire rings. ACTIVITIES: Fishing, Hiking, Rock Climbing, Mountain Biking. OPEN FOR USE: Year Round. CONTACT: LaJara Resource Area (719) 274-8971. NOTE: Canyon campground capacity 75 people. 7.5' TOPOGRAPHIC MAP: Twin Mountains SE.

Map No.	Campground Name	Map Loc.	Fee	No. of Units	Max. Length	Elev.	Toilets	Water	Agency
3	**La Jara Reservoir State Wildlife Area**	D-1	0	Dispersed	Open	9,968'	Yes	Yes	Colorado Division of Wildlife

LOCATION: 20 mi S of Monte Vista on Hwy 15, 1/2 mi W to Ra Jadero Canyon Rd, 12 mi SW to reservoir. FACILITIES: Boat ramp, Pets OK. ACTIVITIES: Fishing, Hiking, Hunting in the fall season. OPEN FOR USE: May through Oct. CONTACT: Colorado Division of Wildlife SE Region (970) 227-5200. NOTE: 635 acre reservoir no concessions, rough access road. 7.5' TOPOGRAPHIC MAPS: Terrace Reservoir.

Map No.	Campground Name	Map Loc.	Fee	No. of Units	Max. Length	Elev.	Toilets	Water	Agency
4	**Alamosa**	C-1	0	10	50'	8,700'	Yes	Yes	Rio Grande National Forest

LOCATION: 12 mi S of Monte Vista on Hwy 15, 17.4 mi W on FDR 250. FACILITIES: Picnic Tables, Pets OK. ACTIVITIES: Fishing, Hiking, 4-Wheeling. OPEN FOR USE: Late May through mid-Sept. CONTACT: Conejos Peak Ranger District (719) 274-8971. NOTE: Camp is along the Alamosa River, NW of Terrace Reservoir - Fishing rated poor - Near trails. 7.5' TOPOGRAPHIC MAP: Greenie Mountain.

Map No.	Campground Name	Map Loc.	Fee	No. of Units	Max. Length	Elev.	Toilets	Water	Agency
5	**Aspen Glade ®**	D-2	$	34	50'	8,500'	Yes	Yes	Rio Grande National Forest

LOCATION: 18 mi W of Antonito on Hwy 17. FACILITIES: Picnic Tables, Pets OK. ACTIVITIES: Fishing, Hiking. OPEN FOR USE: Mid-May through mid-Sept. CONTACT: Conejos Peak Ranger District (719) 274-8971. NOTE: Reservations Needed. Campground is along Conejos River near River Springs Ranger Station. FDT 735 & 737. 7.5' TOPOGRAPHIC MAP: Osier.

Map No.	Campground Name	Map Loc.	Fee	No. of Units	Max. Length	Elev.	Toilets	Water	Agency
6	**Beaver Creek (Lower)**	C-1	$	19	35'	8,400'	Yes	Yes	Rio Grande National Forest

LOCATION: 2.4 mi SW of South Fork on Hwy 160, 3 mi S on FDR 360. FACILITIES: Picnic Tables, Pets OK. ACTIVI-TIES: Fishing, Hiking. OPEN FOR USE: Mid-June through mid-Sept. CONTACT: Divide/ Del Norte Ranger District (719) 657-3321. NOTE: Campground along Beaver Creek and the confluence of the South Fork of the Rio Grande, north of Beaver Creek Reservoir. Tweksberry TH, FDT 842. 7.5' TOPOGRAPHIC MAP: Beaver Creek Reservoir.

Map No.	Campground Name	Map Loc.	Fee	No. of Units	Max. Length	Elev.	Toilets	Water	Agency
7	**Buffalo Pass**	A-1	$	26	25'	9,000'	Yes	Yes	Rio Grande National Forest

LOCATION: 27.6 mi NW of Saguache on Hwy 114, 1.7 mi W on FDR 775. FACILITIES: Picnic Tables, Pets OK. ACTIV-ITIES: Fishing, Hiking, 4-Wheeling. OPEN FOR USE: Late May through late Sept. CONTACT: Saguache Ranger District (719) 655-2547. NOTE: Campground is just below the Continental Divide near North Pass. 7.5' TOPOGRAPHIC MAP: North Pass.

Map No.	Campground Name	Map Loc.	Fee	No. of Units	Max. Length	Elev.	Toilets	Water	Agency
8	**Cathedral**	B-1	0	33	35'	9,400'	Yes	Yes	Rio Grande National Forest

LOCATION: 8.8 mi W of Del Norte on Hwy 160, 1.5 mi N on Cty Rd 18, 3.1 mi N on FDR 650, 7 mi NW on FDR 640. ACTIVITIES: Fishing, Hiking. OPEN FOR USE: Mid-June through mid-Sept. CONTACT: Divide/ Del Norte Ranger District (719) 657-3321. NOTE: Camp is near Cathedral and Embargo Creeks. Cathedral TH, FDT 794. Last 8 miles of road designed as primitive - lots of trails. 7.5' TOPOGRAPHIC MAP: Pine Cone Knob.

Map No.	Campground Name	Map Loc.	Fee	No. of Units	Max. Length	Elev.	Toilets	Water	Agency
9	**Comstock**	C-1	0	8	30'	9,700'	Yes	No	Rio Grande National Forest

LOCATION: 2 mi S of Monte Vista on Hwy 15, 16.5 mi SW on FDR 265. FACILITIES: Picnic Tables, Pets OK. ACTIVI-TIES: Fishing, Hiking. OPEN FOR USE: Late May through late Sept. CONTACT: Divide/ Del Norte Ranger District (719) 657-3321. NOTE: Campground on south fork Rock Creek - near several trails. FDT 703. 7.5' TOPOGRAPHIC MAP: Greenie Mountain.

Map No.	Campground Name	Map Loc.	Fee	No. of Units	Max. Length	Elev.	Toilets	Water	Agency
10	**Conejos**	D-1	$	16	60'	8,700'	Yes	Yes	Rio Grande National Forest

LOCATION: 23 mi W of Antonito on Hwy 17, 7 mi NW on FDR 250. FACILITIES: Picnic Tables, Pets OK. ACTIVI-TIES: Fishing, Hiking. OPEN FOR USE: Mid-May through mid-Sept. CONTACT: Conejos Peak Ranger District (719) 274-8971. NOTE: Camp is along Conejos River adjacent to South San Juan Wilderness. 7.5' TOPOGRAPHIC MAP: Spectacle Lake.

Section 11

Map No.	Campground Name	Map Loc.	Fee	No. of Units	Max. Length	Elev.	Toilets	Water	Agency
11	**Cross Creek**	C-1	$	12	25'	8,800'	Yes	Yes	Rio Grande National Forest

LOCATION: 2.4 mi SW of South Fork on Hwy 160, 6.1 mi S on FDR 360. FACILITIES: Picnic Tables, Boat ramp & Dock, Pets OK. ACTIVITIES: Fishing, Hiking, Boating. OPEN FOR USE: Mid-June thru mid-Sept. CONTACT: Divide/ Del Norte Ranger District (719) 657-3321. NOTE: Campground is near 110 Acre Beaver Creek Reservoir. Cross Creek TH, FDT 812. 7.5' TOPOGRAPHIC MAPS: Beaver Creek Reservoir.

Map No.	Campground Name	Map Loc.	Fee	No. of Units	Max. Length	Elev.	Toilets	Water	Agency
12	**Elk Creek**	D-1	$	34	35'	8,500'	Yes	Yes	Rio Grande National Forest

LOCATION: 23 mi W of Antonito on Hwy 17, 1 mi SW on FDR 128, 200 yards NW on FDR 128. FACILITIES: Picnic Tables, Pets OK. ACTIVITIES: Fishing, Hiking. OPEN FOR USE: Mid-May through mid-Sept. CONTACT: Conejos Peak Ranger District (719) 274-8971. NOTE: Reservations; Camp is at the confluence of Elk Creek and Conejos River and is near the South San Juan Wilderness. Elk Creek TH, FDT 731. 7.5' TOPOGRAPHIC MAP: La Jara Canyon.

Map No.	Campground Name	Map Loc.	Fee	No. of Units	Max. Length	Elev.	Toilets	Water	Agency
13	**Highway Springs**	C-1	$	11	35'	8,400'	Yes	No	Rio Grande National Forest

LOCATION: 5.2 mi SW of South Fork on Hwy 160. FACILITIES: Picnic Tables, Pets OK. ACTIVITIES: Fishing, Hiking. OPEN FOR USE: Early June through mid-Sept. CONTACT: Divide/ Del Norte Ranger District (719) 657-3321. NOTE: Camp is on the South Fork of the Rio Grande River, NW of Beaver Creek Reservoir. 7.5' TOPOGRAPHIC MAP: South Fork West.

Map No.	Campground Name	Map Loc.	Fee	No. of Units	Max. Length	Elev.	Toilets	Water	Agency
14	**Lake Creek**	A-3	$	12	30'	8,200'	Yes	Yes	San Isabel National Forest

LOCATION: 26 mi W of Canon City on Hwy 50 to Texas Creek, 11 mi S on Hwy 69 to Hillside, 3 mi W on FDR 198. FACILITIES: Picnic Tables, Fire Rings, Pets OK. ACTIVITIES: Fishing, Hiking. OPEN FOR USE: Mid-May through late Oct. CONTACT: San Carlos Ranger District (719) 269-8500. NOTE: Campground is near Lake Creek and trailhead for Rainbow Trail. Rainbow Trail is a multiple use trail. 7.5' TOPOGRAPHIC MAP: Cotopaxi.

Map No.	Campground Name	Map Loc.	Fee	No. of Units	Max. Length	Elev.	Toilets	Water	Agency
15	**Lake Fork ®**	D-1	$	18	25'	9,500'	Yes	No	Rio Grande National Forest

LOCATION: 23 mi W of Antonito on Hwy 17, 16 mi NW on FDR 250, W on Lake Fork ranch Rd 0.5 mi. FACILITIES: Picnic Tables, Pets OK. ACTIVITIES: Fishing, Hiking. OPEN FOR USE: Late May through Sept. CONTACT: Conejos Peak Ranger District (719) 274-8971. NOTE: Reservations. Campground on Conejos River near trail to South San Juan Wilderness, Lake Fork Creek, FDT 716. 7.5' TOPOGRAPHIC MAP: Red Mountain.

Map No.	Campground Name	Map Loc.	Fee	No. of Units	Max. Length	Elev.	Toilets	Water	Agency
16	**Luders**	A-1	0	6	25'	9,900'	Yes	No	Rio Grande National Forest

LOCATION: 22 mi NW of Sagauche on Hwy 114, 11 mi NW on FDR 750. FACILITIES: Picnic Tables, Pets OK. ACTIVITIES: Fishing, Hiking, 4-Wheeling. OPEN FOR USE: Late May through late Sept. CONTACT: Saguache Ranger District (719) 655-2547. NOTE: Campground is below Cochetopa Pass along Luders Creek. 7.5' TOPOGRAPHIC MAP: North Pass.

Map No.	Campground Name	Map Loc.	Fee	No. of Units	Max. Length	Elev.	Toilets	Water	Agency
17	**Mix Lake**	C-1	$	22	60'	10,035'	Yes	Yes	Rio Grande National Forest

LOCATION: 23 mi W of Antonito on Hwy 17, 21.6 mi NW on FDR 250, 3/4 mi W on FDR 250 B. FACILITIES: Picnic Tables, Boat Ramp, Pets OK. ACTIVITIES: Fishing, Hiking. OPEN FOR USE: Late May through mid-Sept. CONTACT: Conejos Peak Ranger District (719) 274-8971. NOTE: Campground is near Mix Lake and adjacent to Platoro Reservoir. 25 acre Mix Lake is a put and take rainbow lake - 800 acre Platoro Reservoir - Rated good for rainbow and cutthroats. FDT 759. 7.5' TOPOGRAPHIC MAP: Platoro.

Map No.	Campground Name	Map Loc.	Fee	No. of Units	Max. Length	Elev.	Toilets	Water	Agency
18	**Mogote ®**	D-2	$	41	25'	8,400'	Yes	Yes	Rio Grande National Forest

LOCATION: 15 mi W of Antonito on Hwy 17. FACILITIES: Picnic Tables, Pets OK. ACTIVITIES: Fishing, Hiking. OPEN FOR USE: Mid-May through mid-Nov. CONTACT: Conejos Peak Ranger District (719) 274-8971. NOTE: Camp is along Conejos River at entrance to Rio Grande National Forest. ADJACENT TO MOGOTE GROUP CAMPGROUND. 7.5' TOPOGRAPHIC MAP: Fox Creek.

Map No.	Campground Name	Map Loc.	Fee	No. of Units	Max. Length	Elev.	Toilets	Water	Agency
19	**North Crestone**	A-3	$	13	25'	8,800'	Yes	Yes	Rio Grande National Forest

LOCATION: 12 mi E of Moffat on Hwy 17 to Crestone, 2.2 mi N of Crestone on FDR 950. FACILITIES: Picnic Tables, Pets OK. ACTIVITIES: Fishing, Hiking. OPEN FOR USE: Late May through late Sept.. CONTACT: Saguache Ranger District (719) 655-2547. NOTE: Last 1.5 miles primitive road -rugged trails to lake and stream fishing. North Crestone TH, FDT 744. 7.5' TOPOGRAPHIC MAP: Crestone.

Map No.	Campground Name	Map Loc.	Fee	No. of Units	Max. Length	Elev.	Toilets	Water	Agency
20	**Poso**	B-1	$	11	20'	9,100'	Yes	Yes	Rio Grande National Forest

LOCATION: 10 mi NW of La Garita on Cty Rd 690, 1.5 mi W on FDR 675. FACILITIES: Picnic Tables. ACTIVITIES: Fishing, Hiking. OPEN FOR USE: Late May through late Sept. CONTACT: Saguache Ranger District (719) 655-2547. NOTE: Camp near South Fork of Carnero Creek. Four wheel drive roads in area. 7.5' TOPOGRAPHIC MAP: Lookout Mountain.

Map No.	Campground Name	Map Loc.	Fee	No. of Units	Max. Length	Elev.	Toilets	Water	Agency
21	**Rock Creek**	C-1	0	23	30'	9,200'	Yes	No	Rio Grande National Forest

LOCATION: 2 mi S of Monte Vista on Hwy 15, W 2 mi on Cty Rd 25, S 11 mi to campground. FACILITIES: Picnic Tables, Pets OK. ACTIVITIES: Fishing, Hiking. OPEN FOR USE: Late May through late Sept. CONTACT: Divide/ Del Norte Ranger District (719) 657-3321. NOTE: Campground is near South Fork of Rock Creek and a number of trails. 7.5' TOPOGRAPHIC MAP: Greenie Mountain.

Map No.	Campground Name	Map Loc.	Fee	No. of Units	Max. Length	Elev.	Toilets	Water	Agency
22	**Spectacle Lake**	D-1	$	24	60'	8,700'	Yes	Yes	Rio Grande National Forest

LOCATION: 23 mi W of Antonito on Hwy 17, 7 mi NW on FDR 250. FACILITIES: Picnic Tables, Pets OK. ACTIVITIES: Fishing, Hiking. OPEN FOR USE: Late May through mid-Sept. CONTACT: Conejos Peak Ranger District (719) 274-8971. NOTE: Campground is near Conejos River and adjacent to South San Juan Wilderness. 7.5' TOPOGRAPHIC MAP: Spectacle Lake.

Map No.	Campground Name	Map Loc.	Fee	No. of Units	Max. Length	Elev.	Toilets	Water	Agency
23	**Stone Cellar**	A-1	0	4	25'	9,500'	Yes	Yes	Rio Grande National Forest

LOCATION: 8 mi SE of Gunnison on Hwy 50, 24 mi SE Hwy 114, 5 mi SW on FDR 804, 1 mi SE to FDR 787, 14 mi S on FDR 787. FACILITIES: Picnic Tables, Pets OK. ACTIVITIES: Fishing, Hiking, 4-Wheeling. OPEN FOR USE: Late May through mid-Sept. CONTACT: Saguache Ranger District (719) 655-2547. NOTE: Just east of Stone Cellar Ranger Station - Trailhead to La Garita Wilderness. 7.5' TOPOGRAPHIC MAP: Saguache Park.

Map No.	Campground Name	Map Loc.	Fee	No. of Units	Max. Length	Elev.	Toilets	Water	Agency
24	**Stormking**	B-1	$	11	25'	9,400'	Yes	Yes	Rio Grande National Forest

LOCATION: 14 mi NW of La Garita on Cty Rd 690. FACILITIES: Picnic Tables, Pets OK. ACTIVITIES: Fishing, Hiking. OPEN FOR USE: Late May through late Sept. CONTACT: Saguache Ranger District (719) 655-2547. NOTE: Campground is near Middle Fork of Carnero Creek and at the base of Storm King Mountain. 7.5' TOPOGRAPHIC MAP: Lookout Mountain.

Map No.	Campground Name	Map Loc.	Fee	No. of Units	Max. Length	Elev.	Toilets	Water	Agency
25	**Stunner**	C-1	0	10	45'	9,700'	Yes	No	Rio Grande National Forest

LOCATION: 12 mi S of Monte Vista on Hwy 15, 33 mi W on FDR 250, 1/4 mi SW on FDR 380. FACILITIES: Picnic Tables, Pets OK. ACTIVITIES: Fishing, Hiking. OPEN FOR USE: Late May through mid-Sept. CONTACT: Conejos Peak Ranger District (719) 274-8971. NOTE: Camp is on the Alamosa River and NW of Platoro Reservoir. 7.5' TOPOGRAPHIC MAPS: Summitville/Platoro.

Map No.	Campground Name	Map Loc.	Fee	No. of Units	Max. Length	Elev.	Toilets	Water	Agency
26	**Trujillo Meadows**	D-1	$	50	60'	10,000'	Yes	Yes	Rio Grande National Forest

LOCATION: 32 mi W of Antonito on Hwy 17, 3 mi N on FDR 116. FACILITIES: Picnic Tables, Boat Ramp, Pets OK. ACTIVITIES: Fishing, Hiking. OPEN FOR USE: Mid-May through mid-Sept. CONTACT: Conejos Peak Ranger District (719) 274-8971. NOTE: Camp is beside 70 acre Trujillo Meadows Reservoir. 7.5' TOPOGRAPHIC MAP: Cumbres.

Map No.	Campground Name	Map Loc.	Fee	No. of Units	Max. Length	Elev.	Toilets	Water	Agency
27	**Upper Beaver Creek**	C-1	$	15	35'	8,500'	Yes	Yes	Rio Grande National Forest

LOCATION: 2.4 mi SW of South Fork on Hwy 160, 4 mi S on FDR 360. FACILITIES: Picnic Tables, Boat ramps & docks, Pets OK. ACTIVITIES: Fishing, Hiking. OPEN FOR USE: mid-June through mid-Sept. CONTACT: Divide/Del Norte Ranger District (719) 657-3321. NOTE: On Beaver Creek NW of Beaver Creek Reservoir. 7.5' TOPOGRAPHIC MAP: Beaver Creek Reservoir.

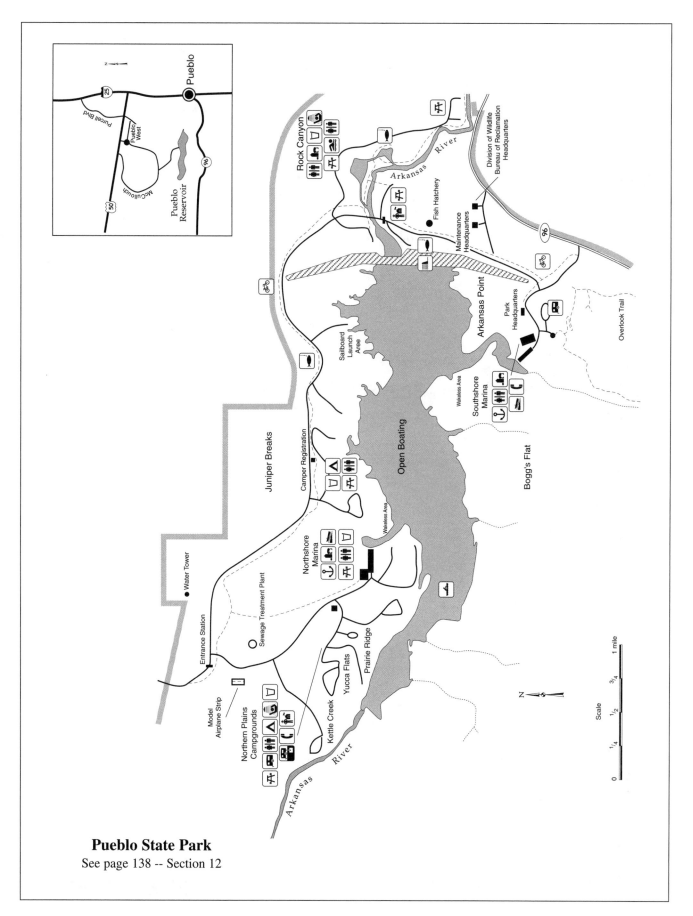

Pueblo State Park

See page 138 -- Section 12

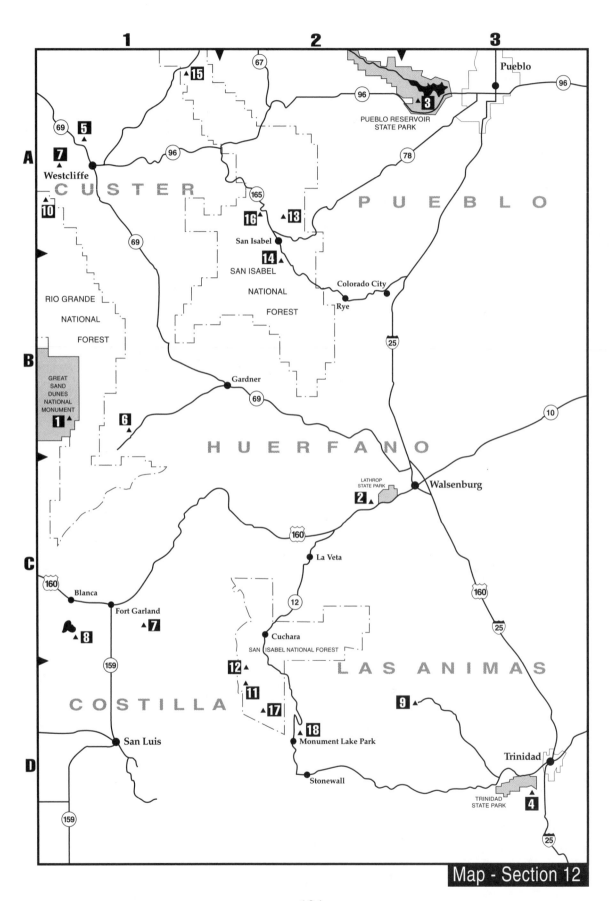

Map - Section 12

Fishing Pier Horseshoe Lake - Lathrop State Park

Section 12

Map No.	Name	Map Loc.	Fee	No. of Units	Max. Length	Elev.	Toilets	Water	Agency
1	Great Sand Dunes National Monument	B-1	$	88	30'	8,175'	Yes	Yes	National Parks Service

Great Sand Dunes, located 38 miles north of Alamosa on Colorado Highway 150, is a place to take a hike, to discover animals and plants, to seek silence and solitude, to take photographs, to ride a horse, to wilderness camp, and, if you like, to run and jump and roll and slide. Your explorations begin at the foot of the dunes; and you can climb as high as you like. If you've ever walked in soft sand on a beach, remember how exhilarating, and how tiring it was? Now imagine walking up a mountain of sand. That's what hiking the Great Sand Dunes is like. Distances can be deceiving in the dunes; often your destination is farther away than it looks. But your efforts will be rewarded with the opportunity to experience the dunes firsthand and to get spectacular views of the San Luis Valley and surrounding mountain ranges.

Although the dunes seem misplaced, they are here because the key ingredients for making dunes - sand, wind, and time - existed here. The Rio Grande, the main river in the San Luis Valley, and the 14,433 foot mountain ranges that border the valley to the west the San Juan's and to the east the Sangre De Cristo's also play major parts in the creation of the Great Sand Dunes.

For centuries, the Rio Grande meandered through the San Luis Valley, much as it does today, carrying sand and other sediments and depositing them in its riverbed and along its shores. Most of the sand was eroded bits and pieces of the San Juan Mountains brought to the Rio Grande by tributary streams. Some of it was eroded particles of rock left in the valley by alpine glaciers during the Ice Age. In time, the Rio Grande changed its course, and these great deposits of sand were exposed to the winds that swept across the broad, flat valley. These winds, blowing toward the northeast, pushed and bounced the grains of sand until the steep Sangre de Cristo Mountains barred the way. Seeking a way over this barrier, the winds surged upward through low mountains passes but leaving the heavier sand at the foot of the mountains. In this way, over thousands of years, the Great Sand Dunes were created.

Plants and Animals
The dunes are a tough environment to survive in, but a few plants and animals do live here. Plants include blowout grass, Indian rice grass, scurfpea, and especially in late summer, the bright yellow prairie sun-flower. These are particularly hardy plants that have adapted to life in the shifting sands. Animals are even more scarce. Kangaroo rats - masters of water conservation - live here, as do two interesting insects found nowhere else on Earth - the Great Sand Dunes tiger beetle and the giant sand treader camel cricket. Other animals, such as mule deer, elk, bobcats, coyotes, ravens, and blackbilled magpies, live on the dunes edge. Many of these animals are nocturnal; look for their tracks.

Camping and Picnicking
The Pinyon Flats Campground is open all year, first-come, first-served. From April to October, tables, grills, water, and restrooms; are provided; the rest of the year water is not available. Backcountry camping is permitted at designated sites and in the dune wilderness; open fires are prohibited and a camping permit is required. Gathering wood is prohibited; buy firewood in the park. A picnic area at the dunes edge has tables, grills, water and restrooms. The Group Campground is open April through October. Three sites that can accommodate 25 to 50 persons.

Trails
A few park trails let you hike or horseback ride in the world away from the dunes the grasslands, pinon juniper woodlands, and ponderosa forests. For information, stop by the information center.

For information write:
Great Sand Dunes National Monument,
Mosca, CO 81146
(719) 378-2312.

Map No.	Name	Map Loc.	Fee	No. of Units	Max. Length	Elev.	Toilets	Water	Agency
2	**Lathrop Reservoir State Park ®**	C-2	$	98	35'	6,410'	Yes	Yes	Colorado State Parks

Lathrop State Park, located 3 miles west of Walsenburg, is an ideal place to relax and camp in the pinon-juniper and high plains grasslands setting typical of south eastern Colorado. Approximately 15 southwest one can see the prominent Spanish Peaks. The early Indians named these peaks "Huajatolla" (Wa-ha-oy-a) and gave them this religious description. "Two breasts as round as woman's and all living things on earth-mankind, beasts and plants derive their substance from that source. The clouds are born there and without clouds there is no rain, and where no rainfalls we have no food and without food we must perish all".

Camping

Lathrop State Park's campgrounds can host up to 98 camping units in addition to the group camping facilities which are available by reservation. Sites in each campground can accommodate tents, campers or trailers. Pinion Campground (79 sites) features showers, laundry facilities and flush toilets. Yucca Campground (19 sites), popular for its nearness to the lake, is a less developed area. Rangers patrol the campground for your safety and to assure quiet

after 10 p.m. Holding tank dump stations are located within each campground.

Fishing

A fishing area designed to accommodate persons with disabilities is located at Martin Lake. Martin and Horseshoe Lakes are stocked with rainbow trout, channel catfish, bass, and crappie. Only the swim beach and boat ramps are closed to fishing, all other areas are open.

Other Activities

Water Sports, Hiking, and Wildlife,

Daily Fee/Annual Pass
For more information contact:
Lathrop State Park
70 County Road 502
Walsenburg, CO 81089
(719) 738-2376

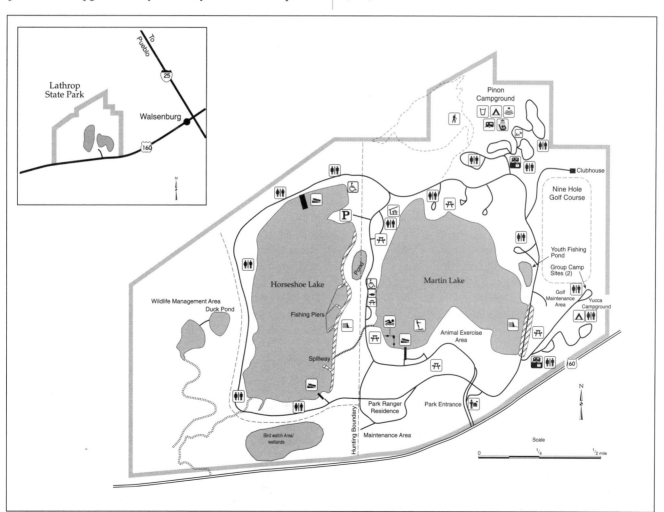

Map No.	Name	Map Loc.	Fee	No. of Units	Max. Length	Elev.	Toilets	Water	Agency
3	**Pueblo State Park ®**	A-3	$	401	45'	4,880'	Yes	Yes	Colorado State Parks

Pueblo State Park, located west of Pueblo, one of Colorado's most popular water sports area, lies in an area of contrast. The high plains around the reservoir appear to stretch endlessly eastward, while the Greenhorn, the Sangre de Cristo and Pikes Peak mountain ranges from a scenic alpine backdrop to the west. Buttes and limestone cliffs rim the irregular 60 mile shoreline (at maximum conservation pool). The Arkansas River feeds the 11 mile-long body of water. The park's low elevation, 4,900 feet allows for a mild climate and a year-round recreation resource. Massive Pueblo Dam (10,500 feet long by 200 feet high) is a major feature of the Frying Pan/Arkansas Project planned and built by US Bureau of Reclamation.

Camping
Pueblo Reservoirs 401 campsites accommodate tents, pick-up campers, motor home's and trailers. Arkansas Point, Prairie Ridge and Yucca Flats campgrounds feature modern toilets, showers, laundry facilities and electricity. Juniper Breaks and Kettle Creek offer primitive facilities featuring vault restrooms and no running water. Group camping facilities are also available. There are dump stations located in the campgrounds and are designated with a sign. See map page 133.

Wildlife
An abundance of wildlife make their home at Lake Pueblo: mule and whitetail deer, bobcats, coyotes, prairie dogs, badgers, cottontail and jack rabbits, beavers and several species of snakes, lizards, and hawks.

Fishing
There is a fishing pond in Rock Canyon, directly below the dam designed especially to accommodate disabled persons. It has a pier and a paved trail that surrounds the pond. Lake Pueblo is an excellent fishery for a variety of warm water species, wipers, and rainbow trout.

Swimming
Swimming is permitted only at the swim beach at Rock Canyon swim area. Facilities include a sand beach, grass picnic area, picnic tables, grills, showers, and water slide

Daily Fee/Annual Pass
For more information contact:
Pueblo State Park
640 Pueblo Reservoir Road
Pueblo, CO 81005 (719) 561-9320

Map No.	Name	Map Loc.	Fee	No. of Units	Max. Length	Elev.	Toilets	Water	Agency
4	**Trinidad State Park ®**	D-3	$	62	35'	6,225'	Yes	Yes	Colorado State Parks

Trinidad State Park, located southwest of Trinidad on Highway 12 lies in the Purgatorie River Valley, an area that has been a popular stopping point for travelers since the early Indian days. Archaeological finds in and around the park, like the tepee rings in the Carpios Ridge Picnic Area and the mountain branch of the historic Santa Fe Trail, which is now one of Trinidad's main streets, are reminders of that early history.

The dam which created Trinidad Lake, was built as an irrigation and flood control project by the US Army Corps of Engineers. The 2,300 acre park, including the 900 acre lake have been managed by the Colorado State Parks since 1980.

Facilities for the Disabled
The Carpios Ridge Campground and the picnic areas have reserved parking spaces and campsites adapted for persons with disabilities. Restrooms, showers, picnic tables and drinking fountains are also accessible.

Camping
The 62 site campgrounds can accommodate recreational vehicles, trailers or tents. Modern facilities include central-ly located water hydrants, a coin-operated laundry, electrical hook-ups, showers and flush toilets. Campsites may he reserved up to 120 days in advance. A holding dump station is located near the campground entrance.See map page 139.

Fishing
Fishing is permitted anywhere on the lake except in the boat launching and docking area. Species caught at Trinidad include: rainbow and brown trout, largemouth bass, channel catfish, walleye, crappie and bluegill.

Hiking/Nature Trails
Two short trails lead from a trailhead located in the campground/picnic area. Neither has water or restroom facilities.

Other Activities
Water Spoils, Hunting, and Wildlife.

Daily Fee/Annual Pass
For more information contact:
Trinidad State Park
32610 Hwy 12
Trinidad, CO 81082
(719) 846-6951

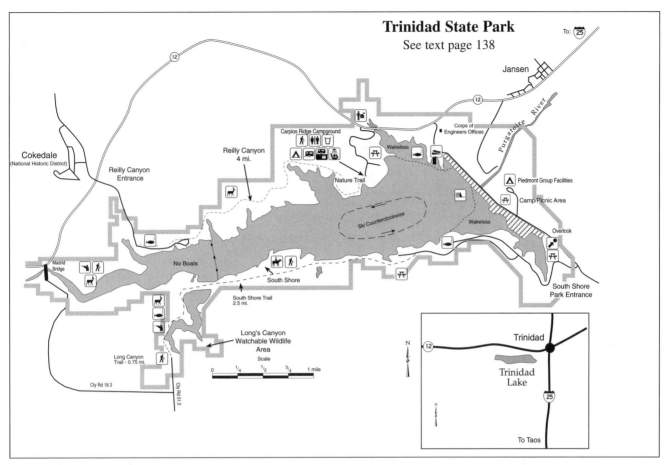

Trinidad State Park
See text page 138

Map No.	Campground Name	Map Loc.	Fee	No. of Units	Max. Length	Elev.	Toilets	Water	Agency
5	**DeWeese State Wildlife Area**	A-1	0	----	----	7,800'	Yes	No	Colorado Division of Wildlife

LOCATION: 5 mi NW of Westcliffe on Hwy 69, N on Copper Gulch Road to access. FACILITIES: Boat Ramp. ACTIVITIES: Fishing, Hunting, Water Sports. Camp in designated area. OPEN FOR USE: Year Round. CONTACT: Colorado Division of Wildlife SE Region (719) 227-5200. NOTE: 780 acre reservoir (CALL FIRST). 7.5' TOPOGRAPHIC MAP: Westcliffe.

Map No.	Campground Name	Map Loc.	Fee	No. of Units	Max. Length	Elev.	Toilets	Water	Agency
6	**Huerfano State Wildlife Area**	B-1	0	Dispersed	Open	7,600'	Yes	No	Colorado Division of Wildlife

LOCATION: 13 mi W of Gardner W on Cty Rd 580. (544 acres.) FACILITIES: Picnic Tables. ACTIVITIES: Fishing, Hunting, Hiking and Wildlife Observation. OPEN FOR USE: Year Round. CONTACT: Colorado Division of Wildlife SE Region (719) 227-5200. NOTE: On Huerfano River (CALL FIRST). 7.5' TOPOGRAPHIC MAP: Red Wing.

Map No.	Campground Name	Map Loc.	Fee	No. of Units	Max. Length	Elev.	Toilets	Water	Agency
7	**Middle Taylor Creek State Wildlife Area**	A-1	0	Dispersed	Open	9,000'	Yes	No	Colorado Division of Wildlife

LOCATION: From Westcliffe, go 8 mi W on Hermit Lakes Road to property. (486 acres.) FACILITIES: Picnic Tables. ACTIVITIES: Fishing, Hunting, Hiking, Wildlife Observation. OPEN FOR USE: Year Round. CONTACT: Colorado Division of Wildlife SE Region (719) 227-5200. NOTE: On Middle Taylor Creek near trails to Upper Lakes. 7.5' TOPOGRAPHIC MAP: Horn Peak (CALL FIRST).

Map No.	Campground Name	Map Loc.	Fee	No. of Units	Max. Length	Elev.	Toilets	Water	Agency
8	**Smith Reservoir State Wildlife Area**	C-1	$	Dispersed	Open	7,721'	Yes	No	Colorado Division of Wildlife

LOCATION: 1/2 mi W of Blanca on Hwy 160 to Airport Road, then 4 mi S to reservoir. FACILITIES: Boat Ramp, Dump Station. ACTIVITIES: Fishing, Hunting, Wildlife Observation. OPEN FOR USE: May through Oct. CONTACT: Colorado Division of Wildlife SW Region (970) 252-6000. NOTE: 700 acre reservoir. Rainbow and brook trout. 7.5' TOPOGRAPHIC MAP: Blanca.

Map No.	Campground Name	Map Loc.	Fee	No. of Units	Max. Length	Elev.	Toilets	Water	Agency
9	**Spanish Peaks State Wildlife Area**	D-3	0		Open	8,100'	Yes	Yes	Colorado Division of Wildlife

LOCATION: 18 mi SW of Aguilar on Cty Rd 41.7 to property. From Trinidad: 7 mi W on Hwy 12 to Cokedale, 18 mi N through Boncarbo, follow signs NW on county roads to property. FACILITIES: None. ACTIVITIES: Hunting, Hiking, Wildlife Observation. . OPEN FOR USE: Year Round. CONTACT: Colorado Division of Wildlife SE Region (719) 227-5200. *NOTE: Roads may not be passable in bad weather. Camp in designated areas only*
7.5' TOPOGRAPHIC MAPS: Weston, Gulmare.

Map No.	Campground Name	Map Loc.	Fee	No. of Units	Max. Length	Elev.	Toilets	Water	Agency
10	**Alvarado**	A-1	$	47	35'	9,000'	Yes	Yes	San Isabel National Forest

LOCATION: 3.5 mi S of Westcliffe on Hwy 69, 5.2 mi W on Cty Rd 140 and 1.3 mi SW on FDR 140 to campground. FACILITIES: Picnic Tables, Fire Rings, Pets OK. ACTIVITIES: Fishing, Hiking, Wildlife Observation. OPEN FOR USE: Mid-May through Oct. CONTACT: San Carlos Ranger District (719) 269-8500. NOTE: 2 mi to Venable Falls. Comanche Venable Loop TH, FDT 1345 & 1347. 7.5' TOPOGRAPHIC MAP: Horn Peak.

Map No.	Campground Name	Map Loc.	Fee	No. of Units	Max. Length	Elev.	Toilets	Water	Agency
11	**Bear Lake**	D-2	$	14	40'	10,500'	Yes	Yes	San Isabel National Forest

LOCATION: 15 mi S of La Veta on Hwy 12, 5.0 mi W on FDR 422. FACILITIES: Picnic Tables, Fire Rings, Pets OK. ACTIVITIES: Fishing, Hiking, Wildlife Observation. OPEN FOR USE: June through Oct. CONTACT: San Carlos Ranger District (719) 269-8500. NOTE: Campground near 8 acre Bear Lake (Short walk from campground). Indian Creek Trailhead, FDT 1300. 7.5' TOPOGRAPHIC MAP: Trinchera Peak.

Map No.	Campground Name	Map Loc.	Fee	No. of Units	Max. Length	Elev.	Toilets	Water	Agency
12	**Blue Lake**	D-2	$	15	40'	10,500'	Yes	Yes	San Isabel National Forest

LOCATION: 15 mi S of La Veta on Hwy 12, 4.0 mi W on FDR 422. FACILITIES: Picnic Tables, Fire Rings, Pets OK. ACTIVITIES: Fishing, Hiking, Wildlife Observation. OPEN FOR USE: June through Sept. CONTACT: San Carlos Ranger District (719) 269-8500. NOTE: Campground is near 5 acre Blue Lake (Short walk from CG) and trails. 7.5' TOPOGRAPHIC MAP: Trinchera Peak.

Map No.	Campground Name	Map Loc.	Fee	No. of Units	Max. Length	Elev.	Toilets	Water	Agency
13	**Davenport**	A-2	$	12	25'	8,500'	Yes	Yes	San Isabel National Forest

LOCATION: 25 mi S of Pueblo on I-25, 18 mi NW on Hwy 165, 1 mi E on FDR 382. FACILITIES: Picnic Tables, Fire Rings. ACTIVITIES: Fishing, Hiking, Wildlife Observation. OPEN FOR USE: Mid-May through Oct. CONTACT: San Carlos Ranger District (719) 269-8500. NOTE: Squirrel Creek Trailhead Trail #1384 is located in CT area. Hwy 165 is now designated as a Scenic By-Way. 7.5' TOPOGRAPHIC MAP: Saint Charles Peak.

Map No.	Campground Name	Map Loc.	Fee	No. of Units	Max. Length	Elev.	Toilets	Water	Agency
14	**Lake Isabelle**	B-2	$			8,600'	Yes	Yes	San Isabel National Forest
a.	La Vista ®			29	50'				
b.	Ponderosa Group ®			---	35'				
c.	Southside ®			8	40'				
d.	St. Charles ®			15	35'				
e.	Spruce Group ®			---	35'				

LOCATION: 25 mi S of Pueblo on I-25, 15 mi NW on Hwy 165 to Lake Isabel. FACILITIES: Picnic Tables, Fire Rings, Pets OK. ACTIVITIES: Fishing, Hiking. OPEN FOR USE: Mid-May through Oct. CONTACT: San Carlos Ranger District (719) 269-8500. NOTE: Reservations; Handicap Accessible; Near Charles River, Lake Isabel and several trails; Reservable sites and 2 group sites. Electrical hook-ups at La Vista CG, fee for day use. 7.5' TOPOGRAPHIC

Map No.	Campground Name	Map Loc.	Fee	No. of Units	Max. Length	Elev.	Toilets	Water	Agency
15	**Oak Creek**	A-1	0	15	25'	7,600'	Yes	Yes	San Isabel National Forest

LOCATION: 12.3 mi SW of Canon City on Cty Rd 143. FACILITIES: Picnic Tables, Pets OK. ACTIVITIES: Fishing, Hiking. OPEN FOR USE: Mid-May through Oct. CONTACT: San Carlos Ranger District (719) 269-8500. NOTE: Campground is near Oak Creek with trail to Lion Canyon. FDT 329. No trash service (pack it out) or drinking water. 7.5' TOPOGRAPHIC MAP: Curley Peak.

Map No.	Campground Name	Map Loc.	Fee	No. of Units	Max. Length	Elev.	Toilets	Water	Agency
16	**Ophir Creek**	A-2	$	31	40'	8,900'	Yes	Yes	San Isabel National Forest

LOCATION: 25 mi S of Pueblo on I-25, 20 mi NW on Hwy 165, 0.5 mi W on FDR 361. FACILITIES: Picnic Tables, Fire Rings, Pets OK. ACTIVITIES: Fishing, Hiking. OPEN FOR USE: Mid-May through late Oct. CONTACT: San Carlos Ranger District (719) 269-8500. NOTE: Campground near Middle Creek. 7.5' TOPOGRAPHIC MAP: Saint Charles Peak.

Map No.	Campground Name	Map Loc.	Fee	No. of Units	Max. Length	Elev.	Toilets	Water	Agency
17	**Purgatoire**	D-2	$	23	40'	9,800'	Yes	Yes	San Isabel National Forest

LOCATION: 23.2 mi S of La Veta on Hwy 12, 4.2 mi W on FDR 34. FACILITIES: Picnic Tables, Fire Rings, Pets OK. ACTIVITIES: Fishing, Hiking. OPEN FOR USE: May through Oct.. CONTACT: San Carlos Ranger District (719) 269-8500. NOTE: Campground is near the North Fork of the Purgatoire River. North Fork Trailhead, FDT 1309. 7.5' TOPO-GRAPHIC MAP: Cucharas Pass.

Map No.	Campground Name	Map Loc.	Fee	No. of Units	Max. Length	Elev.	Toilets	Water	Agency
18	**Monument Lake**	D-2	$	100	22'	9,000'	Yes	Yes	City of Trinidad

LOCATION: 36 mi W of Trinidad on Hwy 12. FACILITIES: Picnic Tables, Firewood, Pets OK ACTIVITIES: Fishing, Hiking, Boating. OPEN FOR USE: Year Round. CONTACT: Monument Lake Resort (719) 868-2226. 7.5' TOPOGRAPH-IC MAP: Stonewall. *19 full service hook-ups.*

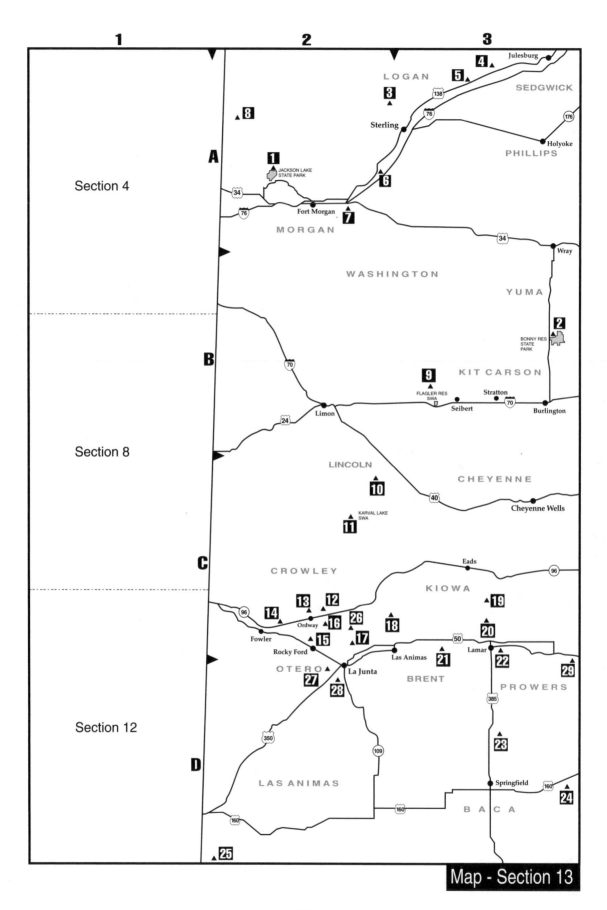

Section 4

Section 8

Section 12

Map - Section 13

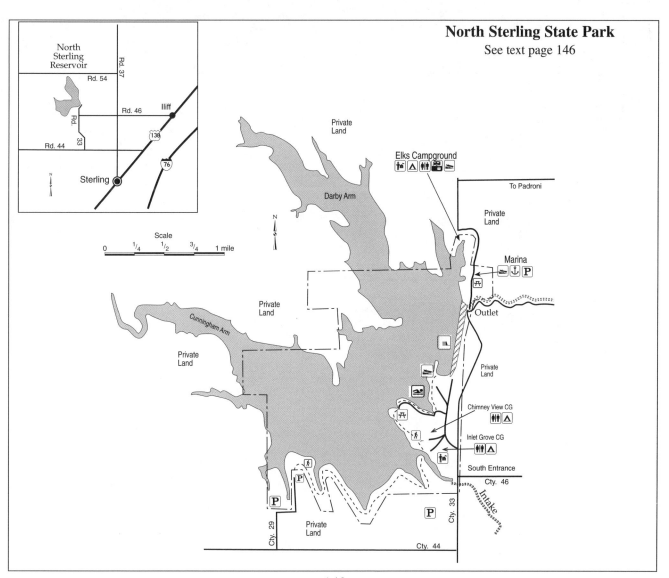

North Sterling State Park

See text page 146

Map No.	Name	Map Loc.	Fee	No. of Units	Max. Length	Elev.	Toilets	Water	Agency
1	**Jackson Lake State Park ®**	A-2	$	262	40'	4,438'	Yes	Yes	Colorado state Parks

Once known primarily for the hunting around its banks, Jackson Lake State Park is now one of Colorado's finest sports sites. Located near Ft. Morgan east of Goodrich on County Road 3, the area is famed for its shore line camping and the large, warm water reservoir with its sandy bottom and beaches. For fun in the sun and unlimited recreational opportunities, Jackson Lake is the place.

Besides providing unlimited recreation, the 2,700 surface-acre lake is an important irrigation reservoir which holds water for the thousands of acres of farm land to the south and the east. The reservoir was built during the turn of the century and incorporates an existing lake. The park has a land area of 440 acres.

Camping
Jackson Lake State Recreation Area has over 180 campsites available for your enjoyment. Most can accommodate campers or trailers and tents. Primitive walk-in and boat-in sites are also obtainable. Facilities include showers, toilets and drinking water. Individual hook-ups are not available at the park.

Wildlife
An abundance of wildlife can be observed and photographed in the park. The list includes: pelicans, eagles, hawks, heron, deer, coyote, waterfowl and numerous shore birds.

Fishing
Jackson Lake is home to walleye, bass, catfish, perch, crappie and drum. Fishing is prohibited in Jackson Lake each year during migratory waterfowl season and from the swim beaches year-round.

Other Activities
Ice boating, ice fishing and ice skating.

Daily Fee/Annual Pass
For more information contact:
Jackson Lake State Park
26363 Road 3
Orchard, CO 80649
(970) 645-2551

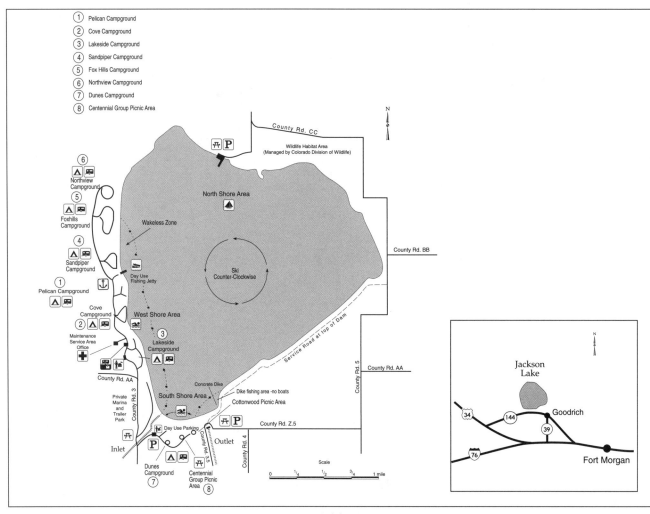

Map No.	Name	Map Loc.	Fee	No. of Units	Max. Length	Elev.	Toilets	Water	Agency
2	**Bonny State Park** ®	B-3	$	190	35'	3,670'	Yes	Yes	Colorado State Parks

Bonny State Park, located about 20 miles north of Burlington on Highway 385, is a recreational oasis in the broad valley of the South Fork of the Republican River, which offers a variety of year round recreational opportunities. Willow trees and large cottonwoods are characteristic of the 3,700 foot elevation and offer colorful vistas in the fall as well as excellent opportunities to observe a variety of birds and animals.

Camping
Bonny State Recreation Area has four campgrounds with 190 camp sites for your enjoyment. Sites within each campground can accommodate tents, motor homes, pickup campers or trailers. The park has no hookups for electricity or water, although water is available in the campgrounds. Damp stations are located at Foster Grove and Wagon Wheel Campgrounds.

Wildlife
Some 7,000 birds representing 250 species have been known to rest at Bonny State Recreation Area during migrations, while some 30 to 50 thousand birds winter in the area.

Fishing
One of the state's finest warm water fisheries, Bonny Reservoir has a thriving population of walleye, northern pike, freshwater drum, white bass, large and smallmouth bass, crappie, bluegill, channel catfish and wipers. A fish cleaning station is located near Wagon Wheel Campground.

Swimming
Two swimming areas are provided at Bonny. A small shallow area is located below the marina store and is within easy walking distance of Wagon Wheel Campground A second, larger and deeper, area is provided at West Beach.

Other Activities
Ice boating, ice fishing and ice skating.

Daily Fee/Annual Pass
For more information contact:
Bonny State Park
30010 County Rd 3
Idalia, CO 80735
(970) 354-7306.

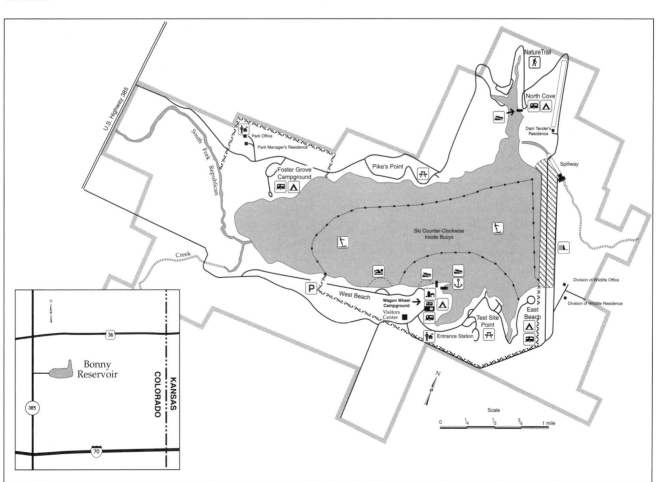

Map No.	Campground Name	Map Loc.	Fee	No. of Units	Max. Length	Elev.	Toilets	Water	Agency
3	**North Sterling State Park ®**	A-2	$	50	40'	4,069'	Yes	Yes	Colorado State Parks

Built during the turn of the century, the reservoir serves as an important irrigation facility along the lower South Platte River Valley. North Sterling reservoir is a boaters paradise, offering a 3,000 acre lake with an interesting array of coves and fingers to explore. An additional 1000 acres of land incorporates modern facilities and support a wide variety of recreational activities when the park is fully developed.

Camping

The Elks Campground can accommodate recreational vehicles, trailers or tents. Electrical hookups, showers, laundry, and a dump station located on the east side of County Road 33, across from Balanced Rock Picnic Area. Dispersed camping is permitted south of the dam, by permit only, in areas not posted against such use. See map page 143.

Other Activities

Warm water fishing, boating, water skiing. Open year around.

Wildlife

A wide variety of wildlife can be found in the area including deer, eagles, pelicans, coyotes, rabbits, and many species of waterfowl and shore birds.

See map page 143.

Daily Fee/Annual Pass
North Sterling Reservoir State Park
24005 County road 330
Sterling, CO 80751
(970) 522-3657

Map No.	Campground Name	Map Loc.	Fee	No. of Units	Max. Length	Elev.	Toilets	Water	Agency
4	**Jumbo Reservoir State Wildlife Area**	A-3	0	Dispersed	Open	3,700'	Yes	Yes	Colorado Division of Wildlife

LOCATION: From I-76 Red Lion exit (#155) 3 mi N to Hwy 138, 1 mi NE to Cty Rd 95, 2 mi N. (1,703 acres.) FACILITIES: Boat ramp. ACTIVITIES: Fishing, Hiking, Hunting. OPEN FOR USE: Year Round. CONTACT: Colorado Division of Wildlife NE Region (970) 472-4300. NOTE: 1600 acre reservoir - Crappie, Bass, Walleye, Largemouth Bass, Carp, Channel Catfish.

Map No.	Campground Name	Map Loc.	Fee	No. of Units	Max. Length	Elev.	Toilets	Water	Agency
5	**Tamarack Ranch State Wildlife Area**	A-3	0		Open	3,700'	Yes	Yes	Colorado Division of Wildlife

LOCATION: I-76 to Crook exit (#149) 1/2 mi N on Hwy 55. FACILITIES: None. ACTIVITIES: Fishing, Hiking. OPEN FOR USE: Year Round. CONTACT: Colorado Division of Wildlife NE Region (970) 472-4300. NOTE: Limited camping. Reservation Hunting. *Designated camping.*

Map No.	Campground Name	Map Loc.	Fee	No. of Units	Max. Length	Elev.	Toilets	Water	Agency
6	**Prewitt Reservoir State Wildlife Area**	A-2	0		Open	4,100'	Yes	No	Colorado Division of Wildlife

LOCATION: 15 mi NE of Brush on Hwy 6, 1 mi E on Wildlife Management Area access Rd.. FACILITIES: Picnic Tables, Boat Ramp, Pets OK. ACTIVITIES: Fishing, Hiking, Hunting in fall. OPEN FOR USE: Year Round. CONTACT: Colorado Division of Wildlife NE Region (970) 472-4300. NOTE: 2500 acre Prewitt Reservoir has warm water fishing. *Designated camping.*

Map No.	Campground Name	Map Loc.	Fee	No. of Units	Max. Length	Elev.	Toilets	Water	Agency
7	**Brush Memorial**	A-2	$	53	Open	4,100'	Yes	Yes	City of Brush

LOCATION: 2 mi S of Brush on Hwy 34 to Clayton Street, 4 blocks S. FACILITIES: Electrical Hookups, Picnic Tables, Dump Station, Showers, Playground, Swimming Pool, Wading Pool, Pets OK. ACTIVITIES: Camping. OPEN FOR USE: May through late Oct. CONTACT: (970) 842-5001. NOTE: A city park with golf course and tennis courts. First Night Free! $10.00/ day after first night - 7 day max. stay. Friendly place to visit.

Map No.	Campground Name	Map Loc.	Fee	No. of Units	Max. Length	Elev.	Toilets	Water	Agency
8	**Crow Valley Recreation Area**	A-2	$	10	35'	4,800'	Yes	Yes	Arapaho/Roosevelt National Forest

LOCATION: 1/2 mi W of Briggsdale on Hwy 14, 1/2 mi N on Cty Rd 77. FACILITIES: Picnic Tables, Pets OK. ACTIVITIES: Camping, Wildlife Viewing, Picnicking, Hiking. OPEN FOR USE: Year-Round most years. CONTACT: Pawnee National Grassland (970) 353-5004. NOTE: Camp is set in Pawnee National Grasslands. The only campground in area. Call for conditions. ***ADJACENT TO STEWART J. ADAMS GROUP & CROW VALLEY GROUP CAMPGROUNDS ®.*** 　♿

Map No.	Campground Name	Map Loc.	Fee	No. of Units	Max. Length	Elev.	Toilets	Water	Agency
9	**Flagler Reservoir State Wildlife Area**	B-3	0	Dispersed	Open	4,700'	Yes	No	Colorado Division of Wildlife

LOCATION: 5 mi E of Flagler on Cty Rd 4. (400 acres.) FACILITIES: Boat Ramp. ACTIVITIES: Fishing, Hiking, Power Boating, Water Skiing, Hunting. OPEN FOR USE: Year Round. CONTACT: Colorado Division of Wildlife SE Region (719) 227-5200. NOTE: Water level fluctuates - 160 acres when full. Warm water fish stocked.

Map No.	Campground Name	Map Loc.	Fee	No. of Units	Max. Length	Elev.	Toilets	Water	Agency
10	**Hugo State Wildlife Area**	C-2	0	Dispersed	Open	5,000'	Yes	No	Colorado Division of Wildlife

LOCATION: 12 mi S of Hugo on Cty Rd 109 to Cty Rd 2G, 2.5 mi E to Cty Rd 21, 1 mi E. (2,240 acres.) FACILITIES: None. ACTIVITIES: Fishing, Hiking, Hunting. OPEN FOR USE: Year Round. CONTACT: Colorado Division of Wildlife SE Region (719) 227-5200. NOTE: 19 ponds stocked with largemouth Bass, Channel Catfish, Bluegill and Rainbow Trout.

Map No.	Campground Name	Map Loc.	Fee	No. of Units	Max. Length	Elev.	Toilets	Water	Agency
11	**Karval Reservoir State Wildlife Area**	C-2	0	Dispersed	Open	4,700'	Yes	No	Colorado Division of Wildlife

LOCATION: From junction of Hwy 94 & Cty Rd 109, go S 10 mi on Cty Rd 109. FACILITIES: Shade Shelters. ACTIVITIES: Fishing, Hunting, Hiking. OPEN FOR USE: Year Round. CONTACT: Colorado Division of Wildlife SE Region (719) 227-5200. NOTE: 25 acres, stocked with Largemouth Bass, Channel Catfish, Bluegill - *Wakeless Boating*.

Map No.	Campground Name	Map Loc.	Fee	No. of Units	Max. Length	Elev.	Toilets	Water	Agency
12	**Lake Henry State Wildlife Area**	C-2	0	Dispersed	Open	4,390'	Yes	No	Colorado Division of Wildlife

LOCATION: 3 mi E of Ordway on Hwy 96, 1 mi N on Cty Rd 20. (1,350 acres.) FACILITIES: Boat Ramps. ACTIVITIES: Fishing, Hiking, Hunting, Power Boating, Sail Boating, Sail Surfing, Waterskiing. OPEN FOR USE: Year Round. CONTACT: Colorado Division of Wildlife SE Region (719) 227-5200. NOTE: 1,125 acre lake - shallow, subject to draw down for irrigation - Channel catfish, walleye, largemouth bass. Call for conditions.

Map No.	Campground Name	Map Loc.	Fee	No. of Units	Max. Length	Elev.	Toilets	Water	Agency
13	**Ordway Reservoir State Wildlife Area**	C-2	0	Dispersed	Open	4,300'	Yes	No	Colorado Division of Wildlife

LOCATION: 2 mi N of Ordway on Hwy 71. FACILITIES:None. ACTIVITIES: Fishing, Hiking. OPEN FOR USE: year round. CONTACT: Colorado Division of Wildlife SE Region (719) 227-5200. NOTE: 28 acre Reservoir - Rainbow and warm water fishing, put and take - No Boating (CALL FIRST).

Map No.	Campground Name	Map Loc.	Fee	No. of Units	Max. Length	Elev.	Toilets	Water	Agency
14	**Olney Springs State Wildlife Area**	C-2	0	Dispersed	Open	4,340'	Yes	No	Colorado Division of Wildlife

LOCATION: 1 mi NW of Olney Springs on Cty Rd 7. (8 acres.) FACILITIES: None. ACTIVITIES: Fishing, Hiking. OPEN FOR USE: Year Round. CONTACT: Colorado Division of Wildlife SE Region (719) 227-5200. NOTE: 6 acre reservoir, largemouth bass, channel catfish - *Primitive campsites.*

Map No.	Campground Name	Map Loc.	Fee	No. of Units	Max. Length	Elev.	Toilets	Water	Agency
15	**McClelland State Wildlife Area**	C-2	0	Dispersed	Open	4,200'	Yes	No	Colorado Division of Wildlife

LOCATION: 2 mi NW of Rocky Ford on Cty Rd 266, cross bridge, turn E for 1.75 mi. on Cty. Road 80.5 1.25 miles further east to 662 acre McClelland Tract. FACILITIES: None ACTIVITIES: Hiking, Hunting. OPEN FOR USE: Year Round. CONTACT: Colorado Division of Wildlife SE Region (719) 227-5200. NOTE: Warm water fishing

Map No.	Campground Name	Map Loc.	Fee	No. of Units	Max. Length	Elev.	Toilets	Water	Agency
16	**Meredith Reservoir State Wildlife Area**	C-2	0	Dispersed	Open	4,220'	Yes	No	Colorado Division of Wildlife

LOCATION: 3 mi E of Ordway on Cty Rd 21. FACILITIES: Boat Ramps. ACTIVITIES: Fishing, Hiking, Hunting, Power Boating, Sail Boarding, Waterskiing. OPEN FOR USE: Year Round. CONTACT: Colorado Division of Wildlife SE Region (719) 227-5200. NOTE: 3200 acre - Shallow (15 feet) Warm water fishing.

Map No.	Campground Name	Map Loc.	Fee	No. of Units	Max. Length	Elev.	Toilets	Water	Agency
17	**Holbrook Reservoir State Wildlife Area**	C-2	0	Dispersed	Open	4,160'	Yes	No	Colorado Division of Wildlife

LOCATION: 3 mi N of Swink on Cty Rd 245, 1/2 mi E on Cty Rd FF. (670 acres.) FACILITIES: Boat Ramps. ACTIVITIES: Fishing, Hiking, Hunting, Power Boating, Sail Boating, Sail Surfing, Waterskiing. OPEN FOR USE: Year Round. CONTACT: Colorado Division of Wildlife SE Region (719) 227-5200. NOTE: One of the few DOW areas that has a decent campground. Shaded pull through sites. Warm water fishing - lake subject to summer draw down - fish early.

Map No.	Campground Name	Map Loc.	Fee	No. of Units	Max. Length	Elev.	Toilets	Water	Agency
18	**Adobe Creek Res State Wildlife Area**	C-2	0	Dispersed	Open	4,128'	Yes	No	Colorado Division of Wildlife

LOCATION: 12 mi N of Las Animas on Cty Rd 10. FACILITIES: Boat Ramps. ACTIVITIES: Fishing, Hiking, Boating, Sail Boating, Sail Surfing, Water Skiing, Hunting. OPEN FOR USE: Year Round CONTACT: Colorado Division of Wildlife SE Region (719) 227-5200. NOTE: 1,200 acre Reservoir, warm water fishing, open, little shade. (CALL FIRST).

Map No.	Campground Name	Map Loc.	Fee	No. of Units	Max. Length	Elev.	Toilets	Water	Agency
19	**Queens State Wildlife Area**	C-3	0	Dispersed	Open	3,800'	Yes	No	Colorado Division of Wildlife

LOCATION: From Eads, 15 mi S on Hwy 287 to Cty Rd C, 3.5 mi E to Upper Queens. FACILITIES: Boat Ramp. ACTIVITIES: Fishing, Boating, Sail Boating, Sail Surfing, Water Skiing. OPEN FOR USE: Year Round. CONTACT: Colorado Division of Wildlife SE Region (719) 227-5200. NOTE: Contains 5 Reservoirs Upper, Lower, Queens, Nee Grande, Nee No she - Warm water fishing - Water levels vary - Irrigation lakes.

Map No.	Campground Name	Map Loc.	Fee	No. of Units	Max. Length	Elev.	Toilets	Water	Agency
20	**Thurston Reservoir State Wildlife Area**	C-3	$	Dispersed	Open	4,200'	Yes	No	Colorado Division of Wildlife

LOCATION: 9 mi N of Lamar on Hwy 196, 1 mi W on Cty Rd. (173 acres.) FACILITIES: Boat Ramps. ACTIVITIES: Fishing, Power Boating, Sail Boating, Sail Surfing, Water Skiing, Hunting. OPEN FOR USE: Year Round. CONTACT: Colorado Division of Wildlife SE Region (719) 227-5200. NOTE: 173 acre reservoir stocked with tiger muskie and channel catfish - difficult shore fishing. (CALL FIRST.)

Map No.	Campground Name	Map Loc.	Fee	No. of Units	Max. Length	Elev.	Toilets	Water	Agency
21	**John Martin Res. State Park**	C-3	$	65	40'	3,851'	Yes	Yes	Colorado State Park

LOCATION: 4 mi S of Hasty on Cty Rd 24. FACILITIES: Picnic Tables, Dump Station, Playground, Swimming, Wading Pool, Pets OK. ACTIVITIES: Fishing, Hiking, Sailing. OPEN FOR USE: Early April through late Oct. CONTACT: Corp of Engineers (719) 336-3476. NOTE: Handicap Accessible; Camp is near John Martin Dam, First class campground, 3,200 acre John Martin Reservoir - Great warm water fishing; NEW STATE PARK 2001 - CALL STATE PARKS OFFICE. ♿ (719) 383-2253.

Map No.	Campground Name	Map Loc.	Fee	No. of Units	Max. Length	Elev.	Toilets	Water	Agency
22	**Mike Higbee State Wildlife Area**	C-3	0	Dispersed	Open	4,100'	Yes	No	Colorado Division of Wildlife

LOCATION: 4 mi E of Lamar on Hwy 50. (876 acres.) FACILITIES: None. ACTIVITIES: Fishing, Hiking, Archery/ Rifle Range, Hunting. OPEN FOR USE: Year Round. CONTACT: Colorado Division of Wildlife SE Region (719) 227-5200. Located on Arkansas River - Self Contained units recommended.

Map No.	Campground Name	Map Loc.	Fee	No. of Units	Max. Length	Elev.	Toilets	Water	Agency
23	**Two Buttes Res State Wildlife Area**	D-3	0	Dispersed	Open	4,300'	Yes	Yes	Colorado Division of Wildlife

LOCATION: 17 mi N of Springfield on US 287/ 385, 3 mi E on access road. FACILITIES: Picnic tables, Dump Station, Boat ramp & Docks, Pets OK. ACTIVITIES: Fishing, Hiking, rock climbing. OPEN FOR USE: Year Round. CONTACT: Colorado Division of Wildlife SE Region (719) 227-5200. NOTE:1,200 acre reservoir warm water fishing. *Note: reservoir may be dry.*

Map No.	Campground Name	Map Loc.	Fee	No. of Units	Max. Length	Elev.	Toilets	Water	Agency
24	Burchfield State Wildlife Area	D-3	0	Dispersed	Open	3,700'	Yes	No	Colorado Division of Wildlife

LOCATION: From Walsh go 11 mi E on Cty Rd DD to property. (178 acres.) FACILITIES: None. ACTIVITIES: Wildlife observation, photography. OPEN FOR USE: May through late Oct. CONTACT: Colorado Division of Wildlife SE Region (719) 227-5200.

Map No.	Campground Name	Map Loc.	Fee	No. of Units	Max. Length	Elev.	Toilets	Water	Agency
25	Lake Dorothey State Wildlife Area	D-2	0	Dispersed	Open	7,600'	Yes	No	Colorado Division of Wildlife

LOCATION: 7 mi NE of Raton, New Mexico on Hwy 72 & 526, 12 mi N up Sugarite Canyon. (4,804 acres.) FACILITIES: None. ACTIVITIES: Fishing, Hiking, Hunting. OPEN FOR USE: Year Round. CONTACT: Colorado Division of Wildlife SE Region (719) 227-5200. NOTE: Rainbow Trout fishing, 4800 acre state wildlife area and 4 acre lake (Artificial lures and flies only). *No camping within 200 yards of lake, 100 yards from stream except in designated areas.*

Map No.	Campground Name	Map Loc.	Fee	No. of Units	Max. Length	Elev.	Toilets	Water	Agency
26	Horse Creek Res. State Wildlife Area	C-2	0	Dispersed	Open	4,000'	Yes	No	Colorado Division of Wildlife

LOCATION: 8 mi N of La Junta on Hwy 109 to Cheraw, 2 mi E on Cty Rd 115 to Cty Rd 33, 7 mi N to reservoir. (2,603 acres.) FACILITIES: Boat Ramps. ACTIVITIES: Fishing, Sail Boating, Power Boating, Hunting. OPEN FOR USE: Year Round. CONTACT: Colorado Division of Wildlife SE Region (719) 227-5200. NOTE: (CALL FIRST).

Map No.	Campground Name	Map Loc.	Fee	No. of Units	Max. Length	Elev.	Toilets	Water	Agency
27	Rocky Ford State Wildlife Area	D-2	0	Dispersed	Open	4,000'	Yes	No	Colorado Division of Wildlife

LOCATION: 2 mi NE of Rocky Ford on Hwy 266, cross river bridge, turn E on Cty Rd 80.5. (550 acres.) FACILITIES: None. ACTIVITIES: Hunting, Hiking, Wildlife Observation, Fishing. OPEN FOR USE: Year Round. CONTACT: Colorado Division of Wildlife SE Region (719) 227-5200. NOTE: Fires Prohibited.

Map No.	Campground Name	Map Loc.	Fee	No. of Units	Max. Length	Elev.	Toilets	Water	Agency
28	Timpas Creek State Wildlife Area	D-2	0	Dispersed	Open	4,000'	Yes	No	Colorado Division of Wildlife

LOCATION: 4 mi S of Rocky Ford on Hwy 71 to Hwy 10, 2 mi E across Timpas Creek Bridge, 1 mi S on Cty Rd 21, 1 mi W on Cty Rd Z to property. (141 acres.) FACILITIES: None. ACTIVITIES: Fishing, hiking, Hunting. OPEN FOR USE: Year Round. CONTACT: Colorado Division of Wildlife SE Region (719) 227-5200. NOTE: (CALL FIRST).

Map No.	Campground Name	Map Loc.	Fee	No. of Units	Max. Length	Elev.	Toilets	Water	Agency
29	Arkansas River State Wildlife Area	D-3	0	Dispersed	Open	3,350'	Yes	No	Colorado Division of Wildlife

LOCATION: 4 mi E of Holly on Hwy 50 to Cty Rd 39, 3/4 mi S across canal 1/2 mi W to Property. (98 acres.) FACILITIES: None. ACTIVITIES: Fishing, Hiking, Hunting. OPEN FOR USE: Year Round. CONTACT: Colorado Division of Wildlife SE Region (719) 227-5200 (CALL FIRST).

ADOBE CRK. RES. SWA	12 mi N of Las Animas on Cty Rd 10	DOW	SE	DSP	0	4,128	148
ALAMOSA	12 mi S of Monte Vista Hwy I5, 18 mi W	RGNF	CPRD	10	0	8,700	128
ALMA SWA	1.5 mi N of Alma on Hwy 9	DOW	SE	DSP	0	10,000	73
ALMONT	11 mi N of Gunnison	GNF	TRRD	10	$	8,000	64
ALTA LAKES	8 mi W of Telluride	UNF	NRD	DSP	0	11,216	116
ALVARADO	9 mi SW of Westcliffe	SINF	SCRD	47	$	9,000	140
AMPHITHEATER ®	1 mi SE of Ouray	UNF	ORD	30	$	8,400	116
ANGEL OF SHAVANO	10 mi NW of Poncha Springs	SINF	SRD	20	$	9,200	74
ANGEL OF SHAVANO GRP ®	10 mi NW of Poncha Springs	SINF	SRD	—	$	9,200	74
ANSEL WATROUS*	25 mi NW of Fort Collins	ARNF	CLRD	19	$	5,800	44
ANTERO RESERVOIR SWA	5 mi SW of Hartsel on Hwy 24	DOW	SE	DSP	0	9,000	73
ARAPAHO BAY, ARAP NRA ®*	E arm of Lake Granby	ARNF	SURD	84	$	8,400	30
ARKANSAS RIVER SWA	E of Holly 4 mi on Hwy 50, 1 mi SE	DOW	SE	DSP	0	3,350	150
ASPEN	21 mi SE of Walden	RNF	PWRD	7	$	8,900	26
ASPEN	5 mi NW of Jefferson	PNF	SKRD	12	$	9,900	74
ASPEN GLADE ®	18 mi W of Antonito	RGNF	CPRD	34	$	8,500	129
ASPEN GLEN	2 mi N of Chambers Lake	ARNF	CLRD	8	$	9,000	32
ASPENGLEN	Rocky Mountain National Park	NPS	RMNP	54	$	8,230	22
AVALANCHE CREEK	1.3 mi SE of Carbondale	WRNF	SORD	13	$	7,400	64

B

BABY DOE ®	E side of Turquoise Res	SINF	LRD	50	$	9,900	85
BARBOUR PONDS, STATE P*	W of I-25 2 mi on Hwy 119	DPOR	NO	60	$	5,000	37
BEAR CREEK LAKE PARK	Morrison Rd @ C470	COL	-	52	$	5,775	95
BEAR LAKE	20 mi S of LaVeta	SINF	SCRD	14	$	10,500	140
BEAR LAKE	13 mi SW of Yampa	RNF	YRD	29	$	9,600	13
BEAR RIVER DISPERSED	13 mi SW of Yampa	RNF	YRD	32	$	9,600	13
BEAVER CREEK RES (Lower)	2 mi SW of So. Fork, to FDR 360, 3 mi	RGNF	DNRD	19	$	8,400	129
BEAVER LAKE	40 mi SW of Montrose	UNF	ORD	11	$	8,800	116
BELLAIRE LAKE*	27 mi W of Livermore	ARNF	CLRD	26	$	8,365	26
BELLE OF COLORADO	E side Turquoise Res	SINF	LRD	19	$	9,900	85
BIG BEND	10 mi W of Rustic	ARNF	CLRD	9	$	7,700	32
BIG BLUE	55 mi SW of Gunnison	GNF	CERD	11	$	9,600	117
BIG CIMARRON	40 mi SE of Montrose	UNF	ORD	10	$	8,600	117
BIG CREEK	E of Grand Junction, Grand Mesa	GMNF	GJRD	26	0	10,100	52
BIG CREEK LAKE ®	6 mi S of Pearl on FDR 600	RNF	PWRD	54	$	8,997	27
BIG DOMINGUEZ	29 mi S of Grand Junction	BLM	GJ	9	$	7,500	51
BIG MEADOWS RES ®	11 mi SW of So. Fork, 2 mi W to Res	RGNF	DNRD	53	$	9,200	117
BIG SOUTH*	4 mi N of Chambers Lake	ARNF	CLRD	4	$	8,440	32
BIG TURKEY	19 mi NW of Woodland Park	PNF	SPRD	10	$	8,000	96
BLACKTAIL CREEK	13 mi E of Toponas	RNF	YRD	8	$	9,100	27
BLANCO RIVER	15 mi SE of Pagosa Springs	SJNF	PARD	6	$	7,200	117
BLISS SWA	45 mi NW of LaPorte	DOW	NE	DSP	0	7,800	24
BLODGETT	3.5 mi SW of Redcliffe	WRNF	HCRD	6	$	8,900	74
BLUE LAKE	18 mi S of LaVeta	SINF	SCRD	15	$	10,500	140
BLUE MOUNTAIN*	2 mi SW of Lake George	PNF	SKRD	21	$	8,200	96
BLUE RIVER	9 mi NW of Dillon	WRNF	DRD	21	$	8,400	27
BLUE SPRUCE	I5 mi NE of Rifle	COR	---	30	0	7,250	17
BOGAN FLATS ®	23 mi S of Carbondale	WRNF	SORD	37	$	7,600	65
BOGAN PLATS GROUP ®	23 mi S of Carbondale	WRNF	SORD	—	$	7,600	65
BONNY RES, STATE P	N of Burlington 23 mi	DPOR	SO	200	$	3,670	145
BOOTLEG	6 mi W of Nathrop	SINF	SRD	6	$	8,400	74
BOYD LAKE STATE PARK	N of Loveland on Cty Rd 11C	DPOR	NO	148	$	4,958	38
BRADFIELD (Riverine)	6 mi E of Cahone	BLM	SJ	22	$	6,400	108
BRIDGE	20 mi NW of Pagosa Springs	SJNF	PARD	19	$	7,800	117
BRISTOL HEAD	28 mi W of Creede	RGNF	CRRD	16	$	9,500	117
BROWNS PARK*	20 mi N of Chambers Lake	ARNF	CLRD	28	$	8,400	27
BROWNS PARK NWR	59 mi NW of Maybell on Hwy 3I8	PAWS	---	DSP	0	5,700	7
BROWNS PARK SWA	53 mi NW of Maybell	DOW	NW	DSP	0	8,100	7
BRUSH MEMORIAL	City of Brush	COB		24	$	4,100	146
BUCKINGHAM	10 mi NW of Nederland	BMP	----	10	$	10,061	44
BUCKS	50 mi E of Meeker	WRNF	BLRD	10	$	9,750	17
BUFFALO ®*	0.5 mi SE of Buffalo Creek	PNF	SPRD	41	$	7,400	96
BUFFALO PASS	30 mi NW of Saguache	RGNF	SARD	24	$	9,000	129
BUFFALO SPRINGS*	7 mi N of Antero Junction	PNF	SKRD	17	$	9,000	75
BURCHFIELD SWA	11 E of Walsh on Cty Rd DD	DOW	SE	DSP	0	3,700	150
BURNING BEAR	5.2 mi NW of Grant	PNF	SPRD	13	$	9,500	75
BURRO BRIDGE	35 mi NE of Dolores	SJNF	DMRD	14	$	9,000	109
BYERS CREEK	7 mi SW of Fraser	ARNF	SURD	6	$	9,360	27

C

Name	Location	Forest	District	Sites	Fee	Elev.	Page
CABIN CANYON	35 mi N of Cortez	SJNF	DMRD	11	$	6,500	109
CAMP DICK	7 mi N of Ward on Hwy 72, W 1 mi	ARNF	BRD	41	$	8,650'	42
CAMP HALE GRP(East Fork)®	17 mi NW of Leadville	WRNF	HCRD	---	$	9,200	75
CAMP HALE MEMORIAL	17 mi NW of Leadville	WRNF	HCRD	21	$	9,200	75
CARP LAKE (COBBETT)	E of Grand Junction, Grand Mesa	GMNF	GJRD	20	$	10,300	52
CARTER LAKE	W of Loveland	LCP	---	190	$	5,760	40
CASCADE ®	9 mi W of Nathrop	SINF	SRD	23	$	9,000	75
CATARACT CREEK	2 mi SW of Green Mountain Res	WRNF	DRD	4	0	8,600	27
CATHEDRAL	20 mi NW of Del Norte	RGNF	DNRD	33	0	9,400	129
CAYTON	6 mi NE of Rico	SJNF	DMRD	27	$	9,400	109
CEBOLLA	18 mi E of Lake City	GNF	CERD	5	$	9,200	118
CEBOLLA CREEK (Riverine)	32 mi SW of Gunnison	BLM	GUN	3	0	9,500	116
CEMENT CREEK	25 mi NE of Gunnison	GNF	TRRD	13	$	9,000	65
CHALK LAKE ®	8 mi S of Nathrop	SINF	SRD	21	$	8,700	75
CHAMBERS LAKE ®*	60 mi W of LaPorte	ARNF	CLRD	52	$	9,200	28
CHAPMAN ®*	25 mi E of Basalt	WRNF	SORD	84	$	8,800	75
CHAPMAN GROUP ®	25 mi E of Basalt	WRNF	SORD	---	$	8,800	75
CHAPMAN RESERVOIR	11 mi SW of Phippsburg	RNF	YRD	12	$	9,400	13
CHATFIELD RES. STATE P	Near Hwy 121 & C470 , Lakewood	DPOR	METR	153	$	5,430	92
CHEROKEE PARK SWA	8 mi W of Red Feathers Lakes	DOW	NE	DSP	0	7,700	41
CHERRY CREEK RES. ST. P	SW Denver on Parker Rd	DPOR	METR	500	$	5,600	93
CHRIS PARK GROUP ®	18 mi N of Durango	SJNF	CRD	---	$	8,000	118
CHUKAR TRAILHEAD	17 mi N of Montrose	BLM	UNC	4	0	5,800	64
CIMARRON, CUR. RECREA*	S side of Res @ Cimarron on Hwy 50	NPS	CUR	22	$	6,906	59
CIMARRONA	25 mi NW of Pagosa Springs	SJNF	PARD	21	$	8,400	118
CLEAR LAKE*	4 mi S of Georgetown	ARNF	CCRD	8	$	10.000	76
COALDALE	4 mi S of Coaldale	SINF	SRD	11	$	8.500	76
COBBETT (CARP LAKE)	E of Grand Junction, Grand Mesa	GMNF	GJRD	20	$	10,300	52
COFFEE POT SPRING	40 mi NE of Glenwood Springs	WRNF	ERD	9	0	9,000	65
COKE OVEN SWA	30 mi E of Basalt	DOW	NW	DSP	0	8,800	73
COLD SPRING	27 mi NE of Gunnison	GNF	TRRD	6	$	9,000	76
COLD SPRINGS	7 mi SW of Yampa	RNF	YRD	5	$	10,400	13
COLD SPRINGS ®*	5 mi N of Black Hawk	ARNF	CCRD	38	$	9,200	42
COLLEGIATE PEAKS ®	11 mi W of Buena Vista	SINF	SRD	56	$	9,800	76
COLORADO*	7 mi N of Woodland Park	PNF	PPRD	81	$	7,800	96
COLO. STATE FOREST; State P	20 mi E of Walden on Hwy 14	DPOR	NO.	105	$	8,500+	24
COLUMBINE	25 mi NE of Nucla	UNF	ORD	6	$	9,000	53
COLUMBINE*	3 mi NW of Central City	ARNF	CCRD	47	$	9,020	42
COMANCHE	2 mi N of Ohio	GNF	CERD	4	0	8,900	76
COMSTOCK	19 mi SW of Monte Vista	RGNF	DNRD	8	0	9,700	129
CONEJOS	30 mi NW of Antonito	RGNF	CPRD	16	$	8,700	129
COTTONWOOD LAKE	E of Grand Junction, Grand Mesa	GMNF	CBRD	42	$	10,000	52
COTTONWOOD LAKE	10.5 mi SW of Buena Vista	SINF	SRD	28	$	9,600	76
COVE	8 mi SW of Lake George	PNF	SKRD	4	$	8,400	96
COW CREEK	16 mi N of Dillon on Hwy 9	WRNF	DRD	DSP	0	8,000	29
COWDREY LAKE SWA	2 mi S of Cowdrey	DOW	NE	DSP	0	7,900	24
CRAG CREST	E of Grand Junction, Grand Mesa	GMNF	GJRD	11	$	10,100	52
CRAWFORD RES STATE P*	1 mi S of Crawford on Hwy 92	DPOR	WEST	70	$	6,600	61
CROSS CREEK	9 mi SW of South Fork	RGNF	DNRD	12	$	8,800	130
CROW VALLEY	1 mi NW of Briggsdale	ARNF	PWRD	7	$	4,500	147
CROW VALLEY OVERFLOW GRP ®	1 mi NW of Briggsdale	ARNF	PWRD	---	$	4,500	147
CUTTHROAT	50 mi E of Meeker	WRNF	BLRD	14	$	9,750	17
CUTTHROAT BAY GROUP ®	NW side of Lake Granby	ARNF	SURD	---	$	8,400	30

D

Name	Location	Forest	District	Sites	Fee	Elev.	Page
DAVENPORT	44 mi W of Pueblo	SINF	SCRD	12	$	8,500	141
DEEP LAKE	NW of Dotsero 27 mi	WRNF	ERD	45	0	10,460	14
DAVIS SPRINGS	16 mi N of Dillon on Hwy 9	WRNF	DRD	7	0	8,000	29
DEER CREEK	10 mi NW of Bailey	PNF	SPRD	13	$	9,000	96
DEER LAKES	13 mi E of Lake City	GNF	CERD	12	$	10,400	118
DEARHAMER	East end Ruedi Reservoir	WRNF	SORD	13	$	7,800	67
DELANEY BUTTE SWA	S of Walden on Cty Rd 12W	DOW	NE	DSP	0	8,300	25
DEVILS HEAD	20 mi SW of Sedalia	PNF	SPRD	21	$	8,800	97
DENVER CREEK*	15 mi NW of Granby	ARNF	SURD	25	$	8,800	28
DE WEESE SWA	5 mi NW of Westcliffe on Hwy 69	DOW	SE	DSP	0	7,800	139
DEXTER	NE side Twin Lakes	SINF	LRD	26	$	9,500	87
DIAMOND J SWA	2 mi N of Walden	DOW	NE	20	0	8,100	25

Name	Location			Sites	Fee	Elev.	Page
DIFFICULT ®	5 mi SE of Aspen	WRNF	ARD	47	$	8,200	65
DIFFICULT GROUP ®	5 mi SE of Aspen	WRNF	ARD	—	$	8.000	65
DINNER STATION ®	32 mi NE of Almont	GNF	TRRD	22	$	9,600	78
DINOSAUR NAT. MON.	NW of Rangley	NPS	DNM	151	$	4,800	6
DIVIDE FORK	22 mi S of Grand Junction	UNF	GJRD	11	0	9,200	52
DOME LAKES SWA	8 mi E of Gunnison, 22 mi S Hwy 114	DOW	SW	DSP	0	9,129	116
DORCHESTER	40 mi NE of Almont	GNF	TRRD	10	$	9,800	78
DOWDY LAKE ®*	27 mi W of Livermore	ARNF	CLRD	62	$	8,365	42
DRY GULCH, CUR REC AREA*	N side Res, Hwy 50	NPS	CUR	10	$	7,519	59
DRY LAKE	6 mi NE of Steamboat Springs	RNF	HBRD	8	$	8.000	14
DUMONT LAKE	1 mi W of Rabbit Ears Summit	RNF	HBRD	22	$	9,508	28
DUTCH GEORGE FLATS	W of Ft. Collins 30 mi	ARNF	CLRD	21	$	6,500	44
E							
EAST ELK CRK OP, CUR REC A*	N side Res, Hwy 50	NPS	CUR	2	$	7,519	59
EAST FORK	10 mi NE of Pagosa Springs	SJNF	PARD	26	$	7,600	118
EAST MARVINE	35 mi SE of Meeker	WRNF	BLRD	7	$	8,500	14
EAST PORTAL, CUR REC AR*	Far W end of recreation area	NPS	CUR	15	$	7,519	59
ECHO LAKE ®*	14 mi SW of Idaho Springs	ARNF	CCRD	18	$	10,600	78
EGGLESTON GROUP ®	E of Grand Junction, Grand Mesa	GMNF	GJRD	6	$	10,100	52
ELBERT CREEK	l0 mi SW of Leadville	SINE	LRD	17	$	10,000	78
ELEVEN MILE RES. STATE P.	11 mi S of Lake George	DPOR	SO	300	$	8,600	94
ELK CREEK. CUR REC AREA	N side of Res @ visitors center	NPS	CUR	179	$	7,519	59
ELK CREEK ®	24 mi W of Antonito	RGNF	CPRD	34	$	8,500	130
ELK CREEK OVERFLOW	24 mi W of Antonito	RGNF	CPRD	10	$	8,500	130
ELK WALLOW	25 mi E of Basalt	WRNF	SORD	7	0	8,800	78
ELLIOT CREEK	16 mi N of Dillon on Hwy 9	WRNF	DRD	64	0	8.000	29
ERICKSON SPRINGS	51 mi NE of Delta	GNF	PRD	18	$	6,800	65
ESCALANTE SWA	4.5 mi NW of Delta	DOW	NW	DSP	0	5,000	51
F							
FAIRGROUNDS	Longmont at Hover & Nelson Rd	BOL	-	52	$	5,000	44
FATHER DYER ®	E side of Turquoise Res	SINF	LRD	25	$	9,900	85
FERRIS CANYON	35 mi N of Cortez	SJNF	DMRD	6	$	6.500	109
FIVE POINTS. ARK. HDWTRS	W of Parkdale on Hwy 50	DPOR	SO	20	$	6,000	72
FLAGLER RES. SWA	E of Flagler 5 mi on Rd 4	DOW	SE	DSP	0	4,700	147
FLATIRON RESERVOIR	NW of Carter Lake	LCP	-	42	$	5,470	40
FLAT ROCKS	15 mi SW of Sedalia	PNF	SPRD	19	$	8,200	97
FLORIDA ®	14 mi N of Durango, 9 mi Cty Rd 243	SJNF	CBRD	20	$	8,500	118
FLORIDA GROUP ®	14 mi N of Durango. 9 mi Cry Rd 243	SJNF	CBRD	—	$	8,500	118
FOURMILE*	8 mi W of Fairplay	PNF	SKRD	14	$	10,800	78
FREEMAN RESERVOIR	22 mi NE of Craig	RNF	HBRD	17	$	8,800	14
FULFORD CAVE	18 mi SE of Eagle	WRNF	ERD	7	$	9,600	79
G							
GARFIELD	18 mi W of Salida	SINF	SRD	11	$	10,000	79
GATEVIEW, CUR REC AREA	S side of Res, Lake Fork Arm	NPS	CUR	7	0	7,519	59
GENEVA PARK	7 mi NW of Grant	PNF	SPRD	26	$	9,800	79
GLACIER BASIN	Rocky Mountain National Park	NPS	RMNP	150	$	8,600	22
GLACIER BASIN GROUP ®	Rocky Mountain National Park	NPS	RMNP	15	$	8,600	22
GOLD CREEK	8 mi N of Ohio City	GNF	CERD	6	$	10,000	79
GOLD PARK	12 mi SW of Redcliffe	WRNF	HCRD	11	$	9,300	79
GOLDEN GATE CANYON ST P	13 mi W of Golden	DPOR	METR	168	$	9,100	39
GOOSE CREEK	13 mi SW of Deckers	PNF	SPRD	10	$	8.100	97
GORE CREEK	6 mi SE of Vail	WRNF	HCRD	25	$	8,700	79
GORE PASS	16 mi E of Toponas	RNF	YRD	12	$	9,500	28
GOTHIC	10 mi N of Crested Butte	GNF	TRRD	4	$	9,600	65
GRAHAM CREEK	Vallecito Reservoir	SJNF	CBRD	25	$	7,900	123
GRANDVIEW*	15 mi SE of Chambers Lake	ARNF	CLRD	8	$	10,220	28
GRANITE	19 mi N of Steamboat S, to Fish Cr Rd	RNF	HBRD	8	$	10,200	28
GREEN MOUNTAIN	8 mi SE of Buffalo Creek	PNF	SPRD	6	$	7,600	97
GREEN RIDGE, ARAP NRA ®*	S side Shadow Mtn. Res	ARNF	SURD	81	$	8,400	30
GRIZZLY CREEK	25 mi SW of Walden	RNF	PWRD	12	$	8,500	29
GROUNDHOG RES. SWA	30 mi N of Dolores	DOW	SW	13	0	8,740	108
GUANELLA PASS ®*	8 mi S of Georgetown	ARNF	CCRD	18	$	10,900	80
H							
HAHNS PEAK LAKE ®	30 mi NW of Steamboat Springs	RNF	HBRD	26	$	8,500	14
HALFMOON	10 mi SW of Leadvllle	SINF	LRD	22	$	9,900	80
HALL VALLEY	8 mi NW of Grant	PNF	SPRD	9	$	9,900	80
HANDCART	8 mi NW of Grant	PNF	SPRD	10	$	9,800	80

Name	Location	Agency	District	Sites	Fee	Elev.	Page
HAPPY MEADOWS	3 mi NW of Lake George	PNF	SKRD	7	$	7,900	97
HAVILAND LAKE ®	17 mi N of Durango	SJNF	CRD	45	$	8,000	119
HAY PRESS	22 mi S of Grand Junction	UNF	GJRD	11	0	9,300	52
HAYDEN CREEK	5 mi SW of Coaldale	SINF	SRD	11	$	8,000	80
HEATON BAY ®	N side Dillon Res on Hwy 9	WRNF	DRD	72	$	9,100	77
HECLA JUNCTION, ARK HDWTR	Between Nathrop and Salida, Hwy 285	DPOR	SO	22	$	7,500	72
HIDDEN LAKES	30 mi SW of Walden	RNF	PWRD	9	$	8,900	29
HIDDEN VALLEY	16 mi SE of Lake City	GNF	CERD	3	$	9,700	119
HIGBEE (MIKE) SWA	4 mi E of Lamar on Hwy 50	DOW	SE	DSP	0	4,100	149
HIGHLINE LAKE STATE P	W of Fruita, exit 15, N to Park	DPOR	WEST	25	$	4,697	49
HIGHWAY SPRINGS	5 mi SW of South Fork	RGNF	DNRD	11	$	8,400	130
HIMES PEAK	48 mi E of Meeker	WRNF	BLRD	11	$	9,000	14
HINMAN	22 mi NW of Steamboat Springs	RNF	HBRD	13	$	7,600	15
HOLBROOK RES. SWA	3 mi N of Swink on Cty Rd 24.5, E .5 mi	DOW	SE	DSP	0	4,160	148
HORNSILVER	3 mi S of Redcliffe	WRNF	HCRD	12	$	8,800	80
HORSE CREEK RES. SWA	2 mi E of Cheraw on Cty Rd 115, N 7 mi	DOW	SE	DSP	0	4,000	150
HORSESHOE	16 mi nw of Dillon	WRNF	DRD	7	$	8,540	29
HORSESHOE	16 mi SW of Yampa	RNF	YRD	7	$	10,000	15
HORSESHOE	7 mi SW of Fairplay	PNF	SKRD	19	$	10,600	81
HORSESHOE	11 mi S of Williams Fork Res	RNF	SURD	7	$	8,540	29
HORSETOOTH RESERVOIR	W of Fort Collins	LCP	---	129	$	5,430	40
HOT SULPHUR SPRINGS SWA	5 mi NW of Hot Sulphur Springs	DOW	NE	DSP	0	7,500	25
HOUSE CREEK ®*	E side of McPhee Res	SJNF	DMRD	51	$	6,924	110
HOUSE CREEK GROUP ®*	E side of McPhee Res	SJNF	DMRD	---	$	6,924	110
HUERFANO SWA	13 mi W of Gardner on Cty Rd 580	DOW	SE	DSP	0	7,600	139
HUGO SWA	14 mi S of Hugo on Hwy 109, 2.2 mi E	DOW	SE	DSP	0	5,000	147

I

Name	Location	Agency	District	Sites	Fee	Elev.	Page
IDLEWILD*	1 mi S of Winter Park	ARNF	SURD	26	$	9,000	29
INDIAN CREEK	l0 mi W of Sedalia	PNF	SPRD	11	$	7.500	97
INDIAN CREEK EQUESTRAIN ®	10 mi W of Sedalia	PNF	SPRD	8	$	7.500	98
INDIAN RUN SWA	18 mi SE of Hamilton	DOW	NW	DSP	0	6,700	13
IRISH CANYON	53 mi N of Maybell	BLM	LSK	3	0	6,000	7
IRON CITY	16 mi W of Nathrop	SINF	SRD	15	$	9,900	81
IRON SPRINGS	27 mi SW of Montrose	UNF	MDRD	7	$	9,500	109
ISLAND ACRES, Co. River SP	Exit 47 on I-70 in Debeque Canyon	DPOR	WEST	53	$	4,700	50
ISLAND LAKE	E of Grand Junction, Grand Mesa	GMNF	GJRD	41	$	10,300	52
IVY CREEK	20 mi SW of Creede	RGNF	CRRD	4	0	9,500	119

J

Name	Location	Agency	District	Sites	Fee	Elev.	Page
JACK GULCH	41 mi W of LaPorte	ARNF	CLRD	71	$	8,100	43
JACKSON CREEK	24 mi S of Sedalia	PNF	SPRD	9	$	8,100	98
JACKSON RES. STATE P	W of Goodrich 2.5 miles	DPOR	NOR	262	$	4,438	144
JEFFERSON CREEK ®*	6 mi NW of Jefferson	PNF	SKRD	17	$	10,100	81
JENSEN SWA	9 mi NE of Meeker	DOW	NW	DSP	0	7,500	13
JOE MOORE RES. SWA	5 mi NE of Mancos	DOW	SW	DSP	0	7,520	108
JOHN MARTIN RESERVOIR STATE P*	S of Hasty 4 mi	COE	---	65	$	3,851	149
JUMBO	E of Grand Junction, Grand Mesa	GMNF	CBRD	26	$	9,800	52
JUMBO RESERVOIR SWA	I-76 Red Lion exit, 3 mi NE	DOW	NW	DSP	0	3,700	146
JUNCTION CREEK*	6 mi NW of Durango	SJNF	CRD	38	$	7.500	110

K

Name	Location	Agency	District	Sites	Fee	Elev.	Page
KARVAL RESERVOIR SWA	S of Karval on Hwy 109 l0 mi	DOW	SE	DSP	0	4,700	147
KELLY DAHL ®*	3 mi S of Nederland	ARNF	BRD	46	$	8,600	43
KELLY FLATS*	7 mi E of Rustic	ARNF	CLRD	23	$	6.750	44
KELSEY ®	8 mi S of Buffalo Creek	PNF	SPRD	17	$	8,000	98
KENOSHA PASS	4.5 mi NE of Jefferson	PNF	SPRD	25	$	10,000	81
KISER CREEK	E of Grand Junction, Grand Mesa	GMNF	GJRD	12	0	10,100	52
KITE LAKE	6 mi NW of Alma	PNF	SKRD	7	$	12,000	81
KLINES FOLLY	27 mi NW of Dotsero	WRNF	ERD	4	0	10,700	15
KROEGER	18 mi NW of Durango	SJNF	MDRD	10	$	9,000	110

L

Name	Location	Agency	District	Sites	Fee	Elev.	Page
LA JARA RESERVOIR SWA	20 mi S,12 mi SW of Monte Vista	DOW	SW	DSP	0	9,968	128
LAKE CREEK	37 mi SW of Canon City	SINF	SCRD	12	$	8,200	130
LAKE DOROTHEY SWA	N of Raton NM 10 mi, l2 mi E up Canyon	DOW	SE	DSP	0	7,600	150
LAKE FORK ®	40 mi W of Antonito	RGNF	CPRD	18	$	9,500	130
LAKE FORK, CUR REC AREA*	S side of Res. Junction Hwy 50 & 92	NPS	CUR	87	$	7,516	59
LAKE HENRY SWA	3 mi E of Ordway on Hwy 96,1 mi N	DOW	SE	DSP	0	4,390	147
LAKE IRWIN ®	10 mi NW of Created Butte	GNF	TRRD	32	$	10,200	66
LAKE JOHN SWA	20 mi NW of Walden	DOW	NE	PVT	$	7,800	25

LAKEVIEW ®	S side Taylor Park Res	GNF	TRRD	46	$	9,330	85
LAKEVIEW ®	NW side Twin Lakes	SINF	LRD	59	$	9,500	87
LATHROP RES STATE PARK	3 mi W of Walsenberg on Hwy 160	DPOR	SO	98	$	6,350	137
LA VISTA ®*	Lake Isabel 39 mi SW of Pueblo	SINE	SCRD	29	$	8,600	141
LINCOLN GULCH	10.5 mi SE of Aspen	WRNF	ARD	7	$	9,600	81
LITTLE BEAR*	E of Grand Junction, Grand Mesa	GMNF	GJRD	36	$	10,200	52
LITTLE MATTIE	N side Ruedi Reservoir	WRNF	SORD	20	$	7,800	67
LITTLE MAUD	N side Ruedi Reservoir	WRNF	SORD	22	$	7,800	67
LITTLE SNAKE SWA	17 mi N of Maybell	DOW	NW	DSP	0	6,900	8
LODGEPOLE ®*	5 mi NW of Jefferson	PNF	SKRD	35	$	9,900	82
LODGEPOLE ®	15 mi NE of Almont	GNF	TRRD	16	$	8,800	82
LON HAGLER SWA	5 mi W of Champion	DOW	NE	DSP	0	5,400	41
LONE CONE SWA	SE of Norwood 25 mi	DOW	SW	DSP	0	7,963	108
LONE ROCK ®*	17 mi SE of Buffalo Creek	PNF	SPRD	19	$	6,400	98
LONG DRAW(RES)	12 mi SE of Chambers Res	ARNF	CLRD	25	$	10,030	30
LONGS PEAK	Rocky Mountain National Park	NPS	RMNP	26	$	9,400	22
LORY STATE PARK ®	West of Fort Collins	DPOR	NE	6	$	6,500	39
LOST LAKE	17 mi SW of Crested Butte	GNF	PRD	11	0	9,600	66
LOST MAN	15 mi SE of Aspen	WRNF	ARD	10	$	10,700	82
LOST PARK*	21 mi NE of Jefferson	PNF	SKRD	10	$	10,000	98
LOST TRAIL	38 mi SW of Creede	RGNF	CRRD	7	0	9,500	119
LOTTIS CREEK	17 mi NE of Almont	GNF	TRRD	27	$	9,000	82
LOWER PIEDRA	45 mi W of Creede	SJNF	PARD	17	$	7,200	119
LOWRY	S side of Dillon Res	WRNF	DRD	29	$	9,300	77
LUDERS CREEK	33 mi NW of Saguache	RGNF	SARD	6	0	9,900	130
LYNX PASS	21 mi E of Yampa	RNF	YRD	11	$	8,900	30
M							
MANCOS STATE PARK	10 mi N of Mancos on FDR 561	DPOR	WEST	33	$	7,800	107
MARSHALL PARK	7 mi SW of Creede	RGNF	CRRD	15	$	8,800	119
MARVINE	35 mi SE of Meeker	WRNF	BLRD	18	$	8,100	15
MAVRESSO	19 mi NE of Dolores	SJNF	DMRD	13	$	7,600	110
MATTERHORN	15 mi SW of Telluride	UNF	GJRD	28	$	9,500	124
MAY QUEEN	NW side Turquoise Res	SINF	LRD	34	$	9,900	85
MC CLELLAND SWA	2 mi NW of Rocky Ford Hwy 266 E 2 mi.	DOW	SE	DSP	0	4,200	148
MCCLURE	29 mi S of Carbondale	GNF	PRD	19	$	8,200	66
MCPHEE ®*	S side McPhee Res near Dolores	SJNF	DMRD	65	$	6,924	110
MCPHEE GROUP ®*	S aide McPhee Res near Dolores	SJNF	DMRD	---	$	6,924	110
MCDONALD FLATS	16 mi N of Dillon on Hwy 9	WRNF	DRD	13	$	8,000	29
MEADOW LAKE	35 mi N of New Castle	WRNF	RRD	10	$	9,600	15
MEADOW RIDGE ®*	S side of Rampart Res	PNF	PPRD	19	$	9,200	100
MEADOWS GROUP ®	6 mi SE of Buffalo Creek	PNF	SPRD	---	$	7,000	98
MEADOWS	15 mi SE of Steamboat Springs	RNF	HBRD	30	$	9,300	31
MEEKER PARK	E of Meeker Park	ARNF	BRD	29	$	8,600'	44
MEREDITH RES. SWA	3 mi E of Ordway	DOW	SE	DSP	0	4,220	148
MERIDIAN	10 mi N of Bailey	PNF	SPRD	18	$	9,000	99
MICHIGAN CREEK*	6 mi NW of Jefferson	PNF	SKRD	13	$	10,000	82
MIDDLE MOUNTAIN	Vallecito Reservoir	SJNF	CBRD	24	$	7,900	123
MIDDLE QUARTZ	20 mi NE of Parlin	GNF	CERD	7	$	10,200	82
MIDDLE TAYLOR CRK SWA	8 mi W of Westcliffe on Hermit Lakes Rd	DOW	SE	DSP	0	9,000	139
MILL CREEK (Riverine)	15 mi SW of Lake City	BLM	GUN	22	$	9,500	116
MILLER CREEK	N of Durango near Lemon Res	SJNF	CBRD	12	$	8,000	120
MIRACLE ROCK	S of Colo. Nat. Monument 20 mi	BLM	GJ	4	0	7,000	51
MIRAMONTE RES. SWA	19 mi SE of Norwood	DOW	SW	DSP	0	7,755	108
MIRROR LAKE	3 mi SE of Tincup	GNF	TRRD	10	$	10,000	83
MIX LAKE	Approx 40 mi S of Monte Vista	RGNF	CPRD	22	$	10,035	131
MIZPAH	6 mi W of Empire	ARNF	CCRD	10	$	9,600	31
MOGOTE GROUP ®	15 mi W of Antonito	RGNF	CPRD	---	$	8,400	131
MOGOTE ®	15 mi W of Antonito	RGNF	CPRD	41	$	8,400	131
MOLLIE B ®	N side of Ruedi Reservoir	WRNF	SORD	26	$	7,800	67
MOLLY BROWN ®*	E side of Turquoise Res	SINF	LRD	49	$	9,900	85
MOLLY GULCH	9 mi SW of Deckers	PNF	SPRD	15	$	7,500	99
MONARCH PARK	20 mi W of Salida	SINF	SRD	38	$	10,500	83
MONUMENT LAKE	36 mi W of Trinidad	COT	---	100	$	9,000	141
MORAINE PARK	Rocky Mountain National Park	NPS	RMNP	247	$	8,150	22
MOREFIELD ®*	Mesa Verde National Monument	NPS	---	477	$	7,000	106
MOSCA	19 mi N of Almont	GNF	TRRD	16	$	10,000	83
MOUNT EVANS SWA	W of Evergreen 10 mi	DOW	CEN	DSP	0	9,500	95

Name	Location	Agency	District	Sites	Fee	Elev.	Page
MOUNT PRINCETON ®	7 mi W of Nathrop	SINF	SRD	17	$	8,000	83
MOUNTAIN PARK ®	8 mi E of Rustic	ARNF	CLRD	55	$	6,650	44
MOUNTAIN PARK GROUP ®*	8 mi E of Rustle	ARNF	CLRD	---	$	6,650	44
MTN. SHEEP POINT (Riverine)	5 mi E of Dove Creek	BLM	SJ	3	$	6,100	108
MUD SPRINGS	S of Colo. Nat. Monument 12 mi	BLM	GJ	12	0	8,000	51
MUELLER STATE PARK	5 mi S of Divide	DPOR	SO	90	$	9,500	95
N							
NARROWS	11 mi E of Rustic	ARNF	CLRD	9	$	6,500	44
NAVAJO RES. STATE PARK*	35 mi W Pagosa Springs, S on Hwy 151	DPOR	WEST	70	$	6,100	114
NORTH BANK	8 mi NE of Almont	GNF	TRRD	17	$	8,000	66
NORTH CANYON	Vallecito Reservoir	SJNF	CBRD	21	$	7,900	123
NORTH CLEAR CREEK	35 mi W of Creede	RGNF	CRRD	25	$	9,900	120
NORTH CRESTONE CREEK	2.5 mi N of Crestone	RGNF	SARD	13	$	8,800	131
NORTH FORK	33 mi E of Meeker	WRNF	BLRD	40	$	7,750	15
NO. FORK OVERFLOW GRP®	33 mi E of Meeker	WRNF	BLRD	---	$	7,750	15
NORTH FORK POUDRE	8 mi W of Red Feather	ARNF	CLRD	9	$	9,150	32
NORTH FORK RESERVOIR	16 mi NW of Poncha Springs	SINF	SRD	8	$	11.000	83
NORTH RIM*	S of Crawford on Black Can Rd	NPS	BCNM	13	$	8,000	58
NORTH STERLING RES. ST P	11 mi N of Sterling	DPOR	NO	50	$	4,069	146
O							
O'HAVER LAKE ®	9 mi SW of Ponacha Springs	SINF	SRD	29	$	9,200	83
OAK CREEK	12 mi SW of Canon City	SINF	SCRD	15	0	7,600	141
OAK RIDGE SWA	20 mi E of Meeker Cty Rd 8 near Buford	DOW	NW	DSP	0	6,995	13
OLIVE RIDGE ®*	15 mi S of Estes Park	ARNF	BRD	56	$	8,350	43
OLNEY SPRINGS RES SWA	1 mi NW of Olney Springs on Cty Rd 7	DOW	SE	DSP	0	4,340	148
OLD TIMER	South side Vallecito Reservoir	SJNF	CBRD	10	$	7,900	123
ONE MILE ®	8 mi N of Almont	GNF	TRRD	25	$	8,600	66
OPHIR CREEK	45 mi SW of Pueblo	SINF	SCRD	31	$	8,900	141
ORDWAY RESERVOIR SWA	2 mi N of Ordway on Hwy 71	DOW	SE	DSP	0	4,300	147
OSPREY	7 mi N of Deckers	PNF	SPRD	10	$	8,100	99
OUZEL	5 mi N of Deckers	PNF	SPRD	13	$	8,000	99
OWL MOUNTAIN SWA	S of Walden 20 mi	DOW	NE	DSP	0	8,200	25
P							
PAINTED ROCKS	8 mi N of Woodland Park	PNF	PPRD	18	$	7,900	99
PALISADE	8 mi NW of South Fork	RGNF	CRRD	12	$	8,300	120
PAONIA STATE PARK*	16 mi E of Paonia on Hwy 133	DPOR	WEST	15	$	6,500	62
PARK CREEK	9 mi SW of South Fork	RGNF	DNRD	16	$	8,500	120
PARRY PEAK	W End Twin Lakes Res	SINF	LRD	26	$	9,500	84
PAWNEE®*	6 mi W of Ward	ARNF	BRD	55	$	10,350	43
PEACEFUL VALLEY	7 mi N of Ward on Hwy 72, W 2.5 mi	ARNF	BRD	17	$	8,500'	43
PEAK ONE®	W side Dillon Res near Frisco	WRNF	DRD	79	$	9,100	77
PENITENTE CANYON	3 mi W of LaGarita	BLM	SL	10	0	7,800	128
PICEANCE SWA	20 mi SW of Meeker	DOW	NW	DSP	0	6,000	8
PICKLE GULCH GROUP®	4 mi N of Black Hawk	ARNF	CCRD	---	$	9,100	43
PIKE COMMUNITY GROUP®	5 mi N of Woodland Park	PNF	PPRD	---	$	7,700	99
PINE COVE	W side of Res near Frisco	WRNF	DRD	55	$	9,100	77
PINE POINT	Vallecito Reservoir	SJNF	CBRD	30	$	7,900	123
PINE RIVER	25 mi NE of Bayfield	SJNF	CBRD	6	$	8,100	120
PINES	25 mi SE of Walden	RNF	PWRD	11	$	9,200	32
PINEWOOD LAKE	W of Carter Lake	LCP	---	16	$	6,580	40
PINYON FLATS	Great Sand Dunes National Mon.	NPS	---	88	$	8,175	136
PITKIN*	18 mi NE of Parlin	GNF	CERD	22	$	9,300	84
PLATTE RIVER	3.5 mi N of Deckers	PNF	SPRD	10	$	6,300	99
PONDEROSA GROUP ®	Lake Isabel, 39 mi SW of Pueblo	SINF	SCRD	---	$	8.600	141
PONDEROSA, CUR REC A	N side Res on Soap Crk Rd	NPS	CUR	21	$	7,519	59
PORTAL	17 mi SE of Aspen	WRNF	ARD	7	$	10,700	84
POSO	12 mi NW of LaGarita	RGNF	SARD	11	$	9,100	131
PRAIRIE POINT	16 mi N of Dillon on Hwy 9	WRNF	DRD	44	$	8,000	29
PREWITT RES SWA	15 mi NE of Brush Hwy 6, 1 mi E	DOW	NE	DSP	0	4,100	146
PRINTER BOY GROUP ®	E side of Turquoise Res	SINF	LRD	---	$	9,900	85
PROSPECTOR*	S side of Dillon Res	WRNF	DRD	107	$	9,100	77
PUEBLO RES STATE P*	W of Pueblo	DPOR	SO	401	$	4,900	138
PUMPHOUSE*	16 mi S of Kremmling	BLM	LSK	14	0	7,000	25
PURGATOIRE	25 mi S of LaVeta	SINF	SCRD	23	$	9,800	141
PURGATORY	22 mi SW of Silverton	SJNF	CRD	14	$	8,800	120

Q

QUARTZ	22 mi NE of Parlin	GNF	CERD	10	$	9,800	84
QUEENS SWA	I5 mi S of Eads on Hwy 287	DOW	SE	DSP	0	3,800	148

R

RABBIT VALLEY	26 mi S of Grand Junction	BLM	GJ	8	0	4,500	51
RADIUM* (Riverine)	25 mi S of Kremmling	BLM	LSK	2	0	7,000	26
RADIUM SWA	15 mi S of Kremmling	DOW	NW	DSP	0	7,000	26
RAILROAD BRIDGE ARK HDW		DPOR	SO	14	$	7,500	72
RAINBOW LAKES	7 mi N of Nederland	ARNF	BRD	16	$	10,000	44
RED BRIDGE (Riverine)	20 mi S of Gunnison, N of Lake CIty	BLM	GUN	7	$	8,000	64
RED CREEK, CURRECANTI REC.	N side of Res, Hwy 50	NPS	CUR	7	$	7,519	59
RED ROCKS GROUP ®	4 mi N of Woodland Park	PNF	PPRD	---	$	8,200	100
REDSTONE*	13 mi S of Carbondale	WRNF	SORD	37	$	7,200	66
RIDGWAY RES STATE P~	2 mi N of Ridgway	DPOR	WEST	187	$	6,880	115
RIFLE FALLS STATE PARK	8 mi NW of Rifle Gap Res	DPOR	WEST	19	$	6,800	62
RIFLE GAP STATE PARK*	7 mi N of Rifle on Hwy 325	DPOR	WEST	47	$	6,000	63
RINCON, ARK HDWTR	Between Salida and Howard, Hwy 5O	DPOR	SO	5	$	7,400	72
RIO BLANCO LAKE SWA	20 mi W of Meeker	DOW	NW	DSP	0	6,000	8
RIO GRANDE	10 mi SW of Creede	RGNF	CRRD	4	0	9,300	121
RIVER HILL	30 mi W of Creede	RGNF	CRRD	20	$	9,200	121
RIVERS END	N side of Taylor Park Res	GNF	TRRD	15	$	9,330	85
RIVERSIDE*	2.5 mi SW of Lake George	PNF	SKRD	19	$	8,000	100
ROAD CANYON	32 mi W of Creede	RGNF	CRRD	6	0	9,500	121
ROBBERS ROOST	5 mi S of Winter Park	ARNF	SURD	11	$	9,826	32
ROCK CREEK	15 mi SW of Monte Vista	RGNF	DNRD	13	0	9,200	131
ROCK CREEK SWA	20 mi NW Kremmling	DOW	NW	DSP	0	9,200	26
ROCKY FORD SWA	2 mi NE of Rocky Ford, E 0.5 mi	DOW	SE	DSP	0	4,000	150
ROSY LANE ®	8 mi NE of Almont	GNF	TRRD	20	$	8,600	67
ROUND MOUNTAIN*	5.5 mi NW of Lake George	PNF	SKRD	17	$	8,500	100
RUBY MTN, ARK HDWTR*	N of Nathrop on Hwy 285	DPOR	SO	20	$	7,500	72
RUEDI MARINA	Ruedi Reservoir	WRNF	CRD	5	4	7,800	67

S

SADDLEHORN*	@Colorado National Monument	NPS	CNM	80	$	5,800	48
SAN LUIS RES STATE PARK*	8 mi E of Moses on Six Mile Rd.	DPOR	SO	51	$	7,525	128
SAWMILL CREEK	25 mi NE of Craig	RNF	HBRD	6	0	9,000	16
SAWMILL GULCH*	l3 mi NW of Granby	ARNF	SURD	5	$	8,780	32
SEEDHOUSE	25 mi NW of Steamboat Springs	RNF	HBRD	25	$	8,000	16
SELKIRK	7 mi NW of Como	PNF	SKRD	15	$	10,500	84
SEYMORE LAKE SWA	18 mi SW of Walden	DOW	NE	DSP	0	8,625	26
SHEEP CORRAL	11 mi SW of Telluride on FDR 623	UNF	NOR	9	0	8,400	121
SHEPARDS RIM	50 mi E of Meeker	WRNF	BLRD	18	$	9,750	17
SHERIFF RESERVOIR	16 mi SW of Oak Creek	RNF	YRD	5	$	9,723	16
SIG CREEK	27 mi SW of Silverton	SJNF	CRD	9	$	9,000	111
SILVER BAR®	7.5 mi W of Aspen	WRNF	ARD	4	$	8,300	68
SILVER BELL ®	7.5 mi W of Aspen	WRNF	ARD	4	$	8,400	68
SILVER DOLLAR ®	E side Turquoise Res	SINF	LRD	45	$	9,900	85
SILVER JACK*	42 mi SE of Montrose	UNF	ORD	60	$	8,900	121
SILVER QUEEN ®	7.5 mi W of Aspen	WRNF	ARD	6	$	9,100	68
SILVER THREAD	29 mi W of Creede	RGNF	CRRD	11	$	9,500	121
SKAGWAY RES. SWA	E of Victor 7 mi on Cty Rd 441	DOW	SE	DSP	0	9,000	95
SLEEPING ELEPHANT*	8 mi N of Chambers Lake	ARNF	CLRD	15	$	7,850	32
SLUMGULLION	9 mi SE of Lake City	GNF	CERD	21	$	11,200	122
SMITH RESERVOIR SWA	4 mi S of Blanca	DOW	SW	DSP	0	7,721	140
SNOWBLIND	7 mi NE of Sargents	GNF	CERD	23	$	9,300	84
SNOWSLIDE	6.5 mi N of Hesperus	SJNF	CRD	12	$	9,000	111
SOAP CREEK	15 mi NW of Gunnison	GNF	TRRD	21	$	7,700	68
SOUTH FORK	22 mi SE of Williams Fork Res	ARNF	SURD	21	$	8,940	34
SOUTH FORK	30 mi SE of Meeker	WRNF	BLRD	18	$	7,600	16
SOUTH MEADOWS*	6 mi N of Woodland Park	PNF	PPRD	64	$	8,000	100
SOUTH MINERAL	9 mi W of Silverton	SJNF	CRD	26	$	10,000	122
SOUTH RIM	N of Hwy 50 on Pinon Springs Rd	NPS	BCNM	102	$	8,400	58
SOUTH SIDE ®	Lake Isabel. 39 mi SW of Pueblo	SINF	SCRD	8	$	8,600	141
SPANISH PEAKS SWA	18 mi SW of Aguilar on Cty Rd 41.7	DOW	SE	DSP	0	8.100	140
SPECTACLE LAKE	30 mi NW of Antonito	RGNF	CPRD	24	$	8,700	131
SPILLWAY	8 mi SW of Lake George	PNF	SKRD	24	$	8,500	101
SPRING CREEK	10 mi NE of Almont	GNF	TRRD	12	$	10,900	68
SPRINGER GULCH	6.6 mi SW of Lake George	PNF	SKRD	15	$	8,300	101

SPRINGDALE	4.5 mi N of Woodland Park	PNF	PPRD	14	$	9,100	101
SPRUCE	17 mi E of Lake City	GNF	CERD	9	$	9,300	122
SPRUCE GROUP ®	Lake Isabel Rec. Area	SINF	SCRD	---	$	8,600	141
SPRUCE GROVE	E of Grand Junction, Grand Mesa	GMNF	CBRD	16	$	9,900	52
SPRUCE GROVE	14 mi NW of Lake George	PNF	SKRD	26	$	8,600	101
ST CHARLES ®	Lake Isabel, 39 mi SW of Pueblo	SINF	SCRD	15	$	8,600	141
ST. LOUIS CREEK	3 mi S of Eraser	ARNF	SURD	18	$	8,900	34
STAGECOACH RES. STATE P*	16 mi S Steamboat Springs	DPOR	NO	100	$	7,250	12
STEAMBOAT LAKE STATE P	27 mi N of Steamboat Springs	DPOR	NO	222	$	8,000	12
STEVENS CREEK, CUR REC	NE side Res, Hwy 50	NPS	CUR	54	$	7,540	59
STEWART ADAMS GROUP ®*	1 mi N of Briggsdale	ARNF	PWRD	---	$	4,500	147
STILLWATER. ARAP NRA ®*	NW end of Lake Granby	ARNF	SURD	127	$	8,400	30
STONE CELLAR	52 mi SE of Gunnison	RGNF	SARD	5	$	9,500	132
STORMKING	14 mi NW of LaGarita	RGNF	SARD	11	$	9,400	132
STOVE PRAIRIE LANDING*	12 mi E of Rustic	ARNF	CLRD	9	$	6,000	44
STUNNER	45 mi SW of Monte Vista	RGNF	CPRD	10	0	9,700	132
SUGARLOAF	23 mi SE of Williams Fork Res	ARNF	SURD	11	$	8,900	34
SUMMIT LAKE	16 mi NE of Steamboat Springs	RNF	HBRD	16	$	10,300	34
SUNSET POINT	Arapaho National Recreation Area	ARNF	SURD	25	$	8,300	30
SUNSHINE	8 mi SW of Telluride	UNF	NRD	15	$	8,700	122
SUPPLY BASIN	27 mi NW of Dotsero	WRNF	ERD	7	0	10,700	16
SWEETWATER LAKE	7 mi N of Dotsero	WRNF	ERD	10	$	7,700	16
SYLVAN LAKE STATE PARK	16 mi S of Eagle	DPOR	WEST	50	$	8,500	73
T							
TABOR ®	E side Turquoise Res	SINF	LRD	20	$	9,900	85
TAMARACK RANCH SWA	I-76 Crook exit, 0.5 mi N on Hwy 55	DOW	NE DSP	0		3,700	146
TARGET TREE	7 mi E of Mancos	SJNF	MDRD	25	$	7,800	111
TARRYALL RES. SWA	15 mi SE of Jefferson on Cty Rd 77	DOW	SE DSP	0		9,000	74
TAYLOR CANYON TENT	8 mi NE of Almont	GNF	TRRD	7	$	8,600	68
TEAL*	27 mi NW of Pagosa Springs	SJNF	PARD	16	$	8,300	122
TEAL LAKE	11 mi W of Hebron	RNF	PWRD	17	$	8.812	34
THE CRAGS	7 mi SE of Divide	PNF	PPRD	17	$	10,100	101
THE GATE (Riverine)	14 mi N of Lake City	BLM	GUN	8	0	8,400	64
THIRTY MILE	37 mi W of Creede	RGNF	CRRD	35	$	9,300	122
THREE FORKS	l3 mi NE of Rifle	WRNF	RRD	4	$	7,600	17
THUNDER RIDGE ®*	S side Rampart Res	PNF	PPRD	21	$	9,200	100
THURSTON RESERVOIR SWA	10 mi NW of Lamar	DOW	SE DSP	0		4,200	149
TIGIWON	9 mi S of I-70 Dowd Junction exit	WRNF	HCRD	9	0	9,900	85
TIGIWON COM. HOUSE GRP®	9 mi S of I-70 Dowd Junction exit	WRNF	HCRD	---	$	9,900	85
TIMBER CREEK	Rocky Mountain National Park	NPS	RMNP	100	$	8,900	22
TIMBERLINE GROUP	6 mi N of Jefferson	PNF	SPRD	---	4	9,000	74
TIMPAS CREEK	8 mi SE of Rocky Ford on Cty Rd Z	DOW	SE DSP	0		4,000	150
TOM BENNETT	W of Kelly Flats CG, S Cty Rd 63E	ARNF	CLRD	12	$	9,000	42
TRAIL CREEK	16 mi NW of Woodland Park	PNF	PPRD	7	0	7,800	101
TRANSFER ®	21 mi NW of Dolores	SJNF	MDRD	13	$	8,500	111
TRANSFER PARK ®	14 mi N of Durango 5 mi N Lemon Res	SJNF	CBRD	25	$	8,600	123
TRAPLINE	50 mi E of Meeker	WRNF	BLRD	13	$	9,750	17
TRINIDAD RES. STATE P*	3 mi W of Trinidad	DPOR	SO	62	$	6,300	138
TRUJILLO MEADOWS*	36 mi NW of Antonito	RGNF	CPRD	50	$	10,000	132
TUCKER PONDS	17 mi SW of South Fork	RGNF	DNRD	16	$	9,600	123
TUNNEL	4 mi N of Chambers Lake	ARNF	CLRD	49	$	8,600	34
TWIN EAGLES TRAILHEAD	15 mi NW of Lake George	PNF	SKRD	9	$	8,550	102
TWIN LAKE	E of Grand Junction, Grand Mesa	GMNF	GJRD	13	0	10,300	52
TWIN PEAKS	3 mi W Twin Lakes Reservoir	SINF	LRD	37	$	9,600	88
TWO BUTTES RES. SWA	17 mi N of Springfield on Hwy 287, E 3 mi	DOW	SE DSP	0		4,300	149
U							
UNION RESERVOIR	E of Longmont	LPD	---	42	$	4,956	42
UPPER BEAVER CREEK	7 mi SW of South Fork	RGNF	DNRD	15	$	8,500	132
UTE GROUP ®	18 mi W of Pagosa Springs	SJNF	PARD	I	$	7,150	123
UTE TRAILHEAD	10 mi NE of Olatha	BLM	UNC	2	0	6,600	64
V							
VALLECITO	3 mi N of Vallecito Reservoir	SJNF	CBRD	80	$	8,000	123
VAUGHN LAKE	SW of Oak Creek 35 mi	RNF	YRD	6	$	9,500	17
VEGA RES STATE PARK*	12 mi E of Colbran on Cty Rd 330	DPOR	WEST	101	$	7,960	63
W							
WALTON CREEK	17 mi SE of Steamboat Springs	RNF	HBRD	14	$	9,400	35
WARD LAKE	E of Grand Junction, Grand Mesa	GMNF	GJRD	27	$	10,200	52

WEIR & JOHNSON	E of Grand Junction, Grand Mesa	GMNF	GJRD	12	0	10,500	52
WELLER	11 mi SE of Aspen	WRNF	ARD	11	$	9,200	88
WEST CHICAGO CREEK ®*	10 mi SW of Idaho Springs	ARNF	CCRD	16	$	9,600	88
WEST DOLORES	20 mi NE of Dolores	SJNF	MDRD	13	$	7,800	111
WEST FORK	15 mi NE of Pagosa Springs	SJNF	PARD	28	$	8,000	124
WEST LAKE*	27 mi W of Livermore, 1 mi S	ARNF	CLRD	29	$	8.200	44
WESTON PASS	16 mi SW of Fairplay	PNF	SKRD	14	$	10,200	88
WHITE OWL	36 mi NW of Dotsero	WRNF	ERD	5	0	9,500	68
WHITE STAR	NW side Twin Lakes (West)	SINF	LRD	64	$	9,500	87
WHITESIDE	2 mi NW of Grant	PNF	SPRD	5	$	8,900	88
WIGWAM*	3 mi S of Deckers	PNF	SPRD	10	$	6,600	102
WILDHORN	22 mi SW of Deckers	PNF	PPRD	9	$	9,100	102
WILLIAMS CREEK®	25 mi NW of Pagosa Springs	SJNF	PARD	65	$	8,300	124
WILLIAMS CREEK	10 mi S of Lake City	GNF	CERD	23	$	9,200	124
WILLIAMS FORK RESERVOIR	SE of Kremmling	DWB	DSP	42	0	7.800	35
WILLOW CREEK, ARAP NRA	W of Lake Granby on Hwy 6 to Reserv.	ARNF	SURD	35	$	8,130	30
WILLOWS	16 mi N of Dillon on Hwy 9	WRNF	DRD	35	0	8,000	29
WINDY POINT GROUP ®	S side Dillon Res	WRNF	DRD	---	$	9,100	77
WOLF CREEK	14 mi NE of Pagosa Springs	SJNF	PARD	26	$	8,000	124
WOLFORD MOUNTAIN RES*	NW of Kremmling 7 mi	CRWC	---	48	$	7,500	35
WOODS LAKE	38 mi S of Ridgway	UNF	NRD	41	$	9,400'	111
WUPPERMAN	5 mi SE of Lake City	HCO	---	40	$	8,000	124
WYE	20 mi W of Colo. Springs	PNF	PPRD	21	$	10,300	102
Y							
YOEMAN PARK	17 mi SE of Eagle	WRNF	ERD	24	$	9,000	88

CAMPGROUND SYMBOLS
*   HANDICAP ACCESSIBLE - ACCESS VARIES WITH EACH CAMPGROUND - CALL FIRST.
®   ON A RESERVATION SYSTEM.
NRA = NATIONAL RECREATION AREA
SP   = STATE PARK
SWA = STATE WILDLIFE AREA
DSP = DISPERSED CAMPING

NOTE: MOST FOREST SERVICE CAMPGROUNDS NOW CHARGE OR SOON WILL CHARGE CAMPING FEES.
SEE AGENCY CODES AND PHONE NUMBERS ON PAGE 89

Colorado Recreation Guide Index

Colorado Outdoor Recreation Guides from Outdoor Books & Maps, Inc.

The Best Of Colorado Bike Trails - 77 bike trails for the entire family.
96 pages   Price $9.95   ISBN 0-930657-28-4

The Best Of Northern Colorado Hiking Trails - 78 trials to historical and scenic sites.
112 pages   Price $12.95   ISBN 0-930657-18-7

The Best Of Western Colorado Hiking Guide - 50 trails to scenic and historical sites.
72 pages   Price $9.95   ISBN 0-930657-17-9

The Complete Colorado Campground Guide - Location and information for 500 campgrounds.
160 pages   Price $14.95   ISBN 0-930657-23-3

The Colorado Lakes and Reservoirs Guide - Maps and information for Colorado's major reservoirs.
160 pages   Price $14.95   ISBN 0-930657-00-4

Fishing Close To Home - Maps and information for 150 fishing spots near metro Denver
40 pages   Price $5.95   ISBN 0-930657-05-5

National Forest Trails Guide Series

Maps, directions and trial descriptions for over 750 trails in scenic Colorado National Forests
National Forest:

Arapaho/Roosevelt	83 trails	96 pages	Price $12.95	ISBN 0-930657-08-X
Grand Mesa/Uncompahgre	53 trails	48 pages	Price $6.95	ISBN 0-930657-09-8
Gunnison	72 trails	160 pages	Price $12.95	ISBN 0-930657-10-1
Pike	71 trails	64 pages	Price $12.95	ISBN 0-930657-11-X
Rio Grande	137 trails	96 pages	Price $9.95	ISBN 0-930657-15-2
Routt	62 trails	64 pages	Price $9.95	ISBN 0-930657-12-8
San Isabel	68 trails	160 pages	Price $12.95	ISBN 0-930657-14-4
San Juan	77 trails	72 pages	Price $9.95	ISBN 0-930657-13-6
White River	150 trails	96 pages	Price $9.95	ISBN 0-930657-16-0

Colorado Fishing Guide (MAP) - Locates 1100 stocked lakes and 168 streams on USGS state map.
42"X28" Map   Price $8.00   ISBN 0-930657-30-6

Colorado Camping & Recreation Guide (MAP) - Info. & location of 500 campgrounds on USGS state map.
42"X28" Map   Price $8.00   ISBN 0-930657-31-4

Best of Rocky Mountain National Park Hiking Trails - Maps and describes 30 trails.
48 pages   Price $9.95   ISBN 0-930657-39-X

Best of Colorado 4-Wheel Drive Roads - A 4WD Road Atlas of 165 4WD roads.
190 pages   Price $15.95   ISBN 0-930657-40-3

Olle's Colorado Fishing Guide & Atlas - Maps and fishing information from mountains to plains.
264 pages   Price $24.95   ISBN 0-9137730-41-1

For information on where to purchase these guides contact:
Outdoor Books & Maps, Inc.
11270 County Road 49   Hudson, CO 80642
Phone: (303) 536-4640, (800) 952-5342 FAX: (303) 536-4641
E Mail: obm@ria.net
OR VISIT OUR WEBSITE: www. outdoorcolorado.com